AF371765

ACHY AFFECTS

ACHY AFFECTS

Crisis and Compositions of Selfhood

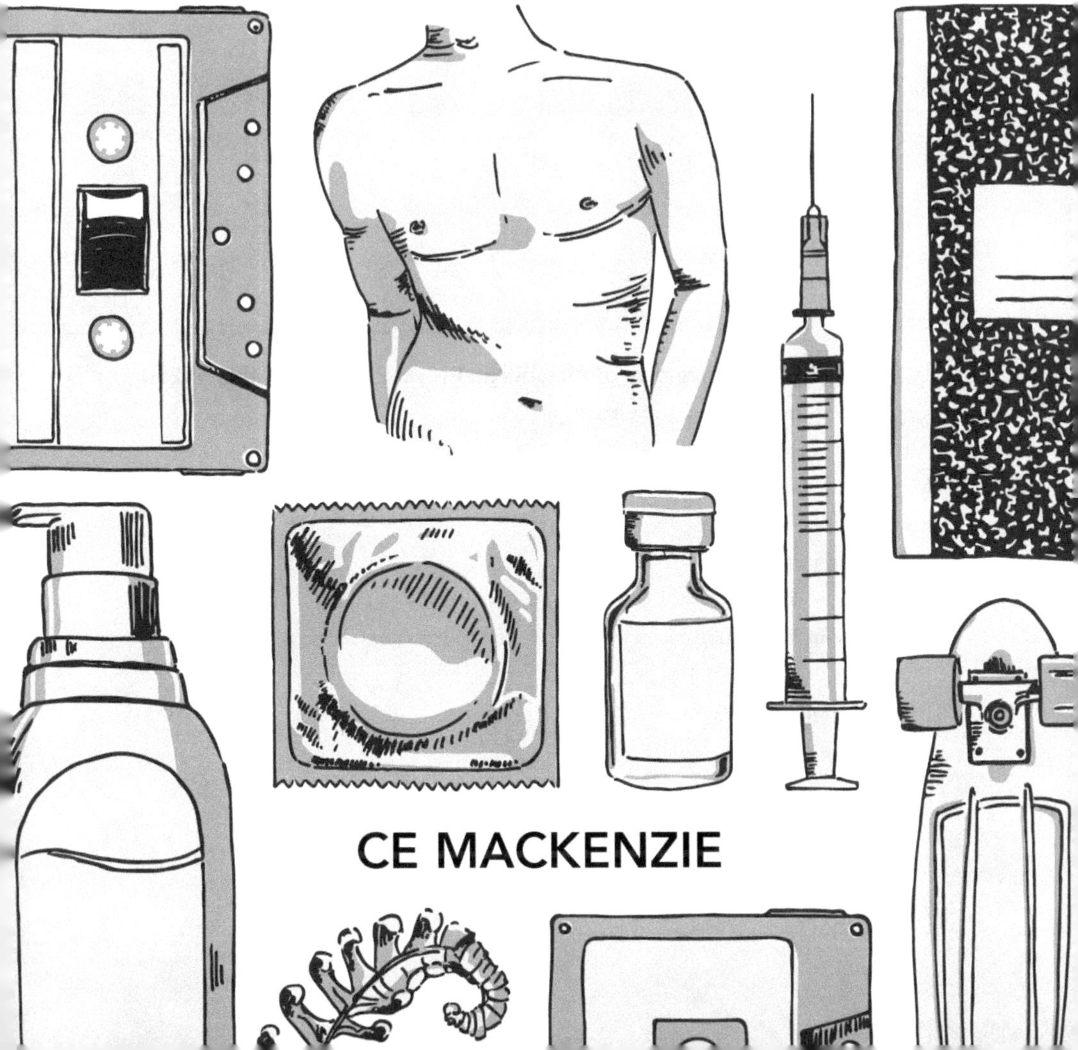

CE MACKENZIE

Published by the University of Pittsburgh Press, Pittsburgh, Pa., 15260

Copyright © 2025, University of Pittsburgh Press

Manufactured in the United States of America

Printed on acid-free paper

10 9 8 7 6 5 4 3 2 1

Cataloging-in-Publication data is available from the Library of Congress

ISBN 13: 978-0-8229-4856-8
ISBN 10: 0-8229-4856-7

Cover art and design by Abbie Adams Studio

For Mary
love and risk

Our feelings are our most genuine paths to knowledge. They are chaotic, sometimes painful, sometimes contradictory, but they come from deep within us.

—Audre Lorde

CONTENTS

CONTENTS

ACKNOWLEDGMENTS

Achy Affects was forged from the daily practice of writing and revising myself over many fraught decades. While I began the project inside the limestone walls of my university, I have always been thinking into these ideas, whether in the glacial streams of interior Alaska or at the seminar table, at syringe exchange or running the dirt ribbons of trail through the forest. Just as many scenes, objects, and passions collated into these pages, there are many who stood next to me, in the classroom or on the alpine ridgeline. That is to say, these acknowledgments not only recognize who helped shape my work, but who helped shape my life and imagination. There are many to thank.

Dr. Cory Holding provided incredible mentorship, support, and presence in my life as I worked through the early stages of this project. She offered generous readings and gentle guidance that has gone on to transform my writing, thinking, and being. But even more, Cory is a good human, a talented teacher, a kind colleague, and a beam of light in the university (and beyond). I am a better thinker for having collaborated with Cory, but also just a better person for knowing her.

Much of this book received renewed energy because of the generous opportunities provided by the University of Pittsburgh's Humanities Center. First, a fellowship in my final year of my doctoral program that not only brought me into community with artists and writers from across the humanities but brought me together with those who also believe in creative, compassionate scholarship. Then, a postdoctoral position that has allowed me to be part of what makes the Humanities Center so meaningful: dissolving the barriers (real and perceived) between the academy and the lives lived outside of campus to create work that is accessible but also beautiful, critical but also communal. I am grateful for Dr. Carla Nappi and Dr. David Marshall, who press for new ways to create and thrive in academic spaces. These two scholars prove that care—for one another, ourselves, and our work—nurtures a vibrant community and sparks ingenuity in our humanities programs. They inspire what I hope to emulate in academia: deep respect for each other and our work.

On that note of inspiration, I am thankful to each mentor who advised me in my writing and research: Dr. Khirsten Scott, Dr. Jules Gill-Peterson, Dr.

Julie Beaulieu, Dr. Shalini Puri, and Dr. Stacey Waite. The scholarship they offer our world and the relationships they provide their students exemplify the kind of university of which I want to be part. There is an academic utopia sounding on the horizon; they are making its arrival possible.

This book is committed to the practice and ethics of harm reduction. I got my start in harm reduction in Oregon working at the HIV Alliance. Patti Hansen oversaw my initial training, followed by two years of volunteering and interning. Patti was my first harm reduction mentor and the first to show me how we can do harm reduction at any time, in any place. That experience inspired an article I published with *Rhetoric of Health and Medicine*, and is now reprinted herein—albeit fragmented and parceled—with permission from University of Florida Press.

Likewise, this book would not be possible without the insights and invitations from those with whom I work at Prevention Point Pittsburgh: Gabby Warner and Moss Visnich, the real deals who never stop believing in an ethics of care. I am grateful for all the shifts and all the trust, for all the knowledge they imparted, for every time I fucked up in the van and they rolled with it, for making me smarter and better at what I do, and for sharing their lives with me.

To my writing colleagues—S. Brook Corfman, Sean Nonnenmacher, and Amanda Awanjo—I am grateful for their insightful edits, positive energy, and empathetic imbibing at cheap happy hours. Go find their writing; these are full-hearted, brilliant human beings. I am in awe of the art they make and the love they give their communities and projects. And for my long-term reader, Heather Dobbins, who has read my writing for over a decade now, challenging and affirming my work simultaneously, and who also said on the streets of Seattle, *life is too short to go unfulfilled. Keep going.* Thank you, Heather.

Thank you to Abbie Adams for creating a gorgeous cover to hold my words. Abbie's incredible artistic vision is matched by her steady friendship to my family. And to my Pittsburgh family, Addie and Colleen (sweet aunties to lil El), and Sophie and Isaac, I am so glad we all are doing life together in this humid city that took me five years to love but that I now call home. Thank you to Daniel Estrada for a friendship anchored in vulnerability, art, and a shared commitment to understanding, not solving, our abiding existentialisms.

To my family: My Dad has prioritized art and wonder since I was very young, introducing me to crucial pieces of literature and music and taking me out into wild spaces. I am grateful to have learned from him that, even though wonder can overwhelm us, it is a through line in life, and a vital one we should not go without. I also want to thank my Mom, a fighter who deserves to recognize her strength and who has shown me exactly all the nerve it takes to recreate our lives. And thank you to my big brother, Colin, my first-ever mentor in this world. Finally, there is much gratitude to extend to my in-laws, my adopted family: John and Ruth, who believe and demonstrate that love moves our world; to my sisters—Sarah, Leah, and Hannah—as well as my nieces and nephew. Together we make a big bunch of laughing, loyal kin who prove love just keeps expanding with every new being brought into our world.

To one of the most important people in my life: Michael. Thank you for letting me write our story. Thank you for believing in a love beyond the scripts, beyond certainty. I am proud of our story, proud to have lived an important era of life with you. Our time together was as beautiful as it was heartbreaking. "The only true currency in this bankrupt world is what you share with someone else when you're uncool." I'm proud to be your uncool someone else.

To the human who summons Rilke to say if we "succeed in loving the expanse between" us, then we will "always see each other as a whole and before an immense sky." You are my argonaut, Mary. My always. I am so proud of us, all the time, for our love and intention, for how we fight for one another and how we laugh every day. You are the best thing to ever happen to me. Our relationship is sacred, is what fills this little sad emo kid with percussive hope. You taught me that to embrace vulnerability is to truly *feel*. And now here I am, writing a whole book on feelings, on love and risk. "Love and risk"—our mantra literally from day one, when we sat on a slouching futon, drinking PBRs, and listening to records in a small, Oregon attic apartment. Thank you for believing in my dreams and protecting them as your own. Thank you for all the mornings you walked our frenetic pup so I could write, and for the drafts upon drafts you read and to which you responded with such insight and kindness. Thank you for creating a life with me, in all the ways. And, my god, thank you for our daughter. She is perfect, and of course she is—she is of you. I love you. Always.

ACHY AFFECTS

INTRODUCTION

Healthy Markets

Tracing Capital through Histories and Compositions of Wellness

I do not believe the story of my scholarship is separate from
the story of my life or the body I live.

—Stacey Waite

Achy Affects surfaces out of chronic longing, from my desire to capture feeling in language yet repetitiously failing. Writing (much like be-ing) aches under the weight of its responsibilities—to get it right, to do no harm—but writing also stings with pleasure, cramping in creativity, vibrating with wonder as the page, as our day, unfolds. *Achy Affects* is about how thought feels, and how composition nurtures this amazing relationship between language and the body, even as we fail. *When in doubt*, one of my past poetry mentors told me, *describe the world*. He was protecting me from the lure of closure and claims. His advice (as I continuously return to it) asks for quiet attention bound up in the body but expanding beyond the parameters of skin. His advice calls for a leave-no-trace poetics. He had me read Rainer Maria Rilke, promised me elegies do more than memorialize, that they invoke feeling and collapse time. Describing the world entangles us in troubled translations, fractured hermeneutics, and fraught processes pocked with human error. But the err is unavoidable. "Leave no trace" means we move carefully through our landscapes—not perfectly, but with the least amount of harm. When I spent two weeks backpacking in Denali National Park, I took a four-hour class on bears, river crossings, and unpredictable weather before receiving a backcountry permit. There is no trail system in Denali—just high brush and arterial glacial streams. "Walk side by side with your partner," the rangers told me, so as to minimize any inadvertent trail-making. "Leave no trace." My partner at the time was Michael, my then husband. Those two weeks I was attuned to everything: the wolves howling, of course, and branches snapping, the bear prints by the tent in the morning, the interminable rain, and the constant buzz of mosquitoes, but also my body. It became just a body in the backcountry. Just movement, muscle, and preservation. I was sinew and synapse, on the cusp of a collapsing marriage. My body was meaningless, and I was grateful for how little it held.

I read Rilke in our tent while the Alaskan sun, mid-August, never fully set. My mentor turned me toward the elegies but Rilke's letters packed smaller, and I was already at low thresholds for the elegiac. Jeans rolled up and propped under my head, I reread his most famous counsel to the young poet: "live the questions."[1] I love this line. Every time I return to it I reabsorb its stun and verity. Rilke advises the young poet to slow his epistemological anguish, to relinquish the satisfaction of telos for the needling delight of process. It's not that we stop searching for answers, Rilke clarifies, but that we stop demanding them.

One hundred yards upwind, Michael hid our bear canister—stuffed with food, ChapStick, toothpaste, and anything else with an inch of scent—under some dense scrub, then stacked our mess kit on top of the canister as a warning call. If an animal got into our gear, the clatter would signal precarity and possible imminence, some heavy force lumbering its way to us. I lay awake listening for that clang, straining my ears against silence. I did not want to get divorced, but I'm gay and trans. And Michael is, well, neither. So while these inchoate severities brimmed often, pressed against skin, they did not breach. Instead, I endured a long, uncertain ache—restless, desiring, and unsure—to which Rilke's calm counsel was at once implosion and balm. To live the questions was to displace knowledge for feeling, to risk everything.

Over a decade later, though I now explicitly identify as queer, I still pang with the thought of *not knowing*. As in, *how did I not know* such an intimate part of myself and how did this illiteracy metabolize as pain? Over a decade later, I still move further into myself, still find myself a mess in process. Out of this private pain—my embodied illiteracy and its material detritus—a public possibility emerged. I wonder, what if we heed Rilke? What if living the questions was a politic, an aesthetic, or the way we honored our bodies and the way we composed our lives?

The Conundrum of Cure: Confronting Telos

When not slogging my heavy pack through the bristled tundra of Alaska's interiors, I lived in Eugene, Oregon, trekking across the tamer wildflower meadows of the Cascades every weekend and working as a barista during the week. I also volunteered with my local harm reduction organization. On Monday nights I joined an outreach crew to stock an old RV with sterile needles, condoms, hot coffee, tampons, Narcan kits,[2] and day-old baked goods. We drove to the edges of downtown Eugene and parked on a dead end next to the railroad tracks, setting up tables and unloading supplies while participants gathered. Often the train thrashed past and I found myself trying to yell over the metal scream of tracks, *Have you exchanged needles with us before?!* Collecting used needles and offering packs of 27- and 29-gauge sterile syringes to new and returning participants, we formed relationships and watched relationships form with people using drugs in our community. Sometimes participants stayed to chat, other times not. But they each left with safer drug-use supplies. Our primary goal was to collect used needles and offer sterile equipment in return. And like most syringe exchanges across the country, ours was a huge force for stymying the spread of HIV and Hep C in the region.

I received hours of training before doing syringe exchange—in STI testing, administering naloxone, and intake forms. But what stuck with me the most was my training in language. In fact, that training came to inform my politics, my abandonment of telos and my investment in process, and my divestment from the individual body as a site of study. At exchange I was trained to speak of process, not results, to expunge shame from the scripts on drug use and instead address current need. For example, the more we say "clean" the more we reinscribe drug use as dirty. The more we celebrate sobriety (something I was explicitly told not to do) the more we reinforce recovery and rehab as the only logical responses to drug use. It is not a new idea that what we say (compose) has direct impact on the material reality of our communities. But it is an idea that requires ongoing attention. Here's another example.

A few years ago the sheriff of Butler County, Ohio, refused to provide lifesaving naloxone (aka Narcan, an FDA-approved nasal spray that immediately reverses an overdose) to his police force and emergency teams, explaining, "All we're doing is reviving them, we're not curing them."[3] Coded in medical telos, "cure" signals a normative expectation of health, that one should always progress toward an acceptable future. Butler County suffers hundreds of overdoses each year, and yet its sheriff suggests *recovery supersedes material lives*—that it is actually better to be dead than alive and using. His statement is founded in eugenics, exposing the historical codependence between healthcare and capitalism, wherein the body is (and has always been) the site of exploration and profit, wherein we come to define health as the ability to ensure solvent futures. Because we have been socially trained to experience distress around those who do not display futural projections of health, we've been taught to pathologize (or criminalize) anything other than the productive. Lorde has already warned us. Ours is "a society where the good is defined in terms of profit rather than in terms of human need."[4] If she is right, and of course she is, then ours is a society that steeps our lives, our very bodies, in capital.

While recognizing the multiple ways we might identify the kinetic tides of capital, I use it to describe a social world saturated by consumption, commodification, and profit—an intricate but enriched network of synaptic exchange charged by soluble possibility. Power shifts along the grid, lighting up some spaces while rendering others dark. Capital has codified the violent and extant legacy of the United States. Establishing itself as a world power through the exploitation of laboring human beings, our capitalist statehood continues to drive our lives into profitable ends and permeate our social worlds to stir profits through any means possible; we must recognize this includes the means of our bodies too. It always has. Our worth is diagnosed and determined by our ability to work, to "give back" to the economy.

Achy Affects is a response this, to the ways capitalism and healthcare convene to rhetorically organize (that is, compose) our bodies into categories of risk, waste, or worth; and it is a response to how capitalism's enforcement of "better" or "more authentic" selves is motivated by money and labor. The good life is a vanishing point: our best selves are just ahead, if only we work hard enough toward overcoming the pain of our marginalized status (even as systems keep us marginalized). Colleen Derkatch explains, "What it means in contemporary Western culture to be 'well' is predicated on the entanglement of seemingly opposed logics that together create an essentially closed rhetorical system where wellness is always a moving target."[5] These opposed logics limit us between two fixed points—sick or well, estranged or connected, dysphoric or euphoric, sober or using—promoting narrow yet dominant narratives of the self; these logics normalize and then commodify outcome. Capital exploits the feeling of euphoria to market it as result, for example, as the desired state and cured condition to dysphoria, what Hil Malatino calls "teleological modes of gendered becoming."[6] But this narrative neglects returns and revisions. It neglects the ongoingness that is my trans body moving through joy and grief simultaneously. And it neglects the significance of relapse in recovery.

How did we get here? There are many ways to answer this question. One is that our vulnerabilities have been curated over centuries of exploitation. Under the (ongoing) practice of imperialism, the US healthcare industry was established through logics of "discovery," often at the cost of non-consenting patients; and it continues to make health compulsory in order to capitulate to capitalism, wherein the body equals profit. "Eugenicists one and all—they considered some body-minds good, using as their criteria whiteness and wealth, heterosexuality and manhood, US citizenship and Christianity, ablebodiedness and ablemindedness," writes Eli Clare. "Other body-minds they deemed bad—marked by defectiveness, degeneracy, deficiency, perversion, feeblemindedness, poverty, criminality, and weakness. They worked to reproduce the 'good' and discard the 'bad.' History is a torrent shaped around them."[7] The torrent torments still. But the "bad" is not just discarded—not in late capitalism. "Bad" must be redeemed and rehabilitated. Rebranded, even. Throughout these chapters I will describe the relationship between capital and US wellness culture broadly conceived and articulated, but I'll start here with the foundations in US healthcare specifically, looking at the ways capital and medicine make singular bodies the exoticized site of knowledge extraction, out of which we get necessitated telos and compulsory health practices.

I will outline a brief history of this relationship between capitalism and the singular body, nurtured as it is by the idea of optimization, to then move toward delinking telos from health, and to finally offer methods of composing bodies with care. *Achy Affects* proceeds from these efforts, specifically on how we might avoid re-marginalizing the marginalized when our political environment diminishes the complexity of so many accumulating cultural crises. For this reason, among many others, I center ache as a transient heuristic.

Our Exhausted, Aspiring Bodies

Michel Foucault famously wrote, "It was the taking charge of life ... that gave power its access even to the body."[8] Foucault of course went on to name this political intervention *biopower*, an "indispensable element in the development of capitalism"[9] that commissions and justifies government or institutional control over our bodies, urging them into labor, urging them into profit and normalizing this process. "A normalizing society is the historical outcome of a technology of power centered on life," he writes.[10] Power operates taxonomically in the normalizing society by imposing category on the broader social imaginary; the body is measured and appraised, qualified and hierarchized. The body is composed. As Big Pharma expands its range of curatives it also expands its range of illness in order to market its products. The more that can be deemed ill, the more that can be made better. The more that can be optimized, the more that can be sold.

Foundations of care in the United States were based on category, the colonial drive to own and make known, to script the flesh as identity. C. Riley Snorton argues this explicit point when he asks, "What does it mean to have a body that has been made into a grammar for whole worlds of meaning?"[11] To answer Snorton's question, it means our hyper-surveilled bodies are hyper-scripted. Foucault further argued that one's behavior and body fortified into fixed identities through cultural shifts in imagination that aligned with disciplinary shifts in the nineteenth and twentieth centuries. We became our behaviors.[12] Gay sex, for example, was no longer registered ephemerally as a temporal act spurred on by feeling, but was compounded into identity: sex became homosexuality. This shift, Foucault tell us, produced cultures of policing founded in binaried regulations—"normal" authorizes deviance, "healthy" informs pathology. While these taxonomical moves occurred within the walls of the clinic where the body exudes knowledge (is coerced into doing so), they quickly found circulation in everyday notions of being and becoming.

As national markets transformed into globalized systems of trade and relationships, as sovereign governments gave way to democratic empires, capitalism permeated Western life, where the "ancient right to *take* life or *let* live was replaced by a power to *foster* life or *disallow* it to the point of death."[13] While social categories were once catalyzed by public institutions such as school, church, the clinic, and courthouse, the market shift invited the individual to regulate social life. We became interventionists, disciplinarians, and regulators. "Distributed throughout the brains and bodies of the citizens,"[14] write Michael Hardt and Antonio Negri, we internalized demands for betterment as moral, taking on the responsibility to be and become healthy, to know ourselves, to know if we are gay, whether we are at risk for addiction, what kind of diseases stream genetically through our kin. This optics of autonomy obliges us toward (re)productive futures while organizing otherness into categories of pathological dissidence. By pacifying its population through the interminable supply and demands of markets, with a politics that places life at its center, healthcare and capitalism establish the worthy body. Under the auspices of the medical-therapeutic industry and scientific objectivity that claims neutrality and positivism, the subject appears through differentiation. What makes us different, makes us.

A present-day example: hepatitis C survives outside the body for up to six weeks, and if contracted can turn chronic in as few as six months. Patients have limited treatment options—among them, painful injections into the stomach with crushing side effects and low clear rates. But a twelve-week course of Sovaldi, taken orally with comparatively mild side effects, boasts 90 percent clearance among patients. After three months, liver enzymes return to normal levels. That is, only if patients can first afford the $1,000-per-capsule price tag and $84,000 for the entire course of treatment, which is not covered by Medicare or Medicaid and only rarely by insurance plans. Other treatments fall into comparable cost brackets while, on average, hepatitis C patients struggle financially, often unemployed, underemployed, and uninsured. Hep C clarifies the parasitic relationship between health and capital in a system that makes incessant demands on the body. With Hep C, the meddling hands of Big Pharma undeniably showcase capital's determinations of health, but what requires further interrogation are the rhetorical methods used by the state to dictate, circulate, and administer these definitions of (and attachments to) healthy bodies. Deeply rooted in historical eugenic principles, and through the teleological language of achievement and progress, US healthcare has justified its interventions by insisting on the body as producer of knowledge. The Hep C patient, stigmatized for a disease contracted by shared drug equipment, must obey medical direction under the intense scrutiny of what their body offers. The submissive patient makes known (often against their will) the difference between clean or contaminated living.

Jasbir Puar explains that our bodies are cataloged "in relation to their success or failure in terms of health, wealth, progressive productivity, upward mobility, enhanced capacity."[15] If we can always be healthier, then we are incited toward the interminable creation of the healthiest body. Health discourse replicates this tired practice of embedding responsibility within the individual body through neoliberal notions of wellness. Inside and outside of the clinic, we find (and acclimatize to) language that moralizes our choices: sobriety, natural childbirth, normal BMI, clean eating, or hitting rock bottom, disordered drinking, born in the wrong body, etc. Language not only reports on the body but, through the compositional habits of the medical-therapeutic industry, it determines the limits of the body.

I will say this here and throughout *Achy Affects*: we need the clinic, the doctor, the surgeon. We need cures and optimized care. We need to be healthy. Rather, I am critical of *how* language is employed and how it influences our ways of thinking about our bodies (and in turn, our selves). In particular, our culture of optimization and constant labor requires us to think of our risky bodies as aspirational, that because we *can* overcome what prevails us, we *must*. The aspirational narrative is the legible narrative, and therefore comes to dominate our expectations of what the body should or can do—from rock bottoms to years sober, from sick to cured, from closets to parades. I lament the loss of multiplicity and the tempering of imagination under such compositional restrictions. Writer, artist, and user of drugs I. Thaca has already said as much: "I do not buy into the idea that eventually I will hit some 'bottom.' Using does not have to entail despair, misery, and heartache. . . . I'm so alone in believing that [using] is a choice that can be consistent with a happy and successful life. That is the hardest part about being a user: not internalizing the belief that I am a piece of shit and trying to live a life of satisfaction and dignity that everyone tells me is impossible."[16]

In addition to telling us we're "pieces of shit," aspirational narratives also strip us of agency and distill us into the simplistic binary in which some have power and others do not. We end up re-marginalizing marginality when focused so solely on telos, on fix, when our language on human life and vulnerability lacks depth, and in a desire for reconciliation with otherness, resists the complexity that makes our communities vibrant and full of possibility. Singling out the marginalized against a center, even as this model might helpfully illuminate how power moves through and dominates vulnerable communities, also circumscribes a center that retains its hegemonic status. Barbara Christian writes, "Constructs like the *center* and *periphery* reveal that tendency to want to make the world less complex by organizing it according to one principle, to fix it through an idea, which is really an ideal."[17] We risk overexposing singular behavior or injury, forcing a world of meaning onto the shoulders of one person or one community of people.

When Dean Spade wants top surgery, his only option requires, of course, medical and therapeutic intervention. He must first secure low-cost counseling, wherein he is forced to provide normalized (aspirational) accounts of his trans experience to be approved for a double mastectomy. I will later go through a very similar experience (see chapter 3). As Spade explains, he must want to "fully" transition before he starts any "alteration."[18] While "fully" implies a teleological demarcation, an end goal, "alteration" implies removal from an original. By understanding gender transition and expression under the aegis of the medical institution, Spade argues, we come to view gender as disorder in need of a coherent solution. Situating his experience within Foucault's notion of the will to knowledge, as a lens through which to analyze the medical-therapeutic industry's regulation of and treatments for trans patients, especially as it has historically sought to reinforce normalized gender categories, Spade draws on his own story to illuminate the material implications of trying to navigate a clinic that will both help and harm him. But he resists these expectations, and through his resistance Spade demonstrates the need for language unconsumed with category and arrivals. He scrutinizes the passing imperative to analyze how authority is given, as default, to the medical-therapeutic community, which only serves to reinforce false concepts such as "real" and "legitimate." Spade's storytelling exposes the prerogatives of successful transition as defined by a binary, questioning what it may mean to allow people agency over their own gender compositions.

While many trans people experience uneasy, incongruent, or painful relationships to our bodies, this is not the whole of it. Emma Heaney describes the "narrative of entrapment" as "the assumption that trans women's very existence *means something* outside itself, something about the gender of a putatively cis general subject, imposes a representational disjuncture between trans self-knowledge and trans *meaning*."[19] The narrative of entrapment produces figures and allegories rather than agency and authors. Heaney is also pressing back against cured states, aspirational templates. "The diagnostic insistence that trans people are uniquely defined by alienation from the body denies the challenge to cis understanding of sex that is posed by trans people who claim the right to determine the sexed and gendered meanings of their own bodies, with or without medical services."[20] Because trans folks are often perceived as alienated from or by our bodies, we are coerced into aspirational narratives and consummate rhetorics. We are called on to produce ourselves, to make ourselves readable, to explain ourselves, to overcome the real and imagined pain of embodiment for an authentic and authenticated destination that is the body. We're never quite enough.

The reality that we cannot escape the systems hurting us means that even when we're not in active pain, we might instead experience chronic ache, because we rely on sources of external power to aid us. Even as we resist an industry's hands on our bodies, we also depend on networks of care. We need care; optimization offers very real sources of survival. So if we're not destroying the clinic and we cannot escape capital, what then are we doing? Well, we're attempting to describe the world without holding it hostage to singular compositions. We're attempting to honor the question the body finds itself in. We're writing into the question of how we might move from healthcare as elite and objective to quotidian and communal. The language we use, on paper and out loud, matters. While we're taught to scrutinize our own bodies to mark their successes and failures, in holding ourselves accountable to others' ideals and expectations, what mostly emerges are feelings: anxiety, shame, caution, pride, eagerness, anger, fear, vulnerability. Those feelings are telling us something. Despite their erratic movements and inconclusive energies, feelings yield knowledge. In fact, feelings, Lorde said, are our most genuine path to knowledge.[21]

Ache and Feeling

I take as fact that our lives are saturated by the pain of capital and that we are exhausted by its expectations on our bodies. But while capital harms us to make us profitable, we are also always deeply feeling creatures, made of more than just pain. We imagine, create, retreat, and work. We love and break up and make terrible decisions, decisions that don't define us but do make us. So often, struggle is cast as singular, and therefore surmountable, a mess to wipe clean. But my body betrays this narrative at every turn. My body is the site of ongoing uncertainty, in process and aching over that reality. And within this specific ache, I recognize those myths—that knowing all of ourselves makes a morality, that overcoming pain is compulsory and therefore possible, and that the good human is the known human—I recognize that these myths fail us.

Audre Lorde should be considered an early affect theorist. When she says there are no new ideas, only new ways of making them felt, she is saying that *thought feels*, which means through the sensations of the skin into the quotidian blink of the day. I can think of no better definition for affect. Our contradicting collage of sensations pulls at our attentions. To listen is to allow feeling its place in our imaginations. "For there are no new ideas. There are only new ways of making them felt—of examining what those ideas feel like being lived on Sunday morning at 7 A.M., after brunch, during wild love, making war, giving birth, mourning our dead—while we suffer the old longings, battle the old warnings and fears of being silent and impotent and alone, while we taste new possibilities and strengths."[22] With *feeling*, there's no contained goal in sight, just the motions of the body existing and having that be enough and worthy of everything. It is the "one day at a time" attitude, which asks for attention, as in, attending to. And when we attend—to our communities but also, importantly, to ourselves—we empower.

Affect studies reflects an allergy to stabilizing taxonomies. It rejects the belief that by outlining the definitive borders of each body—by cataloging pain, deviance, or pathology—we will uncover objectively useful data. Just as often, our bodies are often unknowable. But also, trading bodily knowledge for health services is a poor way to provide care. Indeed, my use of "affect" throughout *Achy Affects* describes the hive of emotions, sensations, and somatic intensities shaping our relationship to the environs within which we find ourselves. The exchange—between internal and external—is always ongoing, porous, and confusing. Language is not first on the scene, but often arrives later, or arrives muddied, adrenal, elusive.

Affect diverts from static analytics toward these messy sensations, from the metaphorized body (i.e., the "trans body" or the "Black body") toward the social worlds that enact power through calculated compositions. In so doing, we will not seek to classify the body to capture its teleological rank, nor locate it on a schematic of prescribed health and determined futures, but instead practice dailyness, offer resources without debt, forgo opinion, and relinquish our attraction to expertise and cred. I believe this form of practice is anti-capitalist, even as it must operate within a capitalist state.

Such focus on feeling (over argument) resituates the scene of accountability: we pull knowledge from systems rather than exploit the individual body to construct social meaning. We invite interruption, stalling the freighted force of knowledge pressed into us by healthcare or punitive systems, by organized or social medias. We meet our imaginations with a bit more generosity. My interest specifically in affect is exactly this relationship to literacy, how sensation intensifies our ways of knowing. My commitment to affect forms the questions propelling this project: how do capitalist logics make communities of people—specifically, queer, trans, and drug-using people—rhetorical spectacles for the purpose of productive futures? How do feelings give attention to bodies without exploiting those bodies for grand narratives? I have been so complicit in this violence, demanding my own body answer all the questions brought against it. And the questions *are* important. These pages are about figuring out how to live in them rather than punctuate them.

So, while moving through the narrative topography of my own life—one riven with failure—I look toward affect to demonstrate how capitalist logics erase complexity to categorize one as either healthy or unhealthy, productive or passive, normative or pathological, dysphoric or euphoric. My effort is toward demobilizing these binaries that structure our social literacies around our bodies, especially as we attempt to talk about vulnerable experiences of embodiment. At syringe exchange, even as I witnessed our bodies exhausted by the compulsory demands of capital—that one pursue recovery at all costs—so also did I see people living dynamic, vibrant lives marked by attention and care. Participants built connections with one another, or they collected free kibble to feed the alley cats; they had jobs or they didn't; they had families or they had chosen families. Pain is not our only story.

This brings us to the *ache* in affect, to how an achy hermeneutics might release us from the call toward mastery. One of feeling's earliest theorizers was Aristotle, who organized emotion through opposites.[23] Anger opposes calm; love opposes hate. This heuristic haunts us still, primarily because language is predominantly made meaningful through converse associations. But this model of antithesis overexposes difference for the sake of legibility. Affect studies has traditionally followed suit, dichotomizing emotions into positive and negative ("bad" or "ugly") feelings to analyze their political manifestations. But in so doing we have naturalized a binaried concept of socialized emotion: we try to overcome what's negative, convert shame to pride, coerce grief into closure. While honoring how affect scholars differentiate emotion,[24] I am interested in moments of contact, how feelings converge to express (inadequately but no less importantly) the intellect and the body in relationship. Because the reality is, even when we stumble into a blissed moment, we might find it still burns. The temporal panic that surrounds happiness is only outdone by the bewilderment of how we managed to find our way into such a moment to begin with. Happy can hurt. This is not to say I question what is warm and good. Let us hold our happy moments as much as possible. Rather, the impulse toward meritocratic culminations—that we overcome the bad to bask in the good—is a bad sell, a total lemon.

Achy is not the same as "bad." Achy hurts, of course; but there is also pining, desire, and nerve. We ache for home. We ache for our lover's interest. We ache for a parent who has only devastated us. We ache for explanation. While ache signals something amiss or lost, it also indicates growth, as in growing pains, a slow change. Ache is chronic and drawn out, an ongoing vibration animated by both the ordinary triggers of being alive and being human, but spurred also by the systemic harms we are made to endure. In this way, ache rejects the notion of positive and negative feelings, a notion that locks us into the narrative of triumph, of overcoming the bad for the good. Instead, ache whirrs within emotional enmeshment, causing us to feel multiple sensations or needs at once; and this multiplicity often better honors the complexity of our situations or compositions. We hurt, but hurt contains many things.

How might we capture the profound currents of living a life shaped by systemic harm, white logic, moral panics, but also fevering beauty, loving connection, and creative ferment? Ache not only illuminates new possibilities for desire, it reckons with our compositional methods, how we compose our work and ourselves. This is what Gary Bowen calls an integrated whole: "It is not a thing in balance, as implied by dichotomies of male/female, gay/straight, and black/white so prevalent in the white way of thinking; but a complete and complex thing which includes an entire rainbow of possibilities—not just the opposite ends of a spectrum."[25] The binary is whiteness. So much critical energy projects onto us (our actions, behaviors, bodies) rather than on systems of thought, how we came to think the way we do and how we might cultivate other ways to wonder. Ache may be one way to understand our lives as not in balance, but complete and complex, as Bowen writes.

I want to rescue us, myself included, from compositions (of all sorts) predicated on telos—an authentic self made compulsory against the backdrop of pain. Cameron Awkward-Rich gives us a place to start. "What would it mean to do minoritarian studies without being driven by the desire to rehabilitate the subjects/objects of our knowledge? What kind of theories would we produce if we noticed pain and, rather than automatically seeking out its source in order to alleviate it, or mining it for resources for perverse or resistant pleasures, we instead took it as a fact of being embodied that is not necessarily loaded with moral weight?"[26] Awkward-Rich asks for theory that refuses to exploit and instead witnesses ache as particular and everyday, and as part of embodiment. He asks us to pay attention without demands for payoff. Our leave-no-trace poetics and harm-reductionist methodologies, our imperfect imprints, are practices of care that we return to and relearn. It is what Hil Malatino calls maintenance work, so that trans and queer people "can get about the work of living."[27] What could be more important than opening up ways for one another to get about the work of living? In so doing, we are still agents of world-making, even as the world makes us.

The Landscapes of *Achy Affects*

I entered the acute pain of divorce unresolved on the decision and making a mess of things to endure the split—beer-backed whiskey at lunch, bad sex with the wrong people, self-isolation. Breaking myself down in order to survive, I pulled the threads of my known self to privilege an inchoate feeling. Happiness, truth, and flourishing—these intoxicating promises did not await me on the other side. There is no other side; I stood on the rim of nothingness that bore everything. I was a wreck. "There are wounds we won't get over," writes Christian Wiman. But we still might be able to "give to our lives a coherence that is not 'closure,' and learn to live with our memories, our families, and ourselves amid a truce that is not peace."[28] *A truce that is not peace*—if this isn't a lyric for my queer body surviving failure, I don't know what is. If this isn't a lyric for everyone living in the fallout of themselves, I don't know what is.

Achy Affects is the watershed of four decades of thoughts, feelings, and memories into the cramped bind of these pages, into the unpunctuated story of coming out and getting divorced and working syringe programs. I follow myself through the dense brush of Alaska's tundra, fold back to witness myself as a child quietly creating but also hiding, converge through my shameful divorce, my coming out, my time spent passing out needles in the streets of Eugene and Pittsburgh, my top surgery, new parenthood. Similarly, my artifacts are beloved items—dusty trails, worn mixtapes, novels with busted bindings, scraps of poetry, old YouTube clips, my body as I make and unmake it. This is intentional. We can do theory in everyday ways, in the everyday. We do not require spectacle to think wildly. We do not need the bodies of queer and trans people, for example, to think and talk about being trans. Instead, I wander through feeling, knowledge, care, gender, failure, sensitivity, street advocacy, and books of poetry to explore what it might mean to compose ourselves against the currents of capital. My years of harm reduction work, my liminal trans body, my travels through high alpine meadows but also through grief and shame, have me here. My writing makes and unmakes me.

Organized into four feelings—wonder, shame, shyness, and nostalgia—I've assembled affects that ache. As in, they hurt, but the pain is not always acute or precarious, is rather yearning or symptomatic of dormant possibility. Summoned in moments of exposure or exhausted nerve, these four feelings are embodied but external, personal but social. Just as they evade and give us ache in their abandon, they also provide shelter, help us grow, not necessarily up, but maybe in horizonal or tactile ways. I deliberately collected feelings that have received a bad rap or have been left unattended. So much has been said on trans anger, for example. But what about trans shyness, the need to say less about ourselves and our bodies? Or, what if being trans meant looking back on our queer childhoods and adolescence, not with regret but through nostalgic affection? My focus on achy affects over binaried argument grants me permission to dwell in a truce that is not peace. I am allowed my failures, my fears standing at the rim of the abyss, my freedom to write into cramped corners.

This work—these pages, my achy days of putting together a life, my political and social mores—means taking on multiples, moving through mixed genres while focused on a central intention: to divest from the body as the producer of social meaning and from ways of knowing that replenish false opposites: authentic or inauthentic, healthy or pathological. As a writer, I've struggled against language as it strikes intentional political paths through our collective social imaginary to form shared and singular imaginations around a cultural issue. Affect is how it feels to live within that issue. But, if we're thinking through embodiment (our feelings, our senses, our sensitivities), and also what we know about those feelings, we will find ourselves ensnared by language and wrecked by translation. Because it is language that makes the map, that follows the trigger of feeling through the body, through our ways of knowing, and out into the world. To describe the world is to become irreparably infatuated with language, despite the many ways it disappoints. *Achy Affects* is my infatuation and my disappointment, but also an articulated vision for caretaking that goes off-map.

Chapter 1, titled "Wonder Drug: Syringe Programs as Sites of Care, Connection, and Renewal," is grounded in my work at Prevention Point Pittsburgh as I assist with their syringe exchange program. In this chapter I rethink precarity within the vibrant space of syringe exchange by analyzing *wonder* as an overlooked affect. Because, as we will see in the second chapter, on shame, mainstream knowledge on the US opioid epidemic often employs rhetorics of spectacle, requires compulsory recovery, and reinforces the racialization of addiction, thereby reducing the participant to a marginalized subject marked only by pain. Instead, as inspired by Kevin Quashie, who writes, "consciousness is not only shaped by struggle but also by revelry, possibility, the wildness of the inner life," I turn to the political potentiality of wonder as the feeling of world-making, being in community, being seen, and having agency.[29] This constructs my methodology, in that a focus on wonder asks us to embrace what we do not know, to center complexity as the object of analysis, rather than subjects or participants. Rather than "study" this program, Prevention Point, in a traditional sense of the word, I attend to the ways wonder nourishes the relationship between our physical bodies and embodied literacy. That is, what we *feel* and what we *know about that feeling*, and how this brings us collectively together in unmastered moments of care. If wonder is horizonal, unconsumed with contained meanings and fixed ends, and capitalism is fully consumed with acquisition, domination, and profit, then wonder and capital are not only antagonists, but they forge discrete epistemological paths.

So much work has already been done on shame and stigma, across disciplines and with varying intentions.[30] I do not replicate that work. I do not redeem shame, to argue for whether it has useful or subversive possibilities. Instead, in the second chapter, titled, "The Spectacle of Shame: Resisting Cure in Crisis," I look at what shame does to our imaginations, how it represses the physical, through our access to healthcare, as well as the desires we might want to follow. I analyze the rhetorical practices circulating through the opioid epidemic to think about the moralization of time and the ongoing racialization of addiction, and how stigma motivates both.

This chapter follows my beginnings with syringe exchange back in Oregon, but also theorizes my own shame. While I have personal connections with addiction, it is not my story to tell. Instead, I hope to show what I have learned about shame through myself and what I am continuing to learn from others at the scene of syringe exchange and drug outreach, how shame constrains us to prevailing rhetorics of success and achievement, and how shame shrunk my story down to only ruins. Erasure, apology, explanation—shame made these the only tools in my compositional toolbox.

So while shame is containment, shyness is possibility. Often, shame and shyness are conflated.[31] But I want to show in my third chapter, titled "Painfully Shy: Trans Feeling and Quiet Refusals," how this very conflation is why we need to do affect studies when we talk about the body: feelings may look similar, but they do wildly different things. With shyness, I press for its usefulness in surviving capital—in moments and murmurs, not as overthrow.

Just as the addicted subject must be en route to recovery, so are trans folks coerced into this same rhetorical paradigm. The trans subject is situated on a path toward the cured state; but rather than sobriety serving as the telos, it's the fully gendered self. In chapter 3, I use shyness to challenge the way trans folks are compelled into aspirational narratives, and describe how these narratives operate according to the logics of capital, that we must be on our way to our best selves. Harm reduction has something to say here—that gendered becoming has no destination. In this way, I am interested in shyness as an affective hermeneutic, in what it teaches us—not about the self or shy person necessarily—but about navigating the demands of a capitalist ecosystem, especially as those demands look like calls for self-optimization, mastery, sociality, and judgment. As a sensitive practice of attention that resists the cacophony of capital, shyness hushes the spectacle made around our bodies and allows us to be in the process of ourselves. As I take a generally positive disposition toward shyness, I cannot deny that to be shy is also to hurt, to be "painfully shy." But what exactly is the source of this pain?

In chapter 4, titled "Nostalgic Potential: The Mixtape Is an Archive, and the Archive Is a Feeling Thing," I then move deeper into the interiors to explore nostalgia as a space of reclamation and agency. Nostalgia was first defined as "homesickness" in the seventeenth century, and was then later reframed as mental illness, as a melancholic attachment to a past (or lost) time. Today, we are stuck in these old tropes and intimidated by political conservatism's current appropriation of this affect. But I believe there are other possibilities in this feeling, even an urgency to reclaiming nostalgia, that we should be serious about extending its potentialities beyond the realm of psychology and politics, to analyze its potential as a resource for survival and identity. I press beyond traditional conceits of nostalgia to argue that we go back not to (or not only to) retrieve a lost object or return to a lost time, but for the relief in return*ing*. I ask, What if nostalgia is not the desire to go back and stay, but to revisit and revel, to re/enact some form of present change? In that way, this achy affect is not reinstating what's lost, but is the feeling of moving back and what that feeling opens, and specifically how it deepens our own sense of agency, literacy, and possibility.

I braid this chapter with my own narrative of trans becoming, how in order to move into future selves, I needed to go back. I frame this through an analysis of my favorite music as a teenager, and how knowledge of the self moves sideways, backwards, and doubles over itself. Finally, I hope to show how this deeply interior feeling swells into something powerful. By being empowered by nostalgia, by exploring our own archives to study the past self and retroactively recognize and give voice, we gain narrative authority over a past that claimed us and learn more about ourselves in our returns.

Chapter 5, "Wild Ache: Composing in Crisis" returns to pain, bends back to the page, toward composition, creation, and revision to explore ache as a method for diffusing the spectacle made around marginalization. Because even as our bodies might collate shame, even as we hurt, we also find quiet shelter under the rain fly or at the table with our families, we are also stunned with wonder. It is the stun and wonder that makes this life survivable, even desirable. This fifth chapter, in honoring the whole of the project, thus examines how we might attenuate the tired binaries that hold our imaginations hostage: we either hurt or we don't; we are oppressed or we oppress; we have agency or it is withheld. Ache allows us to not just describe the world, but to describe *our* world as we encounter it through our skin, to interpret it through the broken poetics, and to live the questions while working toward a future with less harm.

Achy Affects is an experiment and exploration in which I heed Audre Lorde's reminder that there are no new ideas, but new ways of making them felt. I ally with Cameron Awkward-Rich, who privileges process to honor the everyday, and in so doing makes futurity a horizon of hope. I pursue the nostalgic logics of Hil Malatino, who theorizes faux-emo, early-aughts, punk-pop music. Meaning, we can do theory anywhere, not just in elite spaces or with elite objects. I hold close the potential utopias of José Esteban Muñoz, that we protect our futures the moment we un-engineer them, stripping those demands made by our culture of punctuating capital. This kind of imagining is not linear but recursive, a series of returns. The folding and returning creates density, texture, and makes knowledge a thing of multiples. How we know ourselves and how we do not know ourselves, this is only part of the ache. With a world insisting we master our own being, there's *no space* to live the questions. These pages are about the *feeling* of no space and the *feeling* of making space.

Finally, I venerate the advice of my mentor, so I might describe rather than argue, pay witness rather than stake claim. In some ways, these pages reflect my return to a poetic state of mind—line breaks and dashes, cadence and rhythm. Rebecca Lindenberg writes, simply yet profoundly, that poetry is how thought feels.[32] And while these lines of prose are definitively not poetry, I believe poetics has much to offer in how we practice attention, how we nourish interior lives, and how we lose ourselves in language. *Achy Affects* is also about how thought feels and is therefore convicted that it need not be one or the other, theory or life lived, but a collapsing of this false dilemma into many potentialities. "I sensed the possibility of the integration of feeling/knowledge," writes Barbara Christian. "There is, of course, much to be learned from exploring how we know what we know, how we read what we read, and exploration which, of necessity, can have no end."[33] I understand this non-teleological necessity as a renewing commitment to life within the questions.

"Be patient toward all that is unsolved in your heart and try to love the questions themselves."[34] When Rilke goes on to advise the poet to live the questions, to live everything, he also offers this consolation: "Perhaps you will then gradually, without noticing it, live along some distant day into the answer." Rilke doesn't guarantee any outcomes, intimating the inherent faith this project requires, but he offers the distant day as a reminder of more. Perhaps that's key, the answer is (frustratingly, beautifully) non-aspirational.

I am a harm reduction advocate and a writer. I am a stone butch with top surgery scars on my chest. I am a divorcee and happily married. I am a Baptist college alum and a gay, trans nonbinary parent, a drummer, runner, lover of the wild outdoors, even the glacial plains of interior Alaska. I have always been the authentic version of myself, even in crisis, even in delay and despair, even as I work toward other meaningful compositions of my being, expressions of feeling. I am rewriting and revising the same sentences. There's no spoiler here; these chapters offer a simple suggestion: that we see ourselves and one another as already whole, longing toward those horizons formed by our own dreams and desires.

1

Wonder Drug

Syringe Programs as Sites of Care, Connection, and Renewal

Standing up for one's self doesn't have to be triumphant, but
can be, simply, the work of reveling in flowers or blue sky—
the daily practice of understanding what you love and why.

—Kevin Quashie

The more I wonder, the more I love.

—Alice Walker, *The Color Purple*

Gabby and I cranked battery-operated fans and drank bottles of cold water; we complained about the heat and chatted with participants while filling their orders—sterile needles, naloxone, crack pipes, meth bowls. In between bursts of people seeking safer drug use supplies, Gabby explained how Prevention Point Pittsburgh's (PPP) community advocate program works: eight members of our using community receive a monthly stipend for disseminating naloxone (the FDA-approved drug that reverses opioid overdose) throughout their neighborhoods—to friends and family who cannot make it to one of our sites. Our advocates reach places the mobile PPP van cannot. For some, the work perfectly hems into the ebb and flow of their daily lives. "We're all operating on different time and space continuums," Gabby loves to say. Other members are eager to do more; passing out ten boxes of naloxone isn't enough. And there's more work to do. But Gabby lamented how busy they are, how much growth PPP has witnessed in the last few years. We gave out 100 percent more supplies in 2021 than 2020, and 2020 saw its own growth spurt, building 40 percent on the year before.[1] "There's so little time to dream about more," they said. The needs are innumerable and time is scarce. The more our programming expands, the more we need to expand. The more we learn, the more we need to learn. This structural problem—that there is not even time to *dream about more*, much less design, organize, finance, implement, and manage those dreams—feels insurmountable.

Even as I actively write and think against the dominant narratives on drug use, I find in these moments—me sweating in the back of a van, stocking needles, and listening to Gabby—the compulsion toward cohesion and conclusion. I want my writing to capture what it feels like to be in the van (cohesion). I also want to help; and having the answers feels like the best way to help (conclusion). I am desperate for telos, as I suspect many of us are. This chapter is about the affective experience of resisting that telos, even in the face of crisis, even in the face of a crisis without clear end. This chapter is, in this way, about my methods—for writing, thinking, and being in community.

I went into this chapter eager to study the affective possibilities of wonder in community public health programming on drug use and harm reduction. But my second day in the PPP van, our mobile site that we drive from neighborhood to neighborhood, was the day *Roe v. Wade* was overturned. Gabby and I were at our Friday site in an eastern neighborhood of the city; it was one of the hottest days yet, with participants waiting in long lines and under direct sun for water and supplies. As I rolled chore, a small bit of copper wool used for filtering crack, in my hands, as I put pipes and bowls into brown sandwich bags, I reflected on this chapter, flipped it around in my head, pressed on its theoretical semantics, and reckoned with how estranged it was from the reality of the moment I actually occupied. Gathering supplies into green plastic bags, I thought about *Roe* as a reckoning and how "reckoning," as a verb, is kin to recognition. To realize. To see. But reckoning is also a literacy event, a crossed threshold of understanding (the cognition in "recognition").[2] We can't go back. We can't unknow. To reckon with an event is to recognize and re-recognize how little we understand. But the ongoing renewal of recognition disturbs what is engrained; and this is an opportunity.

Eve Tuck and K. Wayne Yang endorse this tension; they encourage us to resist metaphor as a methodological and ethical commitment to keep working. In their piece, "Decolonization Is Not a Metaphor," they write, "He can only make his identity as a settler by making the land produce, and produce excessively, because 'civilization' is defined as production in excess of the 'natural' world (i.e., in excess of the sustainable production already present in the indigenous world)."[3] Part of capital's harassment toward production is to not only stimulate wealth and expansion (though clearly that), but to fantasize toward "easier paths to reconciliation" between settler and indigenous communities.[4] Solidarity *should* be unsettling (wordplay intended).

Our fixation on fix distracts us from the work at hand. The slip into metaphor "turns decolonization into an empty signifier to be filled by any track towards liberation. In reality, the tracks walk all over land/people."[5] Trans theorists argue along similar lines, that theory reshapes the trans person into allegory,[6] relegating one's lived experience to exoticized metaphors of transgression and marginalization. Overexposed yet not seen—this is a method I criticize throughout *Achy Affects*, human beings made into spectacle for the sake of telos and what that telos conjures: knowledge extraction. How do we write while refusing this extraction? How do we work toward liberation while refusing finality? Tuck and Yang argue that freedom is possible, and that while this possibility can be elaborated on through thought and theory, it cannot only be this. It is also particular and felt.[7]

This chapter is grounded in a form of auto-theoretical narrative, captured in fits and starts while assisting Prevention Point Pittsburgh with its syringe program but elaborated on as I returned from shifts and lingered in uneasy feelings and inconclusive thought. Maia Szalavitz, in offering one of the better definitions of harm reduction I've seen, describes it as non-teleological, work that is always evolving, breaching boundaries and disciplines, redefining itself according to current needs. I quote at length from her seminal book, *Undoing Drugs: The Untold Story of Harm Reduction and the Future of Addiction*: "At its core, harm reduction is a movement for the human rights of people who use drugs. However, those rights are impinged upon from every angle—by everything from racist laws and stereotypes that drive criminalization to stigmatizing, punitive, and incompetent 'treatment.' This meant that its ideas needed to be disseminated and understood across multiple disciplines and policy areas."[8] I understand my writing as participating in this dissemination. While so much grinding advocacy and diligent scholarship on the US opioid epidemic is being done in the public health and social work sectors, I offer just a small additional piece to this growing assemblage; I integrate affect studies to encourage a deeper approach to addiction, one that resists capitalistic constructions of the body that demand "productive," profitable futures. My aim in this chapter is to rethink precarity within the vibrant space of syringe programs by analyzing *wonder* as an overlooked affect and as a possible method for resisting telos, attenuating spectacle, and overturning binaried concepts of power (that is, we either have it or we don't). A methodology of wonder circumvents these issues to instead venerate the subject, honor their agency, and say "I see you" without attending to a fix. Wonder also gives us a frame for embracing difference without exploiting difference, for making complexity, rather than the human being, the object of analysis. Which is to say, wonder unsettles while it also renews; and I long to find a way to write into this idea.

All of this comes together to demonstrate why a methods chapter made itself necessary, and why it opens *Achy Affects*: wonder offers a way of being in the world and studying the world that refuses mastery, refuses dominant epistemologies that operate under an agenda of production. Whether in our writing (produce new ideas) or within our own skins (produce better health marks), we feel ourselves relentlessly invited into a kind of *making* that must establish an end, the research paper or portrait of health. Wonder instead stands with us in the myriad of crises, accepting the future as unknown but worth working toward.

I therefore engage forms that hold themselves accountable to the settler need for ease and the capitalist desire for outcome. As a white scholar I recognize (reckon with) myself as especially prone to these influences. In Vlad Glaveanu's summative text on wonder, he writes, "How does wondering help us engage with the possible? By making us aware of the fact that our experience of the world is one among many, and that the perspectives we develop in this world are exactly that—perspectives—not ultimate and singular truths."[9] Glaveanu celebrates particularity while humbling our positionality. We are limited by ourselves. This is not necessarily a problem. In fact, when we reckon with our limits, we welcome ways of thinking that are creative and uninterested in perfection or reconciliation.

This chapter then moves into my unease with prevalent methods of theorizing about marginality in the context of crisis, how capital and theory convene, and how it leads us into methods that demand teleological forms and generate spectacle around a single subject. I then briefly trace wonder through its philosophical history, from Descartes to Sara Ahmed, parsing out its potentials and limitations. This leads me into wonder as a methodological form that stays within the questions, resists punctuating argument, and recesses our theoretical labor so we might instead write affectively about the complex spaces we occupy as researchers, academics, thinkers. Finally, I braid this chapter with stories and descriptions from my work with Prevention

Point Pittsburgh to, as Glaveanu explains, illustrate a perspective that is not ultimate, just one of many.

My Beginnings

I want to be very clear about who I am and how I came into this work, which I hope to accomplish throughout *Achy Affects*; but I also want to be forthright here at the beginning, to locate myself in context. While I have personal, familiar (familial) experiences with addiction, I do not have the lived experience of attending exchange as a participant, of needing supplies such as needles or naloxone. I don't know life on the other side of the van. Instead, I came to this work while living in Oregon, working as a freelance writer. I was vocationally adrift, stringing a living together through temporary writing gigs, and longing for more connection. When I reached out to NEX, the syringe program in Eugene, I signed up to volunteer with their STI testing team, partnering mostly with queer clients seeking health resources. I also started staffing the syringe exchange on Monday nights, when we drove an old RV to the outskirts of town, setting up a table of needles and supplies, and pouring burnt Folgers in a large carafe. I immediately fell in love with work, smitten by the simplicity of meeting needs without condition.

I worked at NEX for two years before leaving Oregon to attend graduate school in Pittsburgh. I planned to study contemporary poetics and queer theory; but after my first year, I ached for those days in the RV and quickly pivoted into health humanities, researching the rhetorics of addiction and crisis in the US public imagination. I also, in a liminal and semi-private way, came out as trans at this time. This reckoning brought me to the current iteration of this book, in which I combine storytelling with theory to more broadly describe how, in this dense climate of capitalism, our bodies are forced relentlessly into explanatory labor.

I hope, in this chapter specifically but in the rest of the book as well, to honor the reality of my subjectivity while not centering only my experience, to also describe (with depth, humility, and ownership of my limits) the community within which I am involved. This form allows me—as Catherine Racine explains in her book on mental health, wonder, and autoethnography—to expose how the "ongoing dominance of 'scientific legitimacy' is entrenched in a positivist, *quantifying, reductive* worldview, despite the emergence of a good number of ideologies challenging its current authority."[10] This change in perspective, Racine says, shifts "the researcher's role from the 'privileged possessor of expert knowledge' to a collaborator and community member allied with her subject."[11] This is important to me, not just for the purpose of devaluing dominant methods of scholarship, but because the central tenet of harm reduction calls us to recognize the user of drugs, not the advocate, as the expert.

Joining Racine, I make my writing a practice for bridging life and theory, to prevent their stratification into parts. Which is another way of saying, I don't see or believe life and theory to be naturally distinct from one another. This form is made possible through the writings of Audre Lorde, Patricia Williams, Gloria Anzaldúa, Christina Sharpe, Saidiya Hartman, Sara Ahmed, and Maggie Nelson, among others. I found in these writers the shared desire to focus on life itself, and how it feels in all its confusion, beauty, and pain. "I do not believe the story of my scholarship is separate from the story of my life or the body I live," writes Stacey Waite.[12]

This is also about accountability. Lorde, in calling back to Paolo Freire, reminds us that the "true focus of revolutionary change is never merely the oppressive situations which we seek to escape, but that piece of the oppressor which is planted deep within each of us."[13] Ann Cvetkovich uses the term "academic memoir" and argues that such a genre, motivated by deconstructive principles, might "expose the material conditions and subject positions that underlie intellectual production."[14] She goes on to also say that this kind of writing "tries to be honest about the ways that activism can sometimes stall out in the routines of daily life, rather than offering revolution as a prescription for change. . . . It suggests that when asking big questions about what gives meaning to our lives, or how art or politics can promote social justice or save the planet, ordinary routines can be a resource."[15] I practice accountability to first describe the world, but to also own the reality that I describe the world as I see and participate in it. This requires vigilance of my complicity within the systems I criticize.

Working in Crisis

My last summer in Oregon we experienced a particularly brutal wildfire season, wherein winds dumped black smoke into the valley for days. The Columbia Gorge ignited during Labor Day weekend after a fifteen-year-old boy and his friends set off fireworks during a burn ban. Many hikers, myself included, were evacuated before the gorge was swiftly overtaken, but the Eagle Creek Fire went on to burn for months, smoldering through winter and even into May, resulting in 50,000 acres of decimation. The teen was fined $36 million for damages, an absurd amount allocated to represent and acquiesce public outrage.[16] I think often of those days, when the Willamette Valley was pressed under a cloud of cindered smoke, when at exchange we passed out needles wearing N95 masks to protect ourselves from the fire's fibers while participants, many unhoused, suffered through the haze, how public health officials said "the most vulnerable should stay indoors at all times." I think about how consequences migrate. I think about the public outrage, its force and attention, that though it was one boy who threw the firecracker, fossil fuel producers and their US congressional accomplices have been throwing a whole damn pyrotechnics show for decades. And I think, This is painfully common. One body blamed, a boy made into a spectacle and gratuitously punished while a community of vulnerable humans quietly suffered in the background. But the systems that assembled and enacted this kinetic moment?

Liz Montegary might call this a "manufactured crisis,"[17] when state and local governing authorities provide an optics of care under duress while, at the same time, diverting our attention to a singular subject and therefore away from systemic harm. Crisis and accountability are pinned to the individual rather than the governing body. Montegary quotes Lauren Berlant to argue that such work "organize[s] the reproduction of life in ways that allow political crises to be cast as conditions of specific bodies and their competence at maintaining health or other conditions of social belonging."[18] As we explored in the introduction, early eugenics told us that the singular body is not only the source of meaning (and money), but responsible for the categorizations projected onto it. The healthcare system has yet to fully divest from this thought, still looking toward behavior and quite literally the skin to make knowledge and define health.

The manufactured crisis does address a real crisis, but by focusing on individual human behavior rather than systemic behavior. Take, for example, the opioid crisis. Undeniably, opioids harm individual persons (though even this depends on the dose) and wider communities (and this depends on public health policy). But this harm is overexposed in order to conceal ongoing and intentional harm wrought by institutional (medical, legal, governing) policy and their influence on the social imaginaries of the people, who then learn to stratify drug use into moral and racialized codes. Studies have shown that the public still primarily blames individual users for addiction, but even that breaks down according to race and class.[19] "Simply put, it appears that heroin users are more believed to be responsible for their poor choices whereas those addicted to prescription pills are more likely to be seen as victims to the practices of prescribing doctors," argues one such study.[20] "Given the different levels of attributions among these two drugs, it begs the question of whether the public views these problems as separate and distinct rather than related."[21] They're related.

The manufactured crisis—and the energy it gathers through intra-connected networks of media, policy, and policing—manifests also in our writing and even in our activism. Trans studies, as an academic discipline but also an ongoing social issue receiving intense political and legal attention, endures a similar struggle. "Trans bodies only seem to become valuable as a warning to others, that is, only once they are made remarkable, in danger, or taken," argues Eliza Steinbock. This goes on to generate "a constant crisis mode of fear and hopelessness, rather than addressing the underlying structural problem of social stigma."[22] By invoking "crisis," one signals a form of time—the quick and urgent invasion of a threatening pathogen—but also designates a population as "those at risk" (the spectacle) and mandates the significance of solution (the telos): the user of drugs must get clean.

The focus on the singular—the trans "body" or the person with addiction—diminishes our imaginary spirit, simplifies our scope for collective complicity (but also collective suffering), and makes difficult our ability to see issues as related, not separate. Take, for example, those harsher judgments on heroin use versus prescription painkillers. The drug one chooses to use, powder or pill, is imbued with classist and racialized perceptions of addiction. Because the United States has an established legacy of criminalizing drug use, because the origins of the opioid epidemic statistically affected white and often rural communities, and because white patients are more likely to be prescribed pain relief, the racialization of opioid use can be traced through methodological efforts to locate the crisis of addiction in the singular despite the multiplicity of factors (I explore this in more depth in chapter 2). In an attempt to understand a complex epidemic through the lens of the individual, so much meaning and responsibility is put on the user of drugs.

I want to return to Cameron Awkward-Rich's question, which I offered in the introduction: "What would it mean to do minoritarian studies without being driven by the desire to rehabilitate the subjects/objects of our knowledge? What kind of theories would we produce if we noticed pain and, rather than automatically seeking out its source in order to alleviate it . . . if we instead took it as a fact of being embodied."[23] I am drawn to his question, as he suggests we embrace rather than discard impossibility to foster new methods of theorizing crisis, methods that refuse to reinscribe the marginalized. Because even the most pained subjects are made not only by their pain—they are beautifully formed by their wonder, their imaginations, and their desire. Awkward-Rich shelters this beauty by affirming ache as everyday. And "everyday" is not meant to minimize pain, especially the kind of pain wrought by systemic injustice. Instead, the everyday is Christina Sharpe's wake work.[24] It asks us how this kind of ache might reveal some of what it means to live within, respond to, maybe even resist the density of capital and its taxonomizing social world.

And also. Awkward-Rich asks quite pointedly, what would it mean not to rehabilitate? What would it mean to not seek comfort in rehab?

So this chapter is about methods—how we do our work, how we approach difference without making that difference exotic, a spectacle, without requiring it to speak its explanation. It is about how we understand our intentions and how that goes on to shape our writing. But this chapter is also about futures, which is to say, the *why* of our work. Why do we work toward creating better worlds by withholding telos? I understand these questions as questions about desire, not outcome, about the reveling,[25] as Kevin Quashie says, that gives us life, inspires us onward and restores us, over and over again.

Wonder and Where to Begin

Rooting wonder to an origin is a difficult task. According to Plato, and as spoken through Socrates, "wonder is the feeling of a philosopher, and philosophy begins in wonder."[26] Which is not to say that wonder begins with Plato, but that wonder begins in each of us. Centuries later, René Descartes would write, "I regard wonder as the first of all the passions. It has no opposite."[27] I love this—wonder as the ember and spark, a primal affect without comparison. Free from an opposite, wonder circumvents the bisection of feeling into positive and negative. Luce Irigaray understood this to mean that wonder is prior to judgment and therefore exempt from hierarchy, that it precedes knowledge even as it is excites imagination.[28] I agree with Irigaray until, unfortunately, she extends this idea into an archaic defense of the difference of sexes, wherein the Other is an object to be demystified. In so doing, wonder serves as a method that foments curiosity around otherness and condones explanatory demands in the face of difference. Here we return to the spectacle, in which our relationship to another reduces to them to their illegibilities. "This concept of wonder is dangerous," writes Iris Marion Young. "It would not be difficult to use it to imagine the other person as exotic."[29] Heeding Young, we will refuse wonder as a tool to embellish difference or demystify otherness into identifiable categories.

Maggie MacLure studies wonder as qualitative methodology in data re-search—a field far outside my own—as "a counterpart" to methods invested in classification and representation, those analyses that "make things stand still and separate out."[30] She goes on to explain how this form of research "is obsessed with sameness and the establishment of fixed, hierarchical relations among entities. It conceives of difference in terms of opposition between al-ready stabilized entities, rather than addressing the manifold movements of difference . . . and therefore cannot open onto the new or the unanticipated."[31] MacLure manages to hold onto difference without cleaving it into opposites, wherein one delineates another. Taking her definition of wonder from Lorraine Daston and Katharine Park's consummate treatise on the affect, *Wonders and the Order of Nature*, wonder, MacLure writes, is "preeminently material: it insists in bodies as well as minds. . . . It is a cognitive passion, 'as much about knowing as about feeling' . . . a passion [that] registered the line between the known and the unknown."[32] That line is ecstatic, that restless yet exciting rec-ognition of limitation (how little I know) and possibility (how much to learn). "We cannot know the world independent of ourselves, but within such vertigi-nous existence, knowing that we do not know, the next step becomes possible," writes Christian Wiman on faith, on what I would instead name wonder.[33]

Like MacLure, Sara Ahmed centers wonder within materiality. Arguing that this affect is too often intellectualized, made sublime when it is also felt and embodied, she writes, "Wonder is a passion that motivates the desire to keep looking; it keeps alive the possibility of freshness, and vitality of a living that can live as if for the first time."[34] Wonder both enlivens the felt self while seeding a grain of poetics in overturned soil, our fever minds racing to catch up to what our bodies already know. Wonder nourishes this relation-ship between our fever minds and buzzing bodies, offering itself as a way to pilot through a data-plastered world. Though this gives wonder a renewable energy, for some, it breeds skeptical hesitations. Glaveanu, for example, takes up after Hannah Arendt to inquire whether we might find in wonder a form of paralysis: "Does it lead to some kind of knowledge or keep us in a perpet-ual state of not knowing? . . . If wonder is not meant to solve problems but, on the contrary, to keep them open, then it risks being, within the Western scientific and philosophical tradition, 'progressively relegated to something like a temporary irritant: a discomfort not to be endured, but rather to be cured—or at least tranquilized.' Arendt warned, in this context, about the wonderer becoming disconnected from his or her social and political reality and, gradually, uncapable of forming opinions or making decisions."[35]

Lest we endanger wonder by creating for it compulsory cures, I must admit I empathize with these anxieties. To get about our work, we need to have some confidence in and knowledge of what we're doing. But I also differentiate the desire to know from the will to know. Michel Foucault tells us that Western theory instituted a never-ending demand for truth that creates systems of power maintained through the notion that knowledge is acquirable.[36] This engenders a will to know that privileges mastery over discomfort. But *a desire* to know understands knowledge as felt and fluid—we seek to learn more because we yearn to.

I, therefore, do not face the "perpetual state of not knowing" with anxiety. This fear of paralysis, of indecision or nonjudgment, materializes from distrust of antisocial behavior. It is a fear of inwardness and interiority, of taking or wasting one's time (I write more about this in my chapter on shyness). This fear is what Tuck and Yang spoke toward: that we will have to, at some point, enter into the uneasy feeling of non-reconciliation to see what might occur without conclusions, opinions, or judgments leading the way. While Plato, Descartes, and Irigaray give me some initial footholds into wonder, I build on Ahmed's insightful descriptions to broaden this affect's genealogy into non-elite spaces of living life where wonder privileges us to non-teleological and auto-renewing forms of imagination. Where wonder nurtures agency in a world that relentlessly works to strip us of agency as *felt*, as something we feel in our bodies and souls, and as lived, something we enact with intention in our communities. This theoretical work parallels the practical work of harm reduction.

Wonder in the Streets and Parking Lots of Pittsburgh

Prevention Point Pittsburgh was founded in 1995 by AIDS activists James Crow and Caroline Acker along with a handful of volunteers. In the late 1980s and early '90s, syringe exchanges were sprouting illegally across major US cities, such as New York, Chicago, and Philadelphia, due in large part to HIV activist groups like ACT UP. Prevention Point established its first site in the historic Hill District, operating underground when police presence and surveillance became too intense. Not until 2002, when the Allegheny County Board of Health finally declared both HIV and hepatitis C to be public health emergencies, did PPP gain legal rights to run its program. This board decision made syringe exchanges legal within county lines, which remains true today—only Allegheny and Philadelphia counties can legally operate exchanges within Pennsylvania's state-wide ban.[37] Many sites operate in similar environments across the United States, forcing residents to cross county or state lines, and to drive long distances or take public transit in order to access safe equipment. Those without easy access to exchange sites rely on organizations like NEXT Distro, an online and mail-based distributor. Or they reuse their equipment or pay for needles online or at the pharmacy, facing stigma and scrutiny.

Pittsburgh was one among many areas suffering the slow collapse of the steel and coal industries, where Purdue Pharma pushed OxyContin hard among other labor communities replete with chronic pain sufferers. As jobs were lost, people were in pain and some grew dependent on their meds. Pittsburgh's location at the intersection of the rust belt and Appalachia makes it indivisible from the origins of the US opioid epidemic. What began with a weekly syringe exchange in the Hill District grew into a schedule of five fully anonymous sites operating throughout the week, each in a different neighborhood, each now offering more than just sterile syringes. PPP facilitates case management assistance and provides drug treatment assistance, risk reduction counseling, overdose prevention, and free HIV and Hep C testing. Likewise, today participants can come to any or all of our sites to find sterile syringes, smoking equipment (pipes, chore, filters), injection works (cottons, alcohol pads, cookers), safer snorting kits, condoms and hygiene items, naloxone, and more. When participants arrive either to our physical site, consisting of a waiting area with two exam rooms, or to our van door at our mobile sites, they first check in with a PPP member who guides them through a short intake form, including what supplies they need. The form is then passed over to me to fill. Some days we have time to linger with each participant, and other days the line is long and we need to move fast. Still, little relationships bloom in those few moments of describing need and offering service.

The first time I worked the PPP van, it was June, and Pittsburgh brimmed with humidity. I crossed the Liberty Bridge, snaked through dense traffic and arrived to a Southside church parking lot right at noon. Fox, one of PPP's outreach specialists, gave me a two-minute rundown on the van while participants knocked on the door and he called back, "Give me another minute." We slipped into synched rhythm as he greeted participants and wrote down their supplies, sliding the order forms over to me, while I tried to move fluidly, organizing smoking equipment from injection works. I quickly memorized where each of our different gauged needles were stored, linking their names and size: 28-gauge, also called halves, also called 50s, because they're the only

50cc syringe we have; 27-gauge, also called pogos, our biggest syringe; but we also stock 31s, 29s, and 25s, called beestings, ultrafines, and blues.

The site was moving smoothly enough in the first half hour, until I confused our sandwich bag of chore for a participant's order. Chore, or Chore Boy, used as a crack pipe filter, is a coarse copper scouring pad that we disentangle, cut into pieces, and hand roll into balls. It is tedious labor to fill a bag and just like that, it was gone. As I tried to avoid obsessing and over-apologizing, despite the childlike heat of shame, of getting in the way, I started cutting new chore, rolling it into balls and dropping them into a new bag. During each lull, I rolled a few pieces and promised myself my fuckup was negligible: we can make more, chore is cheap, and, as Fox said, though with traces of frustration in his voice, I brightened someone's day with my mistake. Yet I failed to overcome the shit feeling of wanting to help but making it worse. This is fragility, no? To center my feeling in that moment is, of course, natural. My body is the body I occupy. To feel ourselves as fragile (vulnerable) is not the issue at hand. But rather, how we respond, whether our work follows the filaments of failure and fragility or whether it keeps on. Wonder asks me to reckon, to enter a state of failure without moralizing, without shame, and in so doing, to avoid overcorrection.

Some of our participants drive up from West Virginia and have since their state essentially banned all syringe programs. In 2021, West Virginia Senate Bill 334 passed state legislature, requiring all operating exchanges to apply to the Office for Health Facility and Licensure and Certification to continue operating. To do so, programs first need the support of the county commission *and* the county sheriff. And even if they receive both, they must conduct a 1:1 exchange and require photo identification.[38] Meaning, *non-anonymous* participants must bring needles to receive needles, and those needles will be traceable to their identities. Justifiably, our West Virginian participants arrive with huge orders, because they bring supplies back for their friends and family. One day, two brothers show up from West Virginia at 3:00 p.m., closing time. Fox and I have to ride the line between care and boundary-setting, which in the end are the same: maintaining a boundary is an act of care in that it, over lengths of time and reiterations, enacts stability. "I'll be here on Thanksgiving," I hear Fox say again and again to participants. To the two brothers, he sighs, says "I'll do this for you today, but in the future you gotta get here on time."

This stability is crucial to establishing trust and long-form relationships. The PPP van rolls into the same parking lots at the same time every week, regardless of heat index or national holidays. Ensuring the correct needles are in each participants' bag—this is also part of building trust. Harm reduction is, at its core, about consistency and unconditionality. In this way, the practice of harm reduction is simple in its terms: rather than insist on recovery or cures, rather than demand determined futures, harm reduction meets people in their moment of need. Harm reduction provides care without requesting one work toward recovery in order to access resources and services. Harm reduction links nonjudgment with non-coercive healthcare, describing drug use as multifaceted and located on a continuum. If traditional healthcare has privileged the cured condition, then harm reduction dismisses the telos of capital time (that there should be some product, some end state) to instead take up the temporal uncertainties of the moment. What does this look like in the van? The protection of repetition over recovery, every time.

On a busy Thursday after the July Fourth holiday, Fox and I gave out 12,620 syringes at the Southside mobile site. "That's got to be a PPP record," he said. Despite the long lines of people waiting, Fox kindly took his time with each participant. He walked them through what an overdose looks like, how to rake your knuckles against someone's sternum to see if they're non-responsive. "If you call 911, don't say it's an overdose. Just say they're unresponsive," he says, wise to the fact that despite the Good Samaritan laws in Pittsburgh, cops will still show.[39]

While Fox smoked during a rare break in activity, he told me the Allegheny Health Network received a $5 million SAMHSA grant a few years ago. SAMHSA (the Substance Abuse and Mental Health Administration) operates within the US Department of Health and Human Services to address issues of mental health and substance use across the country. They outline their opioid relief goals as "combating" the crisis through the "expansion of prevention, treatment, and recovery support services."[40] Meaning, SAMHSA works toward outcome, privileging recovery (sobriety) over reduced harm. Fox told me that the money goes to the Allegheny Health Network, but they don't know how to allocate or utilize it. "None of those doctors or grad students have experience at street level," he said, leaning his body half out of the van to ash into the parking lot. When I asked how those without harm reduction experience get access to such crucial positions of authority, Fox responded flatly, "Education."

Fox and I were talking about knowledge, how some forms are valued over others, how higher-education items on a résumé elevate one into secure positions of regulation and supervision. But, as Fox noted, this is education, not knowledge. (To be clear, I am the person with education, but not knowledge. I'm working on it.) I see from my time in the van how well-equipped Fox is to help our participants. When they don't like the brand of beestings we have available (31-gauged needles used mostly on hands or feet), he advises them on how best to find a new spot for injection. He makes them laugh when he pulls the loop of his suspenders around his bicep into a tourniquet. He tells them that despite what the doctors say, *you can* still use while getting treated for Hep C—"the doctors are lying to you."

I move further into my discomfort: I am a nonexpert who loves both the practice and feel of harm reduction. While I want to share this or share in this, I don't want to co-opt it. I'm trying to reckon with my position as a writer from the university who moves into a community that is both familiar and not mine. I own that I am the grad student Fox criticizes. "Knowing that we do not know makes the next step possible."[41] Owning it allows me to wonder how we might attenuate the distance, share the knowledge, respect expertise outside the confines of the traditional and conventional. Like our other achy affects, wonder is both felt and done. It feels like awe, yes, but it also feels overwhelmed, uncertain, desiring, and elusive. Wonder is an active openness, a position of embracing and inviting uncertainty, the slow or cold take, the run-on sentence or poetic line break.

Liberation Is the Size of a Ball of Chore

A couple years ago, I walked my dog to the Presbyterian churchyard a few blocks from home, one of her favorite neighborhood spots—bustling with bunnies and squirrels, a quiet place to romp with other dogs. On this day, it was just us. The sun was out and beaming its warmth, but the temperature was only just above freezing. Headphones in, I took slow breaths. I was weathering another depressive season. Depression has seized months and years of my life, a genetic inheritance and daily familiarity.

As I took slow breaths, listening to Elliott Smith sing about rose parades, I sensed within the sadness also a gentle strum. Despite the depression, I was not numb, but neither was the strum full or forward-leaning, just thin vibration, the dim hint of vibrance. For years I have tried to train myself away from fixing the depression. While I work toward management—sobriety, running, therapy, family, meds, writing—I resist the pull into telos, that one day I will "feel better," and on that day, I will move into the rest of my life. It requires constant vigilance to keep this idea at bay, to refocus on temporal care. So I tuned into this moment in the churchyard with my dog. In all my threadbare energy, I thought, *I am here*. To survive despite our pain (pain from being alive but also from systemic erasure and harm), we must be able to say *I am here*. It is a short phrase that insists on existence, that says: I take up space, I participate in world-making. *I am here* exists on its own, establishes its own agency. We are its makers.

The feeling of wonder is not just the feeling of awe, the captivation of wild landscapes or the sun falling under the ocean's rim at twilight. Wonder is a quiet strum in a churchyard with a tender hound bounding after rabbits. Meaning, wonder intimates an opening. We might be energized by a song stumbled upon on the radio or by changing the tire on our car. We might be galvanized by caffeine as we muster toward the start of the day, or beer as we linger in the kitchen with friends. But no matter, all of this is taking up space in the world, saying *I am here*.

José Esteban Muñoz promises we protect our futural longings by, counterintuitively, un-engineering the future. While one of our goals at PPP is to help participants envision realistic recovery, it is not the primary goal, which is to reduce harm and overdose and to abate stigma and disease in our community. In so doing, we may not be working toward a future absent addiction, but a future absent the violence surrounding addiction. This kind of temporality, writes Muñoz, is ecstatic and horizonal, "a path and movement to a greater openness to the world."[42]

For Muñoz, who is writing specifically about queerness, our utopic futures are, obviously, not quite here and yet an always existing potentiality. He destabilizes our attachments to liberation *while also working toward liberation*. This is why I call on him now. His understanding of freedom entails willful immersion in an "ontologically humble state, under a conceptual grid in which we do not claim to always already know."[43] This, he argues, might "potentially stave off the ossifying effects of neoliberal ideology,"[44] that which brings us only allegories of and metaphors for liberation. Though criticized for daring to optimistically situate the future as utopic possibility, some of us also choose these optimisms; some of us cultivate these optimisms because we refuse to forfeit our lives into the constraints of one-dimensional narratives of precarity, pain, and otherness.[45] We are more; we deserve more.

I am troubled by the word "liberation." It announces so much telos, too much to make itself viable. What does it take, then, to turn toward ontological humility in order to not only go about our research but also enjoy the aesthetic joys of composition? MacLure offers, "It is this liminal condition, suspended in a threshold between knowing and unknowing, that prevents wonder from being wholly contained or recuperated as knowledge, and thus affords an opening."[46] If we cannot escape the systems in which we are so deeply and forcefully embedded, what do we do? What is liberation, a word with its reach boiled off, when we're burned out? How might wonder become a method for thinking, writing, and dreaming about liberation without simplifying the work of liberation? We roll the chore and refill the bag. As I roll Chore Boy, I think, *Liberation is the size of a ball of chore.* It is the ball of chore. It is the smallest bit of stinging copper wool that brings an inch of less harm into this world. I seem as if I'm romanticizing (or metaphorizing), but I mean to intimate the opposite—that liberatory work is tiny, incremental, repeating. This patient laboring might not satisfy us in the way the collapse of an industrial complex would, but it is what we do while we wait for collapse.

While emotional valves open their mouths when I stand in Pacific Northwest rainforests—the scent of moss, the ferns unfolding their tiny fists, the centricity of time in Douglas firs—I do not wish to relegate wonder to exceptional scenes of the sublime. "I am moved by wonder, certainly, but from a place of innocence to a place of ambivalence and critique—my innocence is *contaminated* through this process."[47] My pumping pathos valves in the old-growth forest mimic my everyday life as a writer, activist, advocate, and academic: when wonder expands, so also does our understanding of complexity; as wonder expands, the more we come to understand how little we know—we are contaminated by our illiteracy. Wonder is a fractal of feeling that enflames our limitations, and then takes pleasure in them. But this is also why it hurts. The sense of excitement incited by growth and change (those painful things) keeps us returning to our work. We have to rewrite the thesis or apologize for our errors; we try and try again.

Another record broken: Gabby looked over the forms from a Friday in August, elbows propped on the van's built-in counter, and calculated. They told me we already saw 100 participants, nearly 70 in the first half of the shift. This sounded right; the moment I jumped into the van, we moved fast. I pulled needles out of boxes, lined up the equipment, filled orders, and sent bags out the back door. For the first hour, Gabby and I didn't say a word to one another—we were that busy. Too busy, I got behind on order forms and a participant walked away with a bag of tampons she didn't ask for. Later, when the activity calmed, Gabby and I laughed at the idea of surprise tampons, but I also dreaded that it meant more mistakes were made. Each Friday was busier than the last, a trend that raised the question of how to meet need when we're ostensibly at capacity. Not surprisingly, I continued to make mistakes each shift.

The next week, a participant complained to Gabby. "Man, y'all forgot my fent strips last week." Meaning, *I* forgot his fentanyl testing strips. He was rightly frustrated. "People are dying out here." I put extra strips in his bag, rechecked his order form twice to ensure I got it right, and jumped out the back door. We're far too busy for me to do much more than pass bags out the back, but I couldn't let it go, especially his words. "People are dying out here." I hopped out of the van, walked up to him chatting with a friend, and interrupted to apologize. "Holler at me if I ever get something wrong, OK?" When he put his arm around my shoulder in a gentle side hug, relief deflated the tension. But I spent weeks wondering what consequences rippled from my serious mistake. I'll never know. Every week I hear about someone who died. Every week I hear about someone saved from naloxone.

Wonder is how we write into openness, resisting easy conclusions and privileging descriptive and narrative emphasis of scenes, systems, and feelings rather than the immutable analytics of a subject-made-object. Throughout *Achy Affects* and with each affect analysis, I attempt to illustrate the mundane and quotidian as worthy sites for doing theory, that the spectacle or spectacular need not animate our writing. This method is particularly common in both addiction and trans studies; whether we marvel at the transgressive performance of the "trans body" (see chapter 3) or grimace at the ways heroin has created "a new face" of addiction (see chapter 2), the spectacle violates embodiment to stimulate (or simulate) knowledge production. This is why I do affect studies. This is why I find myself compelled to speak on behalf of my own "trans body," to refuse overexposing our subject, and why harm reduction captures the kind of community I hope to replicate: relationships bonded through liminality, through shared knowledges, practices, and protection.

Voice, Subject, Spotlight

Late in summer I arrived at the Southside site to find Casey, who usually works the medical van facilitating suboxone, in our supply van. Fox was testing positive for COVID, so Casey stepped in for the afternoon to cover. "Have you done intake in the van before?" they asked. "Does that feel OK?" While I've done intake before, it's never been in the van, where it's faster at ground level. "No problem," I responded. I sat on the cooler in the van's doorway, clipboard in hand, and greeted folks. "Hey, how's it going?" A simple question that will open in any direction. I began with small chat about the dailyness of things, the weather, but also participants' needs. When they said their day was shit, I asked what we could do, if anything. Sometimes it's nothing. I answered questions on what needles we have. "These are the shortest gauge, mostly used on hands and feet." I registered new participants, including those recently settled in the city. "We have fentanyl test strips, but just so you know, most of the heroin here has fent in it."

I'm comfortable with intake except for when it comes to the Narcan forms. Each time we give out Narcan, we're instructed to fill out two pages of paperwork that includes questions such as "What drugs have you done in the past month?" It's crucial we do the paperwork, in that it facilitates ongoing research and gives us new insight into our region's dope supply—how potent new bags are, what to look for, which bags led to overdose, what has tranq in it.[48] I scanned the form quickly, but it was prolix and the line of people was growing. "Hey, should I ask all of these questions, or which are the most important?" I asked, looking up at Casey as they rolled pipes in a sandwich bag. After a beat, we decided to call Fox, who replied, "Man, fuck those questions. Make it a conversation." A classic response from Fox and I admire him for it. But it was my first time giving out Narcan and translating questions into conversation did not come naturally. I understood what Fox meant, why he insisted on conversation over punctuated questions. The former puts participants at ease, relieves them from the idea (the reality) that they're being interrogated. Conversations also engender an affective space wherein we feel that harm reduction and safer use practice is on all of us, not just the user.

At a different site later in the fall, a couple approached the van door to chat with Gabby. They laughed together while waiting in line, elbows playfully checking ribs. "We need more Narcan," they said. "For sure," Gabby replied. "Did you have to use some recently?" We give out dozens of Narcan kits each week, each kit comprised of two doses. The couple described how they were walking through a 7-Eleven parking lot and saw an unresponsive man in his car. They not only could ID an overdose; they not only had Narcan on them; they not only felt uninhibited to knock on his window, open the door, and shake him; they not only used their Narcan on him and saved his life; but they noted what bag of dope he had used. They passed this info on to us so Gabby could add it to our bag board—a whiteboard with the names and notes of the different strains of dope in our region (e.g., "Stranger Danger," found in McKeesport, causes ODs; "Tom and Jerry" causes racing hearts). Gabby responds, "I'm so glad you were there. Thanks for taking care of the community." They say this each time a participant tells us about using Narcan. Each time. Later Gabby leans over to me, reflecting on this story, and says, "Imagine that, a community that cares for itself without the fucking need for cops or doctors."

"You can say 'pass' on any question or make up an answer altogether." I repeat these lines, lines I learned from others working our sites, when I register a new participant to our program. Our new participant forms ask about injection practices, HIV and Hep C status, and length of drug use. The questions are uncomfortable, but the answers helpful. We want our participants to use more safely; knowing if they share needles or if they clean their injection sites affects the information and supplies we might provide. But offering an opt-out, saying "pass" or making up answers (which might skew data) sustains their privacy, their desire (if they have it) to move quickly through our site.

No surprise then that I don't interview any of our participants when writing about my work at PPP. I don't seek any kind of acceptance from the IRB. On the one hand, it should be the voices of participants that drive and form policy decision. It should be their voices we listen to when we want to better understand not just addiction, but their lives in all their assembled, multivalent, knotted beauty. Absolutely. But also, one of the most important aspects of practicing harm reduction is the protection of unconditionality. Regardless of a participant's status, they deserve access to the resources they need without rule or condition. They do not have to give us anything in order to receive supplies and aid, whether it is a promise toward recovery, a detergent bottle filled with used needles, or a completed survey.

The invitation to interview creates conditions and exhausts an already exhausted community. Summerson Carr explains how those who use drugs and those in recovery or rehab services are relentlessly encouraged to *share*.[49] Sharing is made compulsory to healthcare access and consigned to proper recovery: one is lauded as a good participant if they are active, divulging members of the community. But we should question why we require intimacy, what we get from vulnerable sharing that feeds us as researchers or advocates. By inviting a participant to interview, even if they have the option to decline, even if *they desire* an interview, I attenuate our shared space with reciprocality. Which is not to say we don't create meaningful relationships with our participants. We do; but we don't foster those relationships on mutual give and take.

This substantially influences how I write about harm reduction and drug use, what I offer and what I withhold. I long for others to understand the dynamic lives of people who use drugs, especially beyond scripted narratives of powerless addiction. But I long also to protect my participants. They are my priority. They deserve privacy as well as representation and a generosity of attention. They deserve a voice but also the option to opt out, to let others educate themselves. This is difficult, but also an opportunity to move our writing further into complexity, not resolution.

While I began Narcan paperwork for a woman re-upping her supply, she told me her friend died the day before. "They're dropping like flies," she said, exhausted. I felt the need for cohesion rise to the surface; I want to help, to make it better. But I can't. There is no making better a lost life. So I let it go. Instead, I looked her in the eyes and said, "I'm so sorry." And when she started to cry, I held our silent moment together. There's nothing to say and that's OK. I've learned (through my own painful experiences) that when tragedy hits, we do not expect others to make sense of it. What we most need is to be seen and heard. I've written that pain is quotidian (see chapter 4), by which I don't mean trivial or inconsequential. I mean it is every day. Christina Sharpe called it a wake.[50] Crisis without end. There was nothing else to do than be with that woman in that very short, shared moment. She lost someone. We lost someone.

Enabling Possibility, Enabling Life

Overdose is the leading cause of death for Americans under 50.[51] *The* leading cause. A few years ago, an Ohio town attempted to pass three-strikes legislation that would disallow EMS from responding to an overdose victim who had already been Narcan-ed twice before.[52] While most people (around 88 percent) agree Narcan is an important part of emergency kits, about half of people also believe it enables ongoing drug use,[53] that users will take more risks, bigger doses. But Narcan sends one into immediate withdrawal with symptoms such as extreme nausea, body aches, head pain, and more. It's terrible; and no one wants to risk getting Narcan-ed (or overdosing, for that matter). But even this is beside the point. These are human lives who deserve infinite chances to survive. Recently, as a participant waited for his ride, he talked with me and Fox about being out here to get supplies for his brother. "My family and friends think I'm enabling. But you can't save someone who's dead," he said. The first page on our PPP training packet says, "Harm reduction enables choices, possibilities, and opportunities." Harm reduction enables one into a future of infinite potential. "Infinite potential," meaning life itself.

I opened this chapter with an epigraph from Kevin Quashie, who writes, "Standing up for one's self doesn't have to be triumphant, but can be, simply, the work of reveling in flowers or blue sky—the daily practice of understanding what you love and why."[54] I appreciate how Quashie describes reveling as work. Harm reduction, in my opinion, offers one of the more thoughtful ways through the quagmire of American life in this moment. We are over-policed, literally and medically. We suffer the physical and mental consequences of a climate crisis, yet affordable healthcare remains out of reach. We are over-entertained and isolated. We are discarded bits of hustle and stress falling into an ever-expanding economic gap. Harm reduction *sees* the systemic relationship between these issues, and while holding out hope for long-term overhauls it practices a dailyness of care that gets us through a pandemic, a crisis, or even just a shit day. Both intensely temporal—focused on current need and service—and horizonal, in that it works toward futures with a commitment to safety, community, and trust, harm reduction is similar to how we think about our research and our writing without telos, or with delayed or withheld telos. We are, of course, writing and thinking *toward* something, but we let that object evade us so that knowledge drags out in front of us, not for capture but for the experience of dwelling within it. This is wonder renewing itself. Likewise, harm reduction engages the problem by staying within it, by not driving toward over-simplified solutions. It is not a radical politics, harm reduction, though it is hard to convince even progressives the importance of syringe programs. And yet, harm reduction *is* radical because it never abandons the simple claim that our lives have meaning. Without condition. We are here.

2

The Spectacle of Shame

Resisting Cure in Crisis

I didn't yearn for anything but privacy
because it is an embarrassment to be a wound in public.

—Billy-Ray Belcourt

I should have known. Two weeks in Alaskan backcountry, where the sun skimmed the rim of the horizon only to rise back into August sky, brought us as close as we would ever be—two animals bent into the empty space of one another. When making dinner Michael and I sat on our bear canisters facing each other, vigil to our own horizons, scanning for predators. We were careful not to lean into dinner's line of smoke and steam. The fibers on our clothes could hold the scent and call out to animals miles away, even hours later. So, we cooked one hundred yards downwind from camp. And one hundred yards in the other direction, he hid our bear canisters under a fir tree. Midway through our trip Michael and I walked along a high ridgeline of loose scree, moving slow and with caution, using trekking poles to stabilize our footing. We crawled, sediment under our fingernails as the side of the mountain gave way hundreds of feet below to the Savage River. After a half day of this, Michael and I finally came down the ridgeline into a green valley where boulders with mossed backs hunched into earth. But in the same moment of beautiful relief, we saw a sign from park rangers: "Wolf den harboring pups— turn back." We looked at one another, each registering the other's devastation. It would require hours to trek back across the scree in the dim of twilight; it would drain the last of our energy to unfurl mental fortitude in the wake of regression. We turned back.

When Michael and I moved to Oregon six months into our marriage, I was quickly infatuated with the alpine wildflowers, the volcanic obsidian rock fields, the turquoise streams and wet smell of moss, ferns uncurling as early as February, and the quiet calm of the natural world doing its own thing. My first summer in Oregon I knew I wanted even more wild—more remote, more remove. The following spring Michael and I used our tax refunds to book flights to Anchorage. *More wild*. I name this now as desire, as yearning that breaks open into more yearning—a fractal felt in the skin, but also as a state of dreaming that does not exhaust itself.

After weeks in Denali backcountry (what was meant to be a vacation but turned into two weeks of hypervigilance, bushwacking, and sore bodies) Michael and I returned to Oregon with avid appetites. We decided to celebrate our safe return with a homemade meal of salmon, roasted vegetables, garlic couscous, and cheap pinot grigio poured generously into coffee mugs. It was then, finally, after feeling secured by surviving the backcountry with Michael and warmed by two-dollar wine, that I came out to him. Folding into myself under the weight of shame, I told him I was gay, that I had known for a while, but this knowing was diaphanous and delicate, a thin feeling. "Queer desires become an injury to the family," writes Sara Ahmed. "In this way, shame is related to melancholia, and the queer subject takes on the 'badness' as its own, by feeling bad about 'failing' loved others."[1] Michael and I could weather loose scree, wolf dens, and backtracks. We were a team and we loved one another. But it was not enough and I failed him; in my badness and desire, I failed him. *I should have known* became shame's echo.

Foundations of Shame

Shame studies has given us affect studies. Silvan Tomkins, often considered the first contributor to the discipline, devoted three chapters to shame in his seminal volume, *Affect Imagery Consciousness*, published in the early 1960s.[2] Since then, many have followed in his steps to expand affect beyond the field of psychology, to theorize feeling as a political, social, and aesthetic analytic;[3] shame tagged along the entire way. I make of this an attraction to shame, that despite its awkward pain, scholars continue its study because of how much it inflicts and infects, how it fills the space it is in, permeating the cracks and fractures. "The very physicality of shame—how it works on and through bodies—means that shame also involves the de-forming and re-forming of bodily and social spaces," writes Ahmed.[4] Shame contaminates in its hot flush of deviance and blinding exposure, materializing from the depths of us, yet spreading through our multivalent ecosystems as social residue, webbing us to one another in sticky conditions of insecurity, vulnerability, and need. Shame exposes our cultural attachment to the "spectacular truth of bodies,"[5] wherein we look to the skin for meaning, especially if that meaning identifies the pathological, excessive, or abnormal, all categories clarified through the mediation of difference. Shame shapes us; shame destroys us.

In this chapter I join shame studies to argue that shame arrests the animative range of our imaginations, contorting a subject's boundaries, drawing lines around who we dream ourselves to be for the sake of productivity and profit. While wonder inspires creative schemes for surviving crisis, shame shuts us down. When longing toward more wild—exploration, discomfort, multiplicity—shame shrinks us to the tight confines of premediated narratives: once a fuckup, always a fuckup. Eve Sedgwick describes shame as semiotic rupture, in that it "floods into being as a moment, a disruptive moment," as "a form of communication."[6] What does shame communicate? What knowledge does it produce?

In this chapter I take up these questions by analyzing shame's rhetorical manipulations at the intersections of healthcare, drug use, and media. I illustrate how shame is used to coerce people into corrective forms of healthcare by overexposing our decisions, behaviors, and bodies and demanding productive futures. As I've worked syringe exchanges, I've witnessed how historical and social constructions of health in the United States hurt the material realities of all of us, but especially those who use drugs, who, under this regime of wellness and optimization, are exploited to mark the risks of social deviation. At exchange programs we strive to silence shame through care, respect, and an attention on agency rather than expectation. We hold vulnerability and empowerment together, not as opposites. This chapter, then, is not about transforming shame into something more palatable; I am uninterested in rehabilitating aches into arrival. Rather, I am critical of language producing shame and injuring the body by forcing it into demarcated ends. Specifically, national rhetoric around opioid use took up the spectacle, the single subject to conceal the systems of harm—the legacy of the War on Drugs, inhumane drug policies, the profiteering by Big Pharma—to conjure a specific threat: who is it? Who is at risk? And what will we all lose? Again and again, the answer came back coded in whiteness, inspired by capital's dictation of time, and mobilized through shame.

Time Is Money: Becoming a "Productive Member of Society"

The beginnings of my work in harm reduction coincide with the end of my marriage. During the divorce I sought ways to keep busy, so I signed up to volunteer with a local nonprofit (NEX) in Eugene, Oregon, that provided health services to queer people, people who use drugs, and those living with HIV or Hep C. On Mondays I helped at syringe exchange and on Wednesdays I ran the STI testing site. In training to become an outreach worker I learned a lot: how to administer naloxone, how Hep C lives outside the body for up to six weeks, how detergent bottles make useful sharps containers. But most importantly, I learned our most formidable opponent to care was not (or not solely) lack of funding, bad state policy, or the Eugene police, but stigma.[7] In our small Willamette Valley community (like most communities), stigma around drug use prevents easier access to healthcare and community resources. For example, though pharmacies offer syringes and Narcan over the counter, those who use drugs often face judgment and worry about legal repercussions: "I just wouldn't feel comfortable talking about syringes with them [pharmacists] because then they're going to look at me differently every time I go in there," laments a user of drugs in a study that surveyed stigma's effect on utilizing pharmacy resources. "You can just tell by the person's demeanor and their attitude and everything changes towards you, like, kind of just like get me out of the way, and they know what I'm there for type of thing," says another.[8]

Stigma's role in the clinic is both historical and epistemological.[9] One year after Tomkins published his treatise on affect, Erving Goffman famously defined stigma as an "ideology to explain" inferiority, a method to account for danger and rationalize "hate based on differences."[10] This very definition describes a curation of beliefs that center an othered body. Whether it's BMI or bruised injection sites, the medical industry authorizes pathology as a legitimate field of study, through which the category of "health" is reinforced as an imperative, a goal we must relentlessly work toward, but also an ever-changing expectation. Issued through pathologizing rhetoric that sets up the patient to either succeed or fail, stigma indicates one's progress toward (or recession from) the healthy state. We remember that Colleen Derkatch writes, "What it means in contemporary Western culture to be 'well' is predicated on the entanglement of seemingly opposed logics that together create an essentially closed rhetorical system where wellness is always a moving target."[11] Jasbir Puar defines debilitation as a process that situates the body near its own possibilities (what it is or should be) while simultaneously naming that body as failing.[12] At the very expense of our bodies, in order to manipulate our decisions over our bodies, agency is revoked under the auspice of agency given. Shame teaches us these social codes; and we learn that to veer from those codes is dangerous.

We need not venture far to see stigma dictating our bodies in clinical spaces. We most likely need not go beyond our own lives, remembering an event when a healthcare provider told us to do better or dismissed our pain and claims altogether. Bullied by guilt and embarrassment, we shrink under the scolding of state paternalism, that vexed parent leering down at us to facilitate better behavior. Shame makes us feel small; and to feel small is to feel infantilized, reprimanded, and dismissed—the one who knows better putting us in our place while taking control. "Small" also conjures the body as contained, even unseen or unremarkable. Meaning, shame vacillates between an external voice and the internalized echo of that voice. For the person using drugs, stigma ensures that the cessation of use is the only legitimate option for one's relationship to drugs. Even more nefariously, stigma normalizes the racialization of drug use by making a spectacle out of addiction and stratifying people into categories of delinquency (more on this later in the chapter).

The objectives of NEX followed national and international definitions of harm reduction: to provide care and services without coercion, judgment, or demand.[13] Intervention, as a harm reduction principle, has more to do with creating communities through trust than the cessation of drug use; it enacts the belief that we should meet one another where we are—in the process, in the middle of things—to form community around anonymous and free services. Four days a week, NEX offered HIV, Hep C, and STI testing: a swab of the mouth or a finger prick, and then participants waited twenty minutes for results. Many paced the waiting room, crossing from one end to the other, pivoting, and back again. I smiled weakly from my position at the desk to validate without also giving too much attention. But their itch ricocheted around that cramped space, summoning anxiety in the rest of the waiting bodies. Twenty minutes to wait for a test result is too long, and I felt it too. As time spooled out, as the swab soaked in its pool, there was nothing we could do but wait. One night a man arrived during testing hours to ask for a single sterile syringe. The waiting room was full. "They come in packs of ten," I said, handing him the rubber-banded bundle. Tearing one from the rest, he declined the pack to insist this was his last hit. "I'm done with it. On to better days." We remember the sheriff of Butler County, Ohio, who refused to provide naloxone to his emergency teams because, while naloxone saves lives, it doesn't "cure" those lives. His rhetoric demonstrates the fatal implications of an imagination formed by the principles of capitalism. Socially distressed around those who may not project healthy futures, we've been trained into pathologizing the nonproductive.

The man at NEX stayed for my whole shift, drinking Folgers out of a Styrofoam cup and talking through his ache and fever despite flirting with the line of withdrawal. "I'm sorry, I'm sorry," he said, then promising over and again he was "better than this," that this one needle was his last. He made the waiting room look at its shoes with his anxious chatter, his unpredictable gesticulations, the heat he generated through his embarrassment. Whether it was his last hit or not, his struggle surfaced through the affective pressure of shame. His promises were apologies.

Shame is a mobilizing force, extremely useful in sustaining dominant narratives of normative health and directing patients into preordained treatments. From trans people forced to drop weight to receive top surgery to those using drugs who are forced to sober up in order to access Hep C meds, vulnerability is exploited—compressed into the flushed feeling of shame—to motivate one toward desired ends. In both scenarios, the medical professional offers an immutable objective while rescinding his own responsibility for care. Drop weight, get clean, and then receive the services you so desperately need. Because capital cannot compute *process without teleology* (a middle without end), we sense our survival is contingent on labor and secured through the conceit of overcoming failure. This is the story of the body under the coercive forces of wellness culture, US healthcare writ large, and capitalist logics, the body as both vehicle and victim to the American Dream.

To be clear, though healthcare is a corrective and not a collaborative institution, our healthcare teams *do* know more, having trained for years to provide informed care. As I already argued, we are not trying to destroy the clinic but instead to cultivate broader imaginations for care that are not motivated by profit, and to prioritize knowledge beyond the elite, impartial, and nonnegotiable. Under the expanse of healthcare's authority our felt selves diminish, those who know better declaring who we are by how we present. In our most vulnerable conditions and within the clinical space of needed care, who are we to reject our given diagnoses? Capital logics—ways of thinking influenced by the structure and demands of the market—naturalize our attachments to teleological health while also replenishing the ongoing harms wrought by state policy, of which the legacy of the War on Drugs is a flagrant example.

Whether through national policy, mainstream media, or the medical industry, we hear the same drama on drug use rescripted: choosing drugs over family and work, the person who uses is selfish and stalled out, waiting around for a fix, stuck in a habit. Derrida explains this plainly in that it is "always nonwork that is stigmatized."[14] Under the contract of capital, we come to understand time through signposts: educational achievement, vocational stability, property attainment, and familial growth, and in this order. These signposts script pathology from normativity to impose a linear or right way of moving through life—one signpost issues another, while straying from the path indicates deviance or disorder, regression, or relapse. That is, one either works toward healthy futures or stalls out. Elizabeth Freeman argues that the body is the figure through which linear time appears. She calls this chrononormativity, "the use of time to organize individual human bodies toward maximum productivity."[15] As long as we clarify ourselves *and* our future, and as long as those clarifications endorse and ensure capital gain, we're doing the right thing, making the respectable choice, *being* good. We extrapolate "good" to mean many things, including healthy, sober, and responsible. But "good" unequivocally means productive, that we are working and by working securing an economic future. Under the duress of constant capital, we become good beings through the aisles of the market, through the accumulation of unused sick days. Time is money, after all.

Under a false optics of care, capitalism trains us to think in terms of product and productivity, an outcome or happy ending. It is better to be dead than alive and using because we assume drug use renders a failed life. More than 120 people die in the United States each day from an opioid overdose, and more than 100,000 died in 2022 alone;[16] but because of a national imaginary forged by capitalist logics, those deaths get dismissed as expected outcomes of nonproductivity. The language that circulates—through national and local media as well as in policy legislature—codes drug-using communities as wasted and wasting away against ongoing recursions of the "hardworking" citizen. The term "cure" affirms positive outcomes and profitable futures by, for example, forcing those who use drugs to submit to recovery models in order to access lifesaving resources and services (e.g., syringe exchange and anti-craving medications).

When I was training to work with NEX, my first lesson was rhetorical: what we say can have direct impact on our participants' lives. If participants excitedly shared their sobriety with us, we were not encouraged to celebrate alongside them. We could ask how they were feeling but could not congratulate or affirm their sobriety, because that celebration secured a punctuation mark. Such language endorsed outcomes and reinforced cultural expectations of recovery. If the participant relapses (and statistically most do), they may remember that celebratory remark and resist assistance later if needed, apprehensive about disappointing in a culture that is only disappointed with drug use. Similarly, we were trained to challenge the weight of words like "clean" and "addict," how even subtly these reiterations crystallize a broader social understanding of drug use—that it is dirty and antisocial, passive and apathetic. This stigmatizing language not only reinforces stereotypes on drug use, but it makes attaining services more difficult for those not working toward recovery. Federal policy, both its regulations and rhetorics, charts drug use as either criminal or disordered behavior, thereby privileging corrective rehabilitation as the only state response to the opioid crisis.[17]

The Racialization of a Crisis

In late capitalism, as profits now charge through data aggregations, influencer networks, and digital labor, some are left behind; some are still enduring the slow collapse of the steel or coal economies in, say, Appalachia. It is not a coincidence this region also marks the origin of the US opioid epidemic. Purdue Pharma pushed OxyContin hard in poor, rural labor communities replete with chronic pain sufferers, promising in its earliest TV ads that Oxy "gets you back to work."[18] This was just a few years before David Harvey famously pointed out that the West defines sickness as "the inability to work," echoing Derrida's earlier diagnosis of addiction.[19]

While the United States has witnessed (and produced) drug epidemics before, nothing parallels the magnitude of the opioid crisis in terms of overdose numbers, the explosive rate of prescriptions, and new articulations of addiction-catalyzing shame. Indeed, the crack epidemic of the 1980s in many ways cannot be compared to the current opioid crisis, and not just concerning scale, but in terms of state response, cultural discourse and imagination, and public intervention. The crack epidemic unleashed in the 1980s was politically premeditated and rhetorically and violently enacted against communities of color. The government controlled the affective and moral narrative, incarcerating thousands and brutally policing inner-city streets, whether drugs were present or not. The opioid crisis, however, originates not from the organized motions of the US federal government (though the crisis was, of course, later regulated by it) but from the pages of a marketing proposal.

In the late 1980s Purdue Pharma was just another small, privately owned pharmaceutical company. Located in Stamford, Connecticut, and run by the Sackler family, Purdue specialized in laxatives, earwax removal, and an opiate pain reliever for cancer patients called MS Contin. When in the 1990s MS Contin neared the end of its patent, threatening the fiscal future of Purdue, the company brainstormed its next product, one that could be marketed toward chronic pain, one containing the highest concentration of oxycodone to ever hit the market. Relieving pain for up to twelve hours (as opposed to the four to six hours of other over-the-counter narcotics), Purdue branded OxyContin as the drug that helps you regain control over life. *It gets you back to work.*

In 1996 Purdue debuted OxyContin through a comprehensive marketing blitz, employing everything from peppy TV ads to all-expense-paid vacations for busy primary care physicians.[20] Purdue further supplemented its marketing campaign with extensive research into prescription trends, collecting enormous data caches to analyze which doctors prescribed the most opioids and where. From the start, Purdue claimed the risk of addiction as less than 1 percent, though notably their ad materials consistently stated the risk of addiction to opiates (purposefully using the word "opiates" rather than "OxyContin") was minimal. Notwithstanding, this 1 percent statistic was pulled out of context from a dated medical article.[21]

Because OxyContin is a twelve-hour continuous ("Contin" means continuous) release, it was marketed as difficult if not impossible to abuse. But research, including even the internal studies done at Purdue, proved otherwise. Purdue's team found (and then concealed) that once a pill was crushed, 68 percent of the oxycodone could be extracted at once.[22] And with physicians writing 30-, 60-, and even 90-day scripts, dependence formed fast. Within four years of OxyContin's debut, sales at Purdue grew by over $1 billion and the drug became the most frequently prescribed opioid in the United States.[23] The consequences have been devastating. The rise in overdoses and overdose-related deaths skyrocketed simultaneously with OxyContin's expanding prescription coverage.

After years of lawsuits, investigations, and public protesting, in 2007 three Purdue Pharma executives (none part of the Sackler family) pled guilty to federal criminal charges of misleading both physicians and the public about

Oxy's addictive qualities. In 2010 Purdue reformulated the drug to make it more difficult to crush, snort, and inject, while pill mills closed and doctors were held accountable for their prescriptions practices. One of the consequences of the swift change in prescription drug culture was that thousands of withdrawing opioid users were driven toward the cheaper, always available alternative: heroin. In 2010 there were 21,088 deaths from opioid overdose. By 2017, that number more than doubled.[24] Since the release of OxyContin, over a million have died from an opioid overdose.[25]

Across local and national news coverage alike, opioid use has been declared an epidemic, a crisis breaking into wealthy suburbs, "good" schools, and happy families. The racialization of drug use as a state strategy has privileged private wealth, ensured political legacies, and controlled capital through mass incarceration of Black, brown, Indigenous, and queer communities. Fomenting spectacle around white drug use, then, achieves many things simultaneously: it safeguards white drug-users from the War on Drugs legacy; it legitimates a police state that occurs within recovery models and through morally scripted public health initiatives; and it normalizes the demand for protected futures over present need. "Construction of white drug scares, just like those centered on people of color, are about policing boundaries and shoring up cultural expectations based on race and class. Poor, rural methamphetamine users [in this case] violate white expectations of productive, rational citizens fitting with the neoliberal requirements of whiteness."[26] White drug use is composed as a shocking violation of expectations in order to protect penal institutions and sustain harsh drug policies. The racialization of drug use can also be mapped through its history of criminalization, prescriptions trends (white patients are more likely to be prescribed pain relief), and a shift in language: addiction is now a disease breaching the 'burbs.

Public health and rhetoric scholars alike have argued that discourse highlighting "the new face of addiction" directs our collective understanding of opioid use through the imagery of spectacle, stratifying white drug use from non-white use,[27] and that typical news headlines create "a form of narcotic apartheid"[28] by rearticulating social, legal, and political narratives that continue to portray white drug use as a surprise, which reinforces the idea that non-white drug use is expected. These narratives portray white drug use as unplanned and therefore tragic and non-white drug use as measured and therefore criminal.

Since the early days of Oxy, headlines sensationalizing "the new face of addiction" became routine, implicitly conjuring an earlier, "familiar" face of addiction. Of course, this new face is rhetorically and visually coded as young, white, and wealthy—the face representing productive futures. The face of the one who, though descending to the rock bottom of addiction, can always be redeemed through recovery. A recent study confirmed that opioid users are more often offered clinical treatment than those who use crack, for example, since the latter is associated with Black users.[29] Sensationalizing discourse relies on shames to advance the racialization of drugs through an artifice of newness. Shame, therefore, stakes claims on particular futures—chosen futures.

Recovery emerges as the singular model for addressing white drug use and reviving our notions of the healthy, productive citizen. "Rather than simple casting out or disparaging of white opioid users, we see instead attempts to reclaim and restore (through medicalization of their drug use) these white bodies," argue public health scholars Julie Netherland and Helena Hansen.[30] But by moving addiction from the prison cell to the public clinic, we've only traversed institutional terrain, substituting one racist space for another and stabilizing legacies of drug criminalization along the way.

"On the Road to Nowhere"

Among the local, national, and international reports on the US opioid epidemic that span from the late 1990s to the present, I will look at one from a popular news source that aired in 2010. Titled "The New Face of Heroin Addiction," an episode of the long-running ABC News news program *20/20*, profiled heroin use among white, mostly middle-class teenagers in suburban Minneapolis.[31] I chose this piece because of its mainstream popularity and therefore large platform for speaking both about and to middle America, but also its airdate. At this moment in the epidemic, Purdue Pharma had pled guilty to criminally misleading the public about OxyContin's addictive properties and was therefore reformulating the drug to make it difficult to abuse. This swift bottoming-out of the opioid pill market led many to turn toward heroin, as I noted earlier, which was widely available and even more affordable than pills.

This is where *20/20* picks up the story, explaining that rates of heroin use doubled from 2007 to 2010. "Even more surprising" than these numbers, correspondent Christopher Cuomo notes, "may be the face of the new addicts. Tonight you are going to meet kids from families you never thought could fall victim to drugs, families who did everything right." The story then goes on to profile two white youths living with addiction: Ashley and Justin.

Sitting in a bright dining room with Ashley, Cuomo argues, "This is not supposed to happen to you: too smart, too many people who love you, too much money [here Cuomo gesticulates to underscore their suburban setting] and potential." The story then cuts to early home videos in which Ashley is seen as a toddler playing with toys, as a young girl in rollerblades, then as a college student holding a beer. Youth, whiteness, wealth, and traditional family convene to limn Ashley with lost innocence. In voiceover, Cuomo explains how Ashley, like so many college students, experimented with drugs and alcohol in college before developing a dependence on opioids. The trajectory is linearly constructed—transgressing from point A (innocence) to point B (tragedy). In a later scene, Ashley guides Cuomo through her parents' house and into the basement where she lives. "This is your soot?" he asks, noting the black residue (from tar heroin) on doorways and light fixtures. The coerced spectacle of white drug use registers affectively as surprise, threat, and discomfort as cameras track the material residues of the drug, framing addiction as dirt and deviance in the wealthy home. Cuomo's remark "This is not supposed to happen to you" implies that addiction *is* meant to happen to someone.

This profile (like many addiction narratives) focuses on youth, emphasizing early potential in athletics and academics. The innocence of childhood and white adolescence sharpens the danger of an othering substance. And by situating these stories in suburbs, marking the space as unusual, the show compels viewers to imagine borders and the threat of breach. Indeed, the perceived trajectory of drug use—from urban centers to suburban and rural peripheries—appears again and again across media. In the opening scene from this *20/20* piece, Cuomo performs a shocked affect to inform viewers that drugs are moving from the inner city into wealthier neighborhoods. During this specific voiceover, we get clips of dark Minneapolis nights, police cars, and EMS sirens.

Cuomo reports on heroin "ravaging" Ashley inside and out, "changing her voice, damaging her skin." This attention to the body is articulated again later when we are introduced to Justin, also from Minneapolis but now living in Portland, Maine, who is "on the road to nowhere." "The once bright-faced boy who loved the outdoors and planned to follow in his father's footsteps in the family pipe-fitting business, Justin is now a ghost of his former self." This ghost, this boy thinning into specter, symbolizes the braided relationship between capital and respectability. As a direct result of lost income and vocation, Justin's future fades from legibility while his status as productive citizen becomes increasingly incoherent. "When did you stop being like everyone else's ideal kid?" Cuomo asks. Cameras then follow Justin as he waits for his supplier to call back. He is shown as idling for hours alone in the dark, waiting for his fix, wasting time.

Time is constructed in particular ways within Ashley's and Justin's stories. Ashley "soon dropped out of college, quit her job, and began the life of a full-time junkie." Ashley's divergence from her predicted future reinscribes capital time—that we either participate productively in economic life or we stall out. "Full-time" here summons capital's expectations, that labor makes the responsible subject, that drug use only indicates deviation from the workforce and from legible embodiment (since that embodiment is clarified through labor). Users of drugs, including Ashley and Justin, are interpellated as "stuck" to emphasize the pathology of nonlinear subjecthood. While actively using, the subject is unable to be a "productive member of society," though they might yet become one, *if* they choose the (teleo)logical choice: treatment.

"Stuck," as a rhetorical device, implies that what is lost or idling can be redeemed. We can save one who is stuck because, as the story goes, as the white victim of Big Pharma, they were pulled deep into a disease they were never meant to know. Expressions of time—compounded by optimization and advancement rhetorics in medical language—reify people who use drugs as abject, as defective and defecting from the path of financial and emotional prosperity. Discourses that constrain people to a condition of stuck-ness present their full humanness as not yet revoked but possible under recovery. Once the subject takes up the recovery process, a respectable future returns to view.

When Jasbir Puar describes the process of being "evaluated in relation to success or failure in terms of health, wealth, progressive productivity, upward mobility, enhanced capacity," she describes the pathology of being *stuck*, of idling in time.[32] Derrida once asked what it is that we hold against the user of drugs. "He cuts himself off from the world, in exile from reality, far from objective reality and the real life of the city and the community; that he escapes into a world of simulacrum and fiction."[33] Meaning, pathology moves beyond the substance itself; it is the perceived prioritization of and retreat into the interiors, into pleasure or solitude or secrecy, that threatens entrenched notions of well-being. Though "stuck" discourse is undeniably degrading, it generates sympathy by employing rhetorics of loss and grief— lost jobs, estranged families, and abandoned futures—to grade these stories as compelling, to allocate these lives as worth protecting.

Throughout the feature, *20/20* reproduces the stigmatizing "stuck" narrative we see across media coverage of the opioid epidemic: Justin, a user of drugs, did not go to college, has not held a job, has abandoned his family and future vocation. The attention to age also reappears. Justin and Ashley are in their early twenties, headed toward that time in life socially constructed around vocational development, marriage, and family-making, each an imperative mechanism within capital's reproduction of subjecthood. To be "stuck" in early adulthood implies that one occupies space without producing or participating in the development of that (political, social, economic) space. Within capital time, subjects must be mobile, invested in straight trajectories with clear outcomes—careers, property ownership, reproduction. Justin, as this feature frames him, failed at each. The affective register of this *20/20* piece attempts to pathologize the feverish magnitude of the epidemic through the stuck-ness of drug use. The idling user is much more comprehensible (and garishly entertaining) than the myriad mix of institutional machinations that make the epidemic what it truly is. And in this piece, with scant effort made toward deep description, the shame of drug use relegates these two humans to mere allegories of addiction.

The *20/20* story aired over a dozen years ago. Since then, the epidemic has only worsened, with more fatal overdoses each year, the introduction first of fentanyl and then Xylazine in the heroin supply, COVID-19 and the diminishment of accessible resources surrounding the pandemic, the housing crisis, right-wing extremism and its policy work in some of the hardest hit states, and more. Donald Trump's first administration proposed cutting 95 percent of the budget for the Office of National Drug Control Policy while also slashing the Health Resources and Services Administration budget and Medicaid. Twelve percent of those on Medicaid struggle with substance addiction.[34] While some states have closed needle exchanges and limited federal funding toward recovery programs, others are urgently trying to stem a hemorrhaging crisis made worse by judgment and stigma.

In 2020, when Measure 110 passed in Oregon, the Drug Addiction Treatment and Recovery Act decriminalized possession of controlled substances and officially affirmed, "Making people criminals because they suffer from addiction is expensive, ruined lives, and can make access to treatment and recovery more difficult."[35] I celebrated this election result from across the country the same day Biden was declared the winner of the presidential election. Nearly 60 percent of Oregonians voted in favor of Measure 110. I hoped it meant other states would take up the torch. But years later, moods have soured. In July and August 2023, the *New York Times* ran an opinion column and a photo essay within days of each other that reminded me how far we must go in media representation of the opioid crisis. Take, for example, the *Times* photo essay titled "Scenes from a City That Only Hands Out Tickets for Using Fentanyl," by Jan Hoffman.[36] Fascinating to me is the disparity between the article's photographs and its text, how the former highlights humanity, while the latter falls back on sensation; but it is the regeneration of criminality that places this piece alongside countless others struggling to make sense of a public health crisis.

From the title, we are told implicitly that "only" handing out tickets for fentanyl use should astonish us readers. And it does in a country criminalizing drugs. But some nuance is required. As one who has worked with those using drugs in Oregon and Pennsylvania, I've seen that most with an opioid addiction (not all, but most) are not actively seeking to use fentanyl. It's in the supply. The reason, then, that editors at the *Times* chose to use "fentanyl" in the title was to stimulate shock, how it juxtaposes to "only" to suggest an extreme lack of punitive action. The article goes on to profile downtown Portland, Oregon, in 2023, specifically its one-square-mile city center that was the scene of long-standing protests during the Black Lives Matter uprisings in 2020 and one that was hit especially hard by COVID-19. It does not profile any other part of the state, nor does it situate Portland in the housing crisis, which has devastated the West Coast from LA up to Seattle. It does not discuss the racialization of drug use. Most surprisingly, it does not analyze how Measure 110 has changed Oregon's prison system.

What this article *does* do is conflate homelessness with drug use, and criminality with addiction, suggesting the need for punitive action and justifying that action by stimulating incredulity against the backdrop of shame. As in, readers are meant to shake their heads. To be fair, Hoffman's piece profiles different voices of those affected by drug use in downtown Portland. The words from this article are mostly not her own, but those she chose to spotlight. For example, she quotes a user of drugs named Noah Nethers: "'Portland is a homeless drug addict's slice of paradise,' said Noah Nethers, who was living with his girlfriend in a bright orange tent on the sidewalk against a fence of a church, where they shoot and smoke both fentanyl and meth."[37] Noah's tent is reduced to the scene of just shooting up and Noah's life is reduced down to the size of small tarp. Hoffman proceeds to paraphrase the rest of her conversation with Nethers: "He ticked off the advantages: He can do drugs wherever he wants and the cops no longer harass him. There are more dealers, scouting for fresh customers moving to paradise. That means drugs are plentiful and cheap."[38] I want people with addiction to have easy access to affordable drugs. Hopefully safe drugs too, but our country has struggled to successfully maintain safe consumption sites. I also do not want them to be harassed by cops. I would count these as advantages too. But I'm not sure I am meant to, as a reader. I think this article is telling us we're not supposed to want drug users to have any slice of paradise.

In another example, Hoffman writes that downtown retailer "Jennifer Myrl sidesteps needles, shattered glass, and human feces."[39] By including "shattered glass and human feces" alongside needles, Hoffman means for us to take all three objects as mutually inclusive. We are supposed to believe people using drugs are out rioting and shitting in the streets. We are not meant to understand that unhoused people (using drugs or not) do not have access to bathrooms or safe living quarters. Hoffman herself writes, "open-air drug use, long in the shadows, burst into full view," reiterating the implicit, adamant belief that drug use is dirty and deserves ostracization through punitive or moral means. Her *New York Times* article dismisses the wider context of Oregon's drug policy, dehumanizes drug users by dramatizing single users, and justifies stigmatizing language by implying criminality. Four hours south of Portland, a small town called Grants Pass employs ordinances that bar the unhoused from camping on public land. In 2024, the Supreme Court ruled in favor of this ban, legally formalizing the conflation of homelessness and criminality.

Like many families across the United States, mine has not gone untouched by addiction and overdose. Nor have I. This is how I came to understand the way shame manipulates us, clinches our imaginative spirit so that our relationship to the self is taut and contained, rather than expansive and wandering, wondering. Sara Ahmed describes shame as a state of being psychically against one's self, that because shame locates badness within the body, in order to expel the badness, I have to "expel myself from myself."[40] To expel the self from ourselves is ontological death, a form of violence with which we feel forced to comply. Dying while living.

There Is No ~~Easy~~ Answer

In the United States, fifteen states ban syringe services programs (SSPs) while half of the country is under some form of limited access—legislation is ambiguous or SSPs are restricted to designated (usually urban) areas or counties. For example, under Pennsylvania law it is illegal to run a syringe program outside of Allegheny and Philadelphia counties, which operate through city exemption. National drug paraphernalia laws, coupled with intense public scrutiny of exchanges, inhibit most people from reliably accessing sterile syringes and equipment (cookers, cotton, alcohol swabs, Narcan, and more). Likewise, anti-craving medications such as methadone and Suboxone are heavily monitored. Methadone is distributed daily at clinics often relegated to the outskirts of cities; for those taking methadone, for those who may arrive late to work because of a drive across town to their clinic, one missed dose results in full suspension from the program. Furthermore, those on methadone or Suboxone are often not considered sober and thus are disallowed from sharing at NA meetings. The violence of addiction pathology, whether threaded through criminal or medical discourse, manifests clearly in local, state, and national government response to drug use, and the opioid crisis, specifically. Despite these many hurdles—the medical gatekeeping, astringent program regulations, national policy—the single user of drugs is still deemed responsible for not only explaining addiction but carrying the weight of the crisis on their shoulders.

During my time working with NEX in Oregon, I was required to ask, before distributing any packs of needles or supplies, whether our participant wished for information on recovery. "Are you interested in learning about recovery today?" This question was enforced by our funding and augmented our data on regional use. By tracking the using patterns of our participants, and by gesturing toward recovery, we appeased donors who wanted to know their donations went on to generate positive results. But I loathed asking participants about rehab, whether they shared used needles in the past week, when their last STI and HIV tests were. I wanted to pass out supplies without reminding our community of the public's expectations. As I wrote in the last chapter, our participants do not owe us anything. But this is part of our work: the contradictions, that even as we fight stigma we work within the systems still producing it.

These binds are also part of embracing complexity, part of how we navigate a matrix of need and desire, care and boundary. "Harm reduction discourse serves an alternative ethics to the ethics of both criminal justice and the medical discourse underlying public health approaches," writes Susan Shaw.[41] But she also renders caution: "At the same time, harm reduction practices are used to navigate a neoliberal political rationality that relocates responsibility for health to individuals without addressing structural constraints."[42] Harm reduction is not perfect, but it is a practice of looking imperfections directly in the eye.

If capital time requires the rhetoric of being stuck to shame, to racialize and oppress, what then are our options for composing alternative narratives in a climate of crisis and vulnerability? How do we think about the person using drugs not as stuck, but as living and moving and being, as part of our communities, not outliers? Not only are people who use drugs routinely stigmatized through policy and discourse, but they are held captive to this imaginary that marks opioid use as wasted potential and squandered futures. Stories of perseverance, underwritten by the neoliberal appeal to advancement, reestablish meritocracy within the confines of the body, marking difference and demanding participation in capital constructions of social good. We need to move beyond mastery as the method of world-making to envisage an assemblage of experiences, affects, needs, and possibilities that are not contingent on coherency, that do not make demands of futures.

Without a doubt, opioid use has devastated communities across the United States (and beyond, of course), harming individual and social bodies alike. It *does* disrupt families, lead toward economic duress, and inhibit opportunities for material flourishing. But compulsory recovery discourse offers only one way of understanding and reporting on opioid use. The harm of drug use is rhetorically overexposed in order to conceal the sources of intentional violence encouraged through capitalism and its influence on the imaginaries of its people. Under this coercion, we are trained to understand drug use through racialized dichotomies, to classify society into diseased or criminal parts, to see users as spectacles. We should desire a radical imaginative upheaval, not only to serve people who use drugs in their material needs, but to undermine the racialization of all drug use, to unsettle our deeply embedded cultural attachments to health, and to reject shame as a hermeneutic of the body.

During my years at NEX, there was an HIV outbreak in a neighboring county. At that time I was told anyone could receive free testing or a pack of needles, that they didn't need to meet any requirements or fill out any forms. Often these prerequisites drove some participants away. Men would come in for anonymous testing only to learn they first had to disclose certain criteria: whether they had sex with men or used drugs intravenously. The questions were meant to manage our funding, but I watched as some people, stung by shame, turned around and walked defeatedly out the door. During the HIV outbreak, however, we broke with protocol. We gave people fast, free tests and sterile equipment without question, and almost immediately these actions stymied the spread in our and neighboring counties. By suspending our attention to protocol (funding and forms) to attend to the acute present moment, by privileging material need over positivist perspectives, and by changing systemic behavior rather than require change in individual behavior, we protected one another, even into an unknown future. While focused on the temporal exchange between ourselves and our participants—that what we say in the moment matters—we were also actively protecting a future of ongoing relationships, services, and care. We protected futures *even as* we refused to describe those futures. Meaning, we did not enforce recovery or rehab. But what we established rhetorically and materially in the moment conferred ongoing (futural) stability. Our participants can always return to us without explanation or expectation.

Human lives happen within polyvalence, within a humming hive of feelings and needs, isolation and relationships. When Alexander Weheliye defines polyvalence, he describes the expressions we give to "previously nonexistent realities, thoughts, bodies, affects, spaces, actions, ideas, and so on."[43] "Polyvalence" as a biomedical term also refers to antibodies, to the body's fight against pathogens, to the scene of multiple adaptations and life finding its way, even in the grittiest moments. The state invades the body under the guise of care, but its true aim is capital—production and profit. By analyzing and challenging the language that makes this possible, which means not only exposing the pathogen but tracing its mutation under the skin, we might begin to attenuate our investment in health analytics and our attachments to the body as an object from which knowledge is extracted. The project is ongoing, but that's the point. This work refuses predictions for the future and turns instead toward process, the acute care for now, for this moment.

I believe capital wants to stake claims in futures by coercing us into scripted notions of respected labor. *But also*, José Esteban Muñoz's futures consist of aesthetic desires that give life to our current aches and hungers. In that way, the future stokes desire, but that desire is manipulated by capital—ceaseless labor toward the good life—or aesthetically calibrated toward utopia. The multiples. Within the opioid epidemic in particular, the temporal nature of drug use, addiction, and recovery is buried under anxious productivity. Crucial to our work in downtown Eugene was the refusal to place recovery over current need. Meaning, it was more important to see a participant in the dailyness, to offer some coffee and sterile needles and equipment, than it was to demand recovery, even if recovery was still our hope. Studies have shown that people who use syringe exchange programs are five times more likely to enter treatment than those who don't.[44] They are three times more likely to stop using drugs altogether. By emphasizing present care, we allow what is on the horizon (our futures) to illuminate our world without demarcating prescribed paths. By caring for the moment, participants will return for more services, despite relapse. They will begin to associate care with respect, attention, and desire, rather than expectation. Hopefully, over time, this work silences shame and diminishes our internalized pressure to perform health and optimism. Instead, we hold precarity and vulnerability alongside possibility.

The move away from the elite knowledge of the medical industry to instead turn toward process, toward messy convergences of feeling and expression, will be difficult. But I heed Dean Spade when he says we need to focus on "practice and process rather than arrival at a singular point of 'liberation.'"[45] With this in mind, harm reduction—the work we did in downtown Eugene, the practice of providing services without demands, coercion, or expectations to people who use drugs—is not the singular point of liberation, but it does affirm ourselves as in process, as fuckups struck down by wonder, desire, and the longing to live into seemingly impossible futures. It offers us routes around shame rather than the requirement to reform it into palatable feelings or performances.

As participants came from all over the city to our street exchange in Eugene, as we learned about their lives but never their names, I began to recognize how the broader social construction of health wreaks havoc on the material realities of everyone, but especially those who use drugs. At NEX we invited persons using drugs back into our community. Or, perhaps, more to the point, we made an effort to treat them as already part of our community. This invitation and intentional shift in the definition of care not only benefits people who use drugs, but it smothers the flare of shame in all of us to ask us to be gentle in our expectations of what process involves: missteps, relapses, joys, stuck-ness, and setbacks. But I also believe we can translate these ideas beyond street outreach, beyond the primary care office, and into our own felt selves.

Unutterable Hope

Michael and I flew into Anchorage out of Eugene, Oregon, where we had moved the summer before, ditching muted West Michigan less than a year into our marriage. "I need wild," I told him. Moss, meadows, and ribbons of amber trail along whirling opal rivers thrummed an inchoate chord in me, an appetence to both see and be wild. Wild, "to grow or develop without restraint."[46] Before traversing the tangled brush of Alaska's tundra, Michael and I were married on the flat plains of a West Michigan river bend. The city we lived in is considered one of the most religious in the United States—Calvinist and Evangelical, with their doctrines on predestination and omniscience mortaring conservativism into the town's political infrastructure. Michael grew up in the Christian Reformed Church. When exiting his parents' church parking lot, you would face a sign that read, "You are now entering the mission field." I grew up with hippies and Nintendo but attended an Evangelical youth group in high school, followed by a Baptist college that taught creationism in its gen-ed biology classes. We grew into the damning ideologies of original sin, repentance, self-sacrifice, and sexual purity. By the time Michael and I met in our mid-twenties, at a Søren Kierkegaard book club, we had both absconded from our mutual religious pasts by the skin of our teeth.

The wedding was on a bend of the Flat River, a tributary to the Grand River in Michigan, and the reception was held in his parents' backyard. Friends danced on a shiny rented dance floor and tipped their feet into the sky for keg stands. I wore a tight strapless dress that clamped my breath and reddened my ribbed skin. But it was all a show. Michael and I had eloped the week before. Standing under an oak tree with two friends and a minister, we exchanged vows in our jeans. My friend read a poem by Amy Gerstler titled "The Bear-Boy of Lithuania":

> Take my advice, marry an animal. A wooly one is most consoling. Find a fur man, born midwinter. Reared in the mountains. Fond of boxing. Make sure he has black rubbery lips, and a sticky-sweet mouth. A winter sleeper. Pick one who likes to tussle, who clowns around the kitchen, juggles hot baked potatoes, gnaws playfully on a corner of your apron. Not one mocked by his lumbering instincts, or who's forever wrestling with himself, tainted with shame, itchy with chagrin, but a good-tempered beast.[47]

Michael is a wooly one, a fur man born in early summer, reared on the overworked plains of the Christian Reformed Church. Michael's rubbery lips and sticky-sweet mouth were gentle with mine, asking in kindness. We tussled and laughed and clowned around. We read Dostoyevsky together—our two dueling translations open on a shared coffee house table. But then we're caught in Gerstler's lines: both of us in our own ways were stained in shame, which did more than mark: it composed our stories before we lived them.

Shame inhibits, it withholds and reinforces. It essentializes and constrains. So we moved to the damp valley west of the Cascade range, where an attic apartment stamped our marital beginning with a cloudy skylight, wood-paneled walls, and a fridge full of cheap ways to get buzzed. We sat under the yard's fir trees and flipped through the pages of an Oregon backcountry atlas, envisaging variant paths through the backcountry. It wasn't about discovery, that boorish imperialist cliché trumpeting all knowledge as accessible and acquirable. Our dreams were more subtle. And, in the end, extremely painful.

Someone once told me, "Delay is avoidance." And while this feels true on the surface, I lean into its moral intonation and hear the pathologizing of time itself. I think about my days of delay and the circuits of shame; closeted and married, I wasn't waiting and stalling. I was living within the pain of uncertainty. I was setting up my tent, unrolling my mat, and starting campfires. I was unbuckling the hip belt of my pack to safely cross glacial rivers, trading my bulky hiking boots for cheap tennis shoes. Life still happens in the stuck moments, those in which cold currents whorled around my bare ankles. While always tempted to meet shame with pride, and while this is surely a worthy and powerful move, I want to also include uncertainty as a gentle guide for relearning ourselves. Despite the discomfort of the unknown, within this discomfort creativity stirs. When we're not told who we are, we can be anybody. We can compose ourselves.

At times, I am so done with shame, with thinking and writing about it, with living in its shadows. And in other moments, I've barely scratched the surface of shame and the way it inflects our epistemological and emotional selves. "I didn't yearn for anything but privacy because it is an embarrassment to be a wound in public."[48] I keep returning to this poetic line by Billy-Ray Belcourt to sit with the contradictions of the body—that it is both private and public, that it both offers meaning yet has been violently made the producer of meaning. The contradictions seem impossible, but only if I demand they unknot themselves. Within the tangle and tension is also creative criticality, the freedom to fabulate our own scripts and stories. While we may find ourselves in a state of crisis, we take up the radical invitation to dream otherwise.

I should have known. When I say these four words formed a creed that returned to me over and over, I'm talking about rhetoric's recursivity, an echo of language that replenished some fortified idea of my failed self. And while I've often thought of these four words as entrenching a path, compounding a trail into its own dust and wear, I remember to look up, to scan the horizon and let its light orient me. I remember the Denali rangers telling Michael and me to walk side-by-side. Without a trail system, backpackers are asked to walk shoulder to shoulder instead of single file to avoid striking a path where there should only be wild. Such a small shift in practice protects the landscape's delicate ecosystem.

"Our vows didn't say anything about staying married," Michael explained, "just that we would stand by one another through all of life's changes." He told me this mid-divorce, while I was back in West Michigan, informing our parents and coming out. This is what language can do—stabilize meaning even as it modifies meaning. Revision rather than punctuation, creativity over optimization. This is the renewal of a promise through upheaval. This is a commitment to process. This is desire, the skin's fractal that allows us to feel ourselves as possible even in the ruins. It is a way through shame.

It has been many years since coming out over our salmon dinner, and many years since Michael walked me down the aisle when I married my wife. I texted him a couple years ago to tell him I think I'm also trans. He responded with a bitmoji waving the pink-and-blue flag. Michael is one of my best friends now, and I still balked and hesitated about sending him that text. I don't want to come out again. I don't want to come out to all my people again, explaining myself. Explaining my body. Apologizing for my long delay. None of it alleviates the failure. I resist the process even as I know—from my own pained histories—to immerse myself in its mess. Rilke writes:

> We alone
> fly past all things, fugitive as the wind.
> And all things conspire to keep silent about us, half
> out of shame perhaps, half as unutterable hope.[49]

A different translation of his second elegy offers "secret hope" in that last line, but I like "unutterable" better, as it suggests the undecipherable, what cannot be tidied into language. Rilke encourages us to stand still in the unknown, to welcome failure, and in so doing to loosen our demands on what the future holds. My life has summoned heat waves of shame because of my reiterating attempts to know the world and my place in it. Only through feeling have I come to realize that the world (and my queer tenancy) does not require transcription—with its elite knowledges and mastered lines—but amended translations, wherein, with the slightest shift, *secret* becomes *the unutterable*.

3

Painfully Shy

Trans Feeling and Quiet Refusals

> He thought about the difference
> between outside and inside.
> Inside is mine, he thought.
>
> **—Anne Carson, *Autobiography of Red***

Geryon is a shy boy. "Everything about him" is red, including small wings he binds under a leather jacket.[1] But Geryon never flies. Zipping the jacket to his throat, he is cautious and withholding, a diffident animal with mythological roots going back more than a millennium as the beast once slain by Herakles in fulfillment of the tenth labor. But in *Autobiography of Red*, Anne Carson transports Geryon to modern-day suburbia, reviving him into a creature of complexity, interiority, and queer desire. "Everything about him was red" implies otherness, summons blush and flushed cheeks—shame. Carson's Geryon is a young boy-monster, but also an artist writing his autobiography and living with his single mom and his cruel brother. In Carson's version, Geryon is a tender soul, misunderstood by his world and quiet in his desires. He is not killed by Herakles, as he is in Greek mythology, but forced to confront his red alterity under the scope of ruined romance and failure: Herakles is Geryon's first love and first heartbreak.

Carson herself describes *Autobiography of Red*, this novel-in-verse, this poetic hybrid, as a buried box of song lyrics, lectures, and scraps of meat. "You can of course keep shaking the box," writes Carson. "Here. Shake."[2] A shaken box disassembles while it reassembles, bits busted into new patterns or sifting into new reflections of the whole. But the whole is never lost. Rather, the more one shakes the box, the more abundant the possibilities, colliding in collaged disorder. An assemblage. Of course, the pages of *Red* are static, but Carson aggregates varied genres and forms—poetry, story, archive, even pedagogy—that signal our aesthetic need for multiples. In the introduction, for example, Carson opens with a lesson in discourse: "What is an adjective? Nouns name the world. Verbs activate the names. Adjectives come from somewhere else. . . . These small, imported mechanisms are in charge of attaching everything in the world to its place in particularity. They are the latches of being."[3] The particulars nourish aesthetic promise, evincing our lives as more than just categories of events and experiences, but fragmented and whole, and ready to be re-shaken and retold.

My own red autobiography is not new. I take comfort in this, how ordinary it is, my short hair and skinned knees. I was a twelve-year-old tagalong wearing my brother's threadbare tees with Converse sneakers and baggy shorts. He and his friends designated me lookout whenever they lit illicit firecrackers in the school parking lot or smashed an old mailbox; and they let me follow them down to the swimming hole, where we threw big pieces of white bread to the bluegills. The boys would strip their shirts and jump into the warm water in jean shorts, jostling one another under the amber surface. I waited on the clay shore. As much as I wanted to join, my parents had forbidden shirtless swimming earlier in the summer. "You can't take your shirt off like the boys can." When I asked why, I received the standard response conferred to confused children: "You just can't." I learned difference early. I learned difference as ache and want. Jules Gill-Peterson writes, "Being trans in a cis culture means that too many first encounters with oneself come through the shame of exposure."[4] Our encounters with our young queer selves are perilous. As we map the world through rule and arbitration, we are inscribed early and in reiteration by external opinion. The opinion is hot, like a spotlight.

I learned, then, not to ask, to instead lift my cotton shirt over my head while shooting baskets in the privacy of my backyard, where I built and inhabited a whole world of my own imagining. I was practicing layups when a classmate stopped over unannounced, a colorful birthday invitation clasped in her hand. The basketball nested under an arm akimbo, I was in dereliction—topless and burning with a shame I could not translate. I felt the cusp of adolescence making my body strange, even as I did not yet understand why. We remember what Sara Ahmed said of shame, that its "very physicality—how it works on and through bodies—means that shame also involves the de-forming and re-forming of bodily and social spaces."[5] I sensed the deformation, that my boy-child body unsettled these social spaces while also giving others something to read, my body as discourse. Classmates mocked me in my bathing suit during middle school swim class, my arms crossed tightly across my chest; my parents worried over my angles, the lack of soft shape; my teachers told me to speak up; my principal threatened to withhold my high school diploma if I didn't wear a dress to graduation. I was always a quiet child, but then shyness grew into something more than sensitivity. Shy developed in me as I developed in shy to evade the relentless calls for coherence. ("Cohere"—to be united as a whole or to make logical, consistent sense.)

When, at the end of *Autobiography of Red*, Geryon finally strips his jacket, unyokes his red wings and flies, one might misinterpret the scene as the moment of proverbial liberation, that Geryon has overcome his heartache, or has transcended the queerness of his body to exploit its utility. However, this reading would be cursory. Just prior to flight, Geryon has terrible sex with his ex, Herakles—that kind of relapsed hookup that leaves one stung with regret, what Geryon himself calls degrading. Our boy is still a fuckup. So, it's not that Geryon must accept himself to find freedom. And it is not that Geryon must prove he can fly. Instead, alone and adrift in illimitable skies, Geryon describes himself as a "black speck raking his way" as "a memory of our beauty."[6] For a small being against the fiery backdrop of an unstable world, flying is not liberation, but simply a verb. It is a juncture in time, one that convenes a temporal connection between body and movement. As a black speck raking—an adjective in motion—Geryon pierces a moment that contains nothing and everything. He is nothing and everything.

At one point in *Red*, Herakles criticizes Geryon's artwork: *"All your designs are about captivity. . . .* Geryon watched the top of Herakles' head / and felt his limits returning. Nothing to say. Nothing."[7] Herakles sees only Geryon's difference; and in urging him to ostensibly get over it, Herakles pathologizes Geryon's handling of his pain, how he expresses and holds it. What options exist for Geryon? And for us? Are our voices only heard when we overcome or transform our alterities to adopt aspirational stories, heroic tales of the body made over and the self rehabilitated through redeemed failure? Are we only doing well (whatever that means) when we are perceived as on our way to our best, most authentic selves? Are we only responsible citizens through disclosure and explanation, our interiorities brought to light, our confessionals crafted into coherency?

I am curious how shyness teaches us to refuse resolute rhetorics in a world named by nouns. I want to protect Geryon, but also those of us with our wings bound under leather jackets, by elucidating shy's affective potentiality for shaping expression without explanation. Shy skirts the telos of productive (capital) time to instead linger in the quiet delays and deferrals, to shelter us so we might activate our own names and adjectives. As a shy person, I learned to regret and repent for my shyness.[8] I was encouraged to overcome it, to regulate (if not fully disown) it for the sake of propriety, of putting others at ease. This social training cloaked moralism in the rhetoric of disclosure, that to share is to nurture communal well-being. But shyness composes an elemental sense of myself, a deep feeling into which I burrow but also a social tactic I exploit. Shy serves me again and again, as when I navigate the complex, painful landscape of medical assistance to receive gender-based care, wherein I confront the collusion of capitalism and wellness through tenacious expectations to self-divulge. The more offered, the more credible my compositions (spoken and embodied), and the more comprehensible a diagnosis. Finally, alas, the more divulged, the more likely I am to receive care. By delineating my body as hurt, I bypass gatekeeping mechanisms, even as I do not fully feel (or understand) myself as hurt.

This chapter enacts shyness as I forgo exposition to favor storytelling and description, which, of course, proceed from the particularity of my experiences and embodiment. This is an inescapable limitation, and indicative of emotion, that our affects are ours, shivering sensations under our singular skin, even as they are also transmitted and public. My descriptions might fail, tangled up as they are in the nuances of my own body. But failure is an invitation to try again. In this way, in braiding my own story of shy into this analysis, I hope to show exactly this: shy as unsure but also as refuge, refusal, and reattempt.

I will first describe shy's reticent registers before outlining its history of pathologization. I then explore shyness as a practice, how it breaks ulterior paths in a demanding capitalist ecosystem, especially as those demands require extroversion, sociality, aspiration, and judgment, and especially at the scene of trans need. In this chapter I will explain how capital exploits the feeling of euphoria to market it as outcome, as the final and finished state of trans personhood, the cured condition to dysphoric deformity. But this consummate linearity, projected onto and beyond queer and trans experiences, disregards revision and returns. Trans telos erases assemblages of felt energies, focused so solely on the singular subject, their static destination, and all they are obliged into revealing. Shyness clarifies an alternative set of discursive opportunities—language we make, remake, collage, scrap, and revise. We do not have to follow the prescribed scripts, the arc from rock bottom to second chance, from dark closets to public pronouncement. We can dodge or divert, moving sideways out of the spotlight.

A Call for Trans Theory without Telos

There is no singular characterization of shy. It refuses universal containment. Our vocal records and affective performances are gendered, classed, and racialized. Quiet boys are given allowances, their interiorities transcribed as introspection and tenderness while shy girls are withholding, cold, aloof. Those interpretations shift, of course, if the boy appears queerly quiet or the girl stoney silent. In this instance, shy conjures the queer child's hidden threat, just as trans people bear accusations of willful deceit for not disclosing their transness. Shy in American contexts also differs from those parts of the world that venerate quiet as propriety. Studies show, for example, that collectivist cultures value shyness while individualist cultures pathologize it.[9] Because I specifically research US conceptions of wellness and health, I center these markets and those who must endure them while clarifying shy's variable forms across geopolitical lines.

Further, just as shy is pathologized, so too can it preserve privilege, proffering measures of security not afforded by all. I think about the college seminar classroom, where participation can either determine engagement or be read as disruption. Or in the office—whose unfiltered commentary is given grace and who, in speaking up, becomes the killjoy?[10] While some must participate to indicate compliance, others remain silent without repercussion. Who is too loud and who is too quiet? When does silence equal death and when does silence protect life? These questions expose deviating stratifications of shy depending on political context, further foregrounding the need for multiplicity, for imaginations honed to withstand complexity and contradiction. With that said, how then do I proceed to define shy? With conscientious particularity.

I start in the body, where shy is ontological vibration, the tremors and reverberations of our social ecosystems overwhelming our sensorial intake valves. We feel pressed, breaking through seams and into the very edge of ourselves. We feel soaked to the bone. We feel exposed or invisible, seen too deeply yet never enough. We might index shy as anxious, but not always. Because sometimes shyness feels like desire, like having a crush and reveling privately in want without resolution. It might also feel like wonder, to marvel and stand stunned in silence. Shy is not passive. Just as it restrains, it engages. Just as it opts out, it listens in. The shy person reads the room—the moods and gesticulations of others metabolized through porous skin. While our shyness is often interpreted as removal, us quiet kids are actually in the thick of it. Sensitive, attuned, and aware—to feel shy is to connect sincerely with others and ourselves. Replenished by privacy, shy animates curiosity and insulates our interior worlds, especially as our exterior lives are exhausted by overstimulating verbosity.

Shy begins sensorily but can expand politically: by enacting shy we dim the political fervor in which queer folks are pushed under hot spotlights of sensationalized attention. Shy stonewalls. Stalling, lingering, taking a long pause, shy knows all about process. Through diversion, but also witness, listening, and holding, shyness inspires descriptions of our felt queer lives that elude traditional narratives of arrival. In this way, shy is felt and shy is made. By outlining shy as creative charge, we expand its political, public, and aesthetic possibilities to reject or manipulate inscription in a world intimidating us into explanation. To be clear, I'm testifying for shy as one of our multiples, one parcel in a shaken box, one path among many to thwart "single-note portraits of oppression and traumatization" and to blunt the efficacy of sensationalized trans narratives, those that rely on "celebratory tokenization and hypervisibility."[11] The line between seeing (bearing witness) and exposing falls fine; shy knows that line. Shy realizes us as agents, moving and making according to our wills, but also as subjects—forced, coerced, and cajoled into narratives not our own. Meaning, we can do trans studies without a telos. This chapter is a call to do so.

Histories and Pathologies of Shy

Shy surfaces discreetly in literature, is ironically mimetic in that way, hiding behind the legs of bigger affects, namely shame. Silvan Tomkins compares the shy person to an animal playing dead in the face of predatory danger,[12] and observes how it impales us between despair and longing.[13] Charles Darwin also paired shy to shame, calling the former an "odd state of being" wherein the rush of blush into our cheeks betrays us.[14] Shy rarely receives its own indexical entry (a clue to its marginality), so often is it conflated with other affects, folded into dominant emotions such as loneliness, shame, and anxiety. Eve Sedgwick, for example, writes: "Some of the infants, children, and adults in whom shame remains the most available mediator of identity are the ones called (a related word) shy."[15] For Sedgwick, like Darwin, shy is a reaction to a feeling, namely shame: shame hushes us, scolds us into corners, seals us into painful circuits of exposure and concealment, wherein we quietly acquiesce to the lesson being conferred. But by conflating shy and shame, not only is shyness reduced to behavioral response, but it obscures the inverse dynamic: we are shamed for being shy.

The pathologization of shyness in the past century, according to Christopher Lane, led to its current demarcation in the *Diagnostic and Statistical Manual of Mental Disorders* as "acute social anxiety," formally indexed alongside another affect and swept under more recognized emotional conceits. Lane argues we've "narrowed healthy behavior so dramatically" that small emotional blemishes are medically diagnosed as aberrations in need of intervention.[16] The result, or "sad consequence," writes Lane, is the "perhaps unrecoverable loss of emotional range."[17] I too lament loss of range, as range envisages the shaken box: our feelings are not just felt, but enacted, expressed, drawn, sung, doodled in private notebooks, consoled when walking our dogs down to the park, collaged into poetic coffers of meat and scraps. The conflation of shy with anxiety also parallels the rhetorical marriage of "painful" and "shy," such a commonly and casually uttered idiom. If to be shy is to be in or cause pain, what then is the source of this pain? And why do we find it painful to be in the presence of shyness? On the one hand, to *be* painfully shy is to be particularly vigilant, a learned practice of averting danger. After all, pain triggers receptors and excites the nerves to alert of incoming harms. On the other hand, the pathologization of shy originates from another form of anxiety altogether: cultural discomfort with opacity, with the impenetrable and elusive subject. Compounded by capital's investments in a normalizing society, "shy people unsettle others because they unsettle the tacit conventions of social life,"[18] offers Joe Moran. The quiet person must disclose, lest any form of deceit lay dormant.

Criticized as "hard to read" and "painfully shy," the shy person's tender and troubled orientation to their social worlds destabilizes those social worlds by refusing easy transcription. "Painfully shy" reflects the belief that knowledge behaves transactionally, predicated on the notion that intimacy is achieved through the simplistic (daresay, imperialistic) collection of information. That is, knowing ourselves (or one another) takes precedence over other relational modes (seeing, holding, witnessing, attending). We are trained into these habits; our discomfort around opacity is not innate but cultivated to spur what Michel Foucault famously deemed the will to know, that motor of the capitalist state wherein information generates profit. While wonder awakens our imaginations, the will toward knowledge cements kinetic energies to lay simplistic foundations. Foucault argued it is capital's insistence on epistemological mastery that has deepened cultural investment in social category. As capital commissions our imaginary spirit, the notion that knowledge is ours for the taking impels us to be *knowers* rather than *learners*. We are trained early into these habits.

One first learns their shyness through the rhetoric of adults, veiled in explanation or apology. "She's so shy around strangers," I heard repeatedly as I tucked myself behind the legs of my parents. When I was young, they indulged my dodging and blushing; but as I got older, they pushed me by my shoulders. "Don't be rude." "Don't forget to ask questions." "Speak up when you speak with adults." Kathryn Bond Stockton tells us there are modes of growing that are not growing up.[19] The queer child, she writes, upsets traditional conceits of linear development, defying preordained paths into adulthood through "unruly contours of growing."[20] The queer child grows sideways, or in vigor, volume, synaptically, or through deferral. "Where do our stories come from?" asks Jill Stauffer in her book on loneliness. Of course, from our internal sense of self, but just as often "from what other people say to us, from the values and truths produced by whatever cultures surrounds us, and from unspoken affective interactions between persons living alongside one another."[21] Stauffer explains language as transmitter, assembling power through which feelings are structured. Latches of being—language makes our worlds. Told I was shy as a child, I learned that my interior—my dreams, my make-believe, my stories—issued a composite of behaviors, shy, that would not be tolerated past adolescence. Inside was not mine.

The shy child must then mature out of their condition because adulthood requires us to nurture our social and economic worlds. We will participate, create families, and foster domestic spaces that invite others to gather. We will enter the workforce with gregarious energy. We will generate discourse and make meaning. We will create content. As the child ages and is presumed to outgrow their shyness (and other childish behaviors), pathological diagnoses appear alongside shy to account for deviance, this grown human still refusing legibility, this child hiding under the surface. If we failed to grow up into verbosity and we instead grew sideways into quiet ambiguity, then we fail to fulfill our roles as social nurturers, as economic movers and shakers, exiling ourselves within the self, plastered against a wall while life happens, stalling or stalled out. Condemned for not aspiring toward our best, healthiest, most authentic (most gendered) self, we are written into liminality; we are *not yet*. As we saw with dominant depictions of drug use, pathology exceeds the substance. It is not the drug itself that threatens, but the user's retreat into the interiors, their privileging of pleasure or solitude or secrecy. Derrida asks what is it that we hold against the user of drugs? "He cuts himself off from the world, in exile from reality, far from objective reality and the real life of the city and the community; that he escapes into a world of simulacrum and fiction."[22] He might also be describing a wallflower.

I've inhabited my shy body for four decades now. As a child I was often asked to "make my shy face." I'd bow my head but look upward with doe eyes, performing what I was told about shyness—it is demure, infantile, and pained. But adults thought it was cute, this obliged offering of interior feeling. However, I never grew out of shyness, just further into its sensitive registers to deflect, like Geryon, wrongful attention. To stonewall. To turn stone butch. Moran writes, "Perhaps some element of shyness, as our modern-day sociobiologists suggest, makes evolutionary sense. But surely its most human quality is that it often makes no sense at all."[23]

Though we believe that to be human is to be a sense-making animal, we find ourselves unsatisfied by the mythos of this claim. Why am I unhappy after top surgery? Has the procedure not produced needed notions of myself? Did it cut me open or suture me shut? I am teaching myself to let go of these closed questions of external demarcation, to instead care for what's inside, what's mine. Said simply, by Christian Wiman, "We are forever driven to become conscious of a wholeness from which consciousness exiles us."[24] The project will always fail. We will always be, in some form, exiled. Forever. And yet, we do not despair.

Trans Storytelling

Propped on an exam table, "mommy-makeover" pamphlets adorning the walls, I sunk into a thin paper vest and pulled its excess around my chest like a robe, concealing what I inevitably had to share. "So, tell me about your ideas on gender," the doctor asked. He was earnest. His question came after a series of others about my exercise habits, recreational drug use, and family health. I knew to anticipate this question. The exam room was stark and small. My surgeon sat on a stool at my feet, waiting, my wife in the corner, attentive. Whereas others might have memorized and practiced a measured response, I instead sat in silence, unable to find my way outside of my own honesty—I had no fucking clue. "Um, I'm non-binary. Trans non-binary. I have a therapist." Uncertainty brimmed through my loose scree of language as I balked through a few unrehearsed lines about fluidity and premeditation—I've already been to therapy. "Sorry," I said, apologizing for my incoherence when I wished my quiet said enough, said, "I'm aching for something else." Said, "Can you help me?" "Can you help me, not diagnose me, not expect me to feel better?" I thought about syringe exchange when I gathered boxes of needles and dropped them into a black bag with cookers, ties, and cottons, how it took only a few minutes to mark the participant's needs on a half-slip of paper, gather the items from a shelf, bag them, and hand them off. It's possible to do healthcare without explanation. It's possible to provide care ex nihilo, no explanation needed.

My doctor pivoted to ask what I wanted my chest to look like. "What kind of nipples do you want?" As he asked, he focused on my areolas while his hands traced from sternum to armpit, drawing an invisible blade across skin, summoning an imminent male line of pectoral muscle. We fell into the same rhetorical quandary. I never considered the multiple ways one might sculpt a masc chest. I also had little practice talking about such vulnerable parts of my body. When the PA arrived late, he caught her up by compressing our conversation into cogent bits. Of course he did; she was taking notes, uploading them to a portal: "Discussed treatment options for surgical intervention for circum periareolar mastectomy with possible liposuction bilaterally for gender-affirming surgical intervention. Photos taken today. Informed consent reviewed." Our exchange fractured into medical codes and insurance claims; all that falter was left as detritus.

As explored, by nature of living within inescapable capitalism, our relationship to time is manipulated through decrees for optimization and aspiration. To be a good citizen is to secure and protect our futures by making healthy choices and donning happy attitudes. The addicted subject must be en route to recovery, must articulate his trajectory as linear, as proceeding from rock bottom toward cure, toward clean. This performance is public and discursive—an external articulation of overcoming internal addiction, through which one gains credible status for care. But this trope implies that hard work earns peace and prosperity as the body becomes "healthier" and more authentically itself. It pathologizes private (interior) effort by deeming illogical any other narrative than the aspirational. "What is your ultimate goal?" my surgeon asked. "All your designs are about captivity," Herakles lectures Geryon.

The dominant narrative forced on trans folks mobilizes this same rhetorical construct. While we may be slowly spurning the language of disorder (and only is this true in privileged spaces), the trans subject is still situated on a path toward the cured state. But rather than sobriety serving as the telos, it is the fully gendered self—euphoria as a static destination achieved through semantic labor and medical assistance. Hil Malatino writes, "The future is always better than the present, a site of promise, deliverance; transition is framed as a period of trial and potential duress that is rewarded with the experience of harmony, good feeling, corporeal comfort."[25] While neither Malatino nor I wish to undermine euphoria—our euphoric moments secure survival and give joy—I *do* hope to undermine compulsory trans destinations to instead idle within uncured compositions, in adjectives and assemblages. Integral to process is regression, to mess up, to stall in mediocrity and the everyday pathos of being alive and having a body. This where we live most of our lives, in the messy slippage of a day, and yet that mess is pathologized.

Malatino, like myself, relies on community for care. After his top surgery, alongside friends who sent meals and checked in during the long weeks of recovery, he admits to having to "unlearn the shame that has been attached to asking for, offering, and accepting help when we've been full-body immersed in the mythos of neoliberal, entrepreneurial self-making."[26] For Malatino, care and shame not only rub up against capitalism, but are, in many ways, informed by it (see the previous chapter). Late capitalism not only requires and reproduces the image of the self-made achiever, but this image of mastery generates the newest forms of profit.[27] Just as we cannot evade capital, we cannot evade its forceful call for "self-making." It permeates our cultural forms of storytelling; we exist to overcome and by overcoming we are made. Maintenance of the American ethos relies on the retelling of this saga because it holds us accountable to no one: we are solely responsible for our outcomes. We are bootstrappers whose wealth and power matches our efforts of labor (never theft nor scheming). Trans feeling has been co-opted into this self-making machinery to reinforce our bodies as teleological. By understanding gender transition and expression under the aegis of capitalism and medicine, gender is always disorder (even if not in name) in need of a coherent fix.

I want to consider Dean Spade's experience seeking top surgery without expressing name or pronoun shifts, and without a history of hormone replacement therapy. The process he undergoes reflects, foremost, the excessive arbitrations trans people must assuage to receive care: at least a year of therapy, a history of articulated gender "incongruence" (expressed for six months or longer), the cognitive aptitude to make healthcare decisions, lab tests, letters of recommendation (from a therapist, psychiatrist, primary care physician). One must quit smoking and drug use, and so much more. When Spade cannot attest to incongruence, he finds himself forcibly delayed by bureaucratic red tape, evidence that time is never on our side, even when we're actively trying to unstick ourselves. Spade must deign aspirational accounts of his transgender experience, that he desires to advance from one gender to another, the one aspired to. Pressured to legitimize binary gender categories, Spade is denied care until he capitulates to the industry's requirement for teleological descriptions of his body. His providers require discursive proof that he occupies a disjunctive, dysphoric state and wishes to overcome those negative feelings for the positive. "In order to be deemed real, I need to want to pass as male all the time, and not feel ambivalent about this."[28] Spade's own voice fails to sufficiently prove his needs, because even as he is assured, he is ambivalent.

"Their work is, in essence, semiotic work," writes Summerson Carr, who researches conventional addiction narratives in the medical-therapeutic industry.[29] Rather than compose their own stories, participants bend to the will of rehab programs, which require cliché stories of hitting rock bottoms and overcoming dramatized failure. Participants learn how to talk about themselves, addiction, and recovery using explicit forms that ensure mobility through and graduation from recovery programs. Rewarded for clear, confessional language and formulaic story arcs, participants learn that disclosure begets access. Carr argues that the focus on disclosure, especially by therapists and certified health workers (i.e., gatekeepers who grant access to crucial services and resources), results from the conception that addiction is "a disease of denial—which afflicts the ability to read and render inner states in words."[30] The person who uses drugs is divorced from their true sense of self. It is recovery—from disease and/or criminal behavior—that saves them, and not just from failure, but from that false self. "One discovers," Carr writes, "that drug rehabilitation commonly revolves around rehabilitating the drug user's relationship with language. Following linear plotlines that proceed from a denoted dirty past to an anticipated clean future . . . recovery narratives . . . are the most highly valued signs of professional efficacy."[31] This teleological trajectory, codified through "linear plotlines," compresses knowledge into dire dogma, into certainty one must achieve and articulate. We must know ourselves. We must explain ourselves; otherwise we languish in denial, lost and confused.

This divulgent form of discourse continues to dominate the collective impression of what it means to be queer, but especially to be trans—that we must be in motion toward something *more* authentic. When my doctor asked about my ideas of gender, when I offered notes about therapy and pronouns, I gamed the system back, reciting the right script to ensure surgery. I wondered if this makes me complicit and worried it does. But I played the game to access healthcare services and avoid wrongful attention in the process. I spoke with regret in past tense, with pain and urgency in present tense, and with hope in future tense. Coaxed toward our best selves, our best bodies beam on the horizon, but we must first gather the strength to overcome our own ruins and riven bits. "The future is always better than the present."[32]

While historically "euphoria" was used in medical-therapeutic spaces as a diagnostic tool—patients were perceived as healthy through the visage of happiness and effortless embodiment[33]—the term has evolved to describe physiological bliss. In the contemporary Western imagination, "euphoria" now intimates a gendered telos, the finish line for which our hurt bodies long. Under the authority of the medical industry and compounded by capital, euphoria is exploited to market outcome, the desired state and cured condition to dysphoria. While not critical of euphoria in its material possibilities, I am instead skeptical of its use against trans people. Emma Heaney warns us that aspirational narratives of gender, those that tell us being trans *must mean* something, coerce us into believing we must overcome dysphoria in a heroic effort to attain the consummate self.[34] This narrative produces allegories rather than agency, endorses cured states rather than undulating transitions. Paisley Currah asks, "Are transsexual people born in the wrong body, or is it the wrong body narrative imposed by a medical establishment and legal architecture intent on maintaining the rigid border between male and female, even as they develop diagnoses and criteria that would allow one to move morphologically and/or legally from one gender to another?"[35] Documented as alienated from or by our bodies, because we might need medical and therapeutic assistance to ease some discontinuities, the "wrong body narrative" forces overcorrection; it overexposes our ambivalence to conjure pain as only overcome, never witnessed. The vanishing point pulls us in.

While the medical-therapeutic industry identifies euphoria as a diagnostic goal for the treatment of gender dysphoria, a goal with real material benefit, users of drugs do not receive the same generosity for their euphoric needs. Euphoria for some, not all. Euphoria for those deemed reliable, responsible owners of healing bodies.

Though the aspirational model is deeply entrenched in trans composition, I want to be very clear that many trans folks *do* desire the affective experience of arrival. Deservedly so. For some trans folks, linearity ensures survival. Binary gender ensures survival. This is precisely my point; there is no singular trans experience. We are a messy assemblage. One might classify my top surgery as just such a pitch toward authenticity. Without a doubt, I underwent such an intense procedure with the notion of *feeling better*, of adjustment or attunement, of hoping to stand up straight. But also, so many other expressions of being trans exist, those unfolding in arctic tundras or in climbing gyms, those utilizing poetic forms or collaged mediums. Rather than the story of making the self better, I wonder how shyness is part of transition, trans feeling, and trans being. What if the telos of trans is not the authentic self, explained and contained, but a creative current in which we are always authentically composing and revising. Because shy honors feeling and not just language, inchoate sensations are as credible as the contours of argument. We can embrace ambivalence rather than eliminate it.

Trans storytelling is, then, just storytelling wherein the narrator fluently authors and authorizes their own assembled serials of selfhood. Just as we are artisans of our bodies, so are we of our stories.

Shy in a Hospital Bed

The anesthesiologist didn't have me count down from ten. Instead, she said, "You're going to feel lightheaded." As soon as I was gone, I was back, in bed in the post-op recovery room, my doctor's hand on my shoulder. "We need to admit you," he said. He waited for the haze to clear in my eyes. "We're worried your lung might have suffered a laceration and air is escaping into your chest." My memories after surgery are soupy and nonsequential, as I recovered in the temporary post-op bed, waiting for an open hospital room: the nurses playfully ragged each other, their shifts each coming to a close; my doctor studied X-rays in the corner, lifting the glossy black film to light; my throat sore from the breathing tube; and ice chips in a Styrofoam cup. I was, in that moment, euphoric. I was grateful for the warm blanket and ice water, for my nurses and their care under such duress of vulnerability.

But the nurses also confessed confusion around "the language." The nurse who inserted a new IV, this one pumping antibiotics, missed the vein in my arm before prodding the back of my hand. She admitted she was anxious of being reported for using "wrong words." She told me the hospital makes her watch instructional videos on caring for trans patients. Another nurse, who slipped compression socks on my feet, asked why some patients don't want nipples. "Even real guys have nipples," she said confused. Many on my care team used the wrong pronouns, vacillating between "she" and "he" because while the former comes naturally given my small body and feminine cheekbones, the latter is the perception of my aspired destination.

My surgeon's practice was new. Located in wealthy suburbs north of Pittsburgh, Pennsylvania, his unit had performed only a few top surgeries before mine. In that way, my body brought us together in the post-op room, wherein novelty (for them) and fatigue (for me) converged. As I recovered from anesthetics and waited for my overnight bed, that room filled with a strange energy. I was silent in its center, the reason we were all there, why many of the nurses stayed beyond shift hours to clock out. We waited on X-rays, on whether my lung would collapse or hold out. My surgeon came around to check and recheck my breathing, pressing his fingers on my chest as I gasped in pain. The nurses chatted to one another, many as if I could not hear them. With my throat tight from the breathing tube, plus the balm of morphine, I slipped into their presumed silence and into shy vigil. I witnessed their connections among one another, their collegial familiarity. One nurse's little girl came running into the room, surprising her mom at the end of the day with a bear hug. I witnessed community and kinship. But as I waited, I also witnessed how they quickly abandoned the discomfort of my pronouns for the ease of "she/her." In front of me, they laughed over the grammatical oddity of "they/them." I was ghost, specter, the first-person dreamer unnoticed despite all the ways the bright lights of the unit fell on me. Flush from the heat of surgery and narcotics, I was overwhelmed with gratitude for their care, even as they also, simultaneously, demonstrated carelessness.

My surgeon, all even-keeled kindness, good with pronouns but also with nerves, comforted my wife when he told her about my lung and the laceration, how I was on oxygen and needed to stay overnight. He arrived early the next morning and explained the team was still learning. While he again listened to the quiet pops my chest continued to make, I remembered a couple weeks earlier I taught my composition class the importance of process—in our writing but also as a social practice. If we accept others' sideways journeys and messy processes (if we accept the same for ourselves), then we make space for growth—intellectual, political, and artistic growth. We wait, painful as it is, because connection takes time. But then, I hedged. "Sometimes it's not about the journey," I told my class. "Sometimes we need people to get to the damn destination." As much as I resist these destinations, I still recognize their necessity and protections. This is not about pitting the present against the future, but instead about how present ministration makes the future possible. Just as we refuse to force recovery on our syringe exchange participants, tending only to immediate need, we protect our ongoing relationships with those participants. They are more likely to return to exchange and more likely to enter recovery facilities *when we do not* insist on either.

Dani, Cathy, and Ginny oversaw my overnight hours, refilling my IV and dropping off pain pills. Like in the post-op room, the same pronoun alarm occured. Each nursed confessed their fear of "the language," of how to talk about gender, of doing it wrong during the frenetic moment of care. They were afraid of being reported. The provision of care was not, then, unilateral, nurse to patient. We shyly passed it back and forth, through delicate conversation wherein we all wavered between vulnerability and withholding. While I perhaps did not prefer this, tired as I was, I understood it. "My mom was a NICU nurse," I told them. "She did twelve-hour shifts for thirty years." Rather than explain the language, rather than explain another's desire to forgo nipples, or the grammatical logics of non-binary pronouns, I told my caretakers about my mom, working long shifts in a Detroit hospital, how she had retired only earlier that year right before COVID hit.

The lost hours of my hospital room filled instead with unarticulated feelings, transmitted between doctors, nurses, patient. Power shifting in each interaction and along multiple directions persuaded me into shy registers of gratitude but also unease. I didn't report anyone for misgendering or inappropriate questions about nipple placement, not to protect my surgical team from legal or institutional repercussions, but to protect myself by initiating connection across difference in the space of care. I'm not sure it was the best decision. It is just the one I made, with all my privilege and vulnerability, protection and dispossession. The anxious nursing team and me with my bandaged chest—we shared in the failures and limitations of language, what it might do to us. Exposure goes both ways.

The morning I was discharged, my doctor came in to make sure my lungs expanded without leaks. Stethoscope dangling from his ears, when he saw the tattoo of Ferdinand the Bull on my right bicep he excitedly said, "Ferdinand! That's my daughter's favorite book!" Ferdinand, the shy bull who prefers wonder and wildflowers, admits, "I like it better here where I can just sit quietly and smell the flowers." Ferdinand is a quiet, gentle creature, kin to sad Geryon, but when stung by a bee he responds wildly to the pain, causing others to mistake him as fierce, a fighting bull. The others are wrong, and Ferdinand is forced to take on their error.

I got the tattoo just weeks before surgery, to honor this shy bull but also as homage to Elliott Smith, my favorite musician, who also inked Ferdinand on his right bicep. When I was in the tattoo shop, lying on my stomach with my arm slung back, I followed the slow pulse of orange and purple fish as they swam circles in a large tank behind my artist. For the first time I didn't feel pain from the needle, but peace. My artist admitted the fish are there to calm her clients but then went on to argue the pain of a tattoo is mental. I always balk at this sentiment, that pain can be manipulated by our psychic willpower, that we are responsible for what we feel despite the needle charging ink into our skin, sometimes rattling a bone. I still balk. But I also appreciate the opportunity to experience peace and pain at the same time, that one does not extinguish another.

Beyond Representation: The Mile I'm In

Even as I do it here to myself, positioning the trans person within clinic walls replicates a tired scene of trans representation. Of course, clinical spaces provoke dissonance among queer and trans patients. Of course, the medical-therapeutic industry continues to authorize dominant narratives of trans experience. I do not wish to repeat this harm, to reinforce the trans person as a medical metaphor for achievement, but to instead assemble shy into compositional forms, to shunt tedious reruns of trans portrayals relying on metaphors,[36] "bad objects,"[37] or revelations of "spectacular truth."[38] As trans people, we rely on the clinic; it tears us down, then helps us thrive. It gives life—hormone replacement, anxiety meds, IUDs, fertility treatments, scans and tests and prophylactics. It takes life—predatory insurance, unnecessary forms that embellish and overstate, skeptical practitioners. The clinic is not all one thing, no monolith but multiplicities of care, concern, indifference, harm, connection, and dissolution, all circulating in a contained space.

While trans representation—as it appears in industry, media, and policy—expands depictions (and therefore understanding) of trans life, overexposure diminishes, deepening ruts that reify old tropes of transgression. For example, when social life (especially media: academic articles, news clips, tweets and reels) pronounces that trans women of color suffer violence at higher rates than other queer people (and other trans people), violence is further entrenched into being trans and being a woman of color. The statistics are tragically accurate, but by themselves they reduce lives to the coldness of dull numbers. Life scraped from bare life is just *bare*, with violence centralized, not human experience.[39]

The racialization of drug use relies on moralizing rhetoric and sensationalized storytelling to claim addiction has a "new face," thereby conjuring a conventional figure of drug use. Jules Gill-Peterson notes this discursive pattern in trans representations as well, specifically in how it constructs our notions of trans childhood. "The new face of transgender" applies a plasticity meant to reinforce whiteness: "The discourse of plasticity has prescribed one narrow form of futurity through whiteness for trans children, while simultaneously denying any future at all to those who are structurally barred from its highly managed shelter."[40] The abstraction of interchangeability—one drug user represents all drug users, one trans person represents all trans people—mobilizes white, sovereign self-designation and white self-discovery through the blurring of all trans and/or Black humans into interchangeable caricature. Saidiya Hartman explains that this interchange, what she calls "fungibility," imprisons the body as "an abstract and empty vessel vulnerable to the projection of others' feelings, ideas, desires, and values; and, as property, the dispossessed body of the enslaved is the surrogate for the master's body since it guarantees his disembodied universality and acts as the sign of his power and dominion."[41] The meaningfulness of being trans becomes just that, to supply meaning, to attrite into an empty vessel for political convenience.

In deauthorizing the body as the site of totalized meaning (even as that singular body reaches out in need), we must deauthorize reductive prescriptions for representation. In another piece, Gill-Peterson writes, "In the era of trans hypervisibility, the mere presence of a Black or Brown trans woman is supposed to leap into good politics. The trans woman of color appears as a symbol, invoked as the figure in whose name activism, or intersectional consciousness, is conducted. But the trans woman of color is still just that: *a figure for other people*."[42] In order for this figure to succeed, to continue *figure-ing* for the purpose of political and cultural gain, the trans woman of color must continue to suffer. This is *the* definition of trans misogyny, composed from overly medicalized narratives on trans experience and reductive attention wrought by capital's commodification of identity in medical and political marketplaces.

So, how might we replace representation with multiplicity? More stories, more description, and more feeling, but also more contradiction: we deserve representation *and* privacy, the chance to explain ourselves as well as the opportunity to stay silent. Trans representations, for example, "do not simply re-present an already existing reality but are also doors into making new futures possible,"[43] *if* those descriptions and translations of trans life re-narrate the scene of pain, marginalization, and precarity to account for more. Paradoxically, "more" might mean less. In thinking the body, in thinking of being trans, we might turn toward what Jeanne Vaccaro describes as "felt matters," ways of thinking without "succumbing to additive logics."[44] Instead, we "map transgender embodiment as a set of relations among movement, speed, expansion, and excess."[45] I add shyness in prioritizing a "theory of embodiment that does not seek totality or coherence of self."[46] My transness is not an object signifying political or cultural dissent, even as I witness it interpreted as so. My body just *is*, quietly ongoing, involuntarily but no less joyfully taking up space in the world. Rather, I activate shyness as dissent, refusing (when possible) harmful discursions and shielding my body from speculation or scrutinization. I think of Geryon in the sky, his red body gliding against the line of the horizon. He is nothing and everything. Carson said adjectives are imported, meaning foreign, through which novel, strange images—images to be regarded, not appropriated—arrive from another world.

The fight for liberation is often sounded through megaphones and marches. While our loud voices interrupt capital's equilibrium to demand immediate attention and redress (e.g., silence = death), there are also many manners of protest.[47] Kevin Quashie argues this explicit point in his important text *The Sovereignty of Quiet*: "The quiet subject is a subject who surrenders, a subject whose consciousness is not only shaped by struggle but also by revelry, possibility, the wildness of the inner life. Quietness is not a performance of a withholding; instead, it is an expressiveness that is not necessarily legible, at least not in a world that privileges public expressiveness. Neither is quiet about resistance. It is surrender, a giving into, a falling into self. The outer world cannot be avoided or ignored, but one does not only have to yield to its vagaries. One can be quiet."[48] While "shy" and "quiet" are not precise synonyms, I collude with Quashie to propose that shyness, even in its affective aches, provides means of living within capitalism that escape explanatory labor. Because, even as marginalized subjects who suffer both quotidian and institutional harms, our whole lives are not oriented toward "fighting the social world."[49] In this way, shy is a mode of expression that facilitates more modes of expression. Shy is not always the right move, but it is an underrated move.

Shy, as a sensorial form of composition, is an alternative to aspirational discourse and the "narrative of entrapment,"[50] the production of figures or academic metaphors. We do not need to comply with linear storytelling that limns an outcome. If the entrapment narrative curates allegories rather than authors, shy begets minute descriptions of being trans as we experience it on any given day, as both pain and pleasure, witness and refusal, as quotidian as walking through the farmer's market and feeling the sun on our chest. Or, we forsake description altogether, giving way to uncertainty and making that uncertainty felt, shared, focal. Shy licenses new sonics for self-expression; I describe myself without explaining myself. I determine my own gendered meanings of my body through the privacy afforded by stalled moments and muddled murmurs. I draw shaggy-haired boys and lose myself in the inked flow state (see chapter 4). My estranged relationship to my body arouses ache, a deep suffering of dissonance at times, but also a longing for ongoingness. Shyness helps us survive the feeling (and realities) of surveillance as we stand with our backs safely against the wall. Shyness affirms us even as we flutter around in confusion, that we are right to listen to our intuition when it tells us to wait.

In that sense, shy might mean we don't "come out," not in language, even as we do socially, psychically. Shy might mean we withhold information: "I'm trans. I have a therapist," rather than "I have no fucking clue." Shy might mean we lie, like at syringe exchange. "You can say 'pass' on any question or make up answers altogether." Shy might mean diversion. "My mom worked twelve-hour shifts." Shy might mean we let mess into our stories, end those stories with question marks, or a simple "I dunno." Shy is self-protection. We refuse to inscribe ourselves to instead make risky decisions because of gut feeling and need—without explanation or apology—then see how it plays out. We stall and wait and waste time. We resist therapy for years then attend therapy for years. We play and tussle with loved ones and experience vulnerability in domestic security. We write our futures. We assemble, authorize, archive. We toss our old journals in black garbage bags.

Through shyness, by yielding and relearning, I become a better (meaning, more generous) listener. Because, as Gill-Peterson writes, "everyone but trans women have monopolized the meaning of trans femininity,"[51] and I refuse to play a part in that monopoly, or any monopoly. My transness does not forfeit me of accountability. And I hope it never will. Instead, I long to revise my understanding of how different humans experience harm (and beauty) in our world. I long to read, listen, and write. I long to sit shyly with openness toward confrontation and correction, in order to better care for others. Compassion is nurtured through constant renovation of our imaginations. It is a quiet renovation. To realize my errors is to work toward the reduction of harm.

Trans persons deserve gender self-determination, however that manifests, however much that changes. We are all in process. We all regress or grow at angles into corners, against walls. Shy allows it. Our futures do not need to be the site of the best self, just the site of the self, alive and authorial. Cameron Awkward-Rich argues for futures outside of capital's conceit of productive futurity when he writes, "At the same time, transness, at minimum, is the insistence on the human capacity for once unimaginable change. . . . I had to cultivate—actively cultivate—a kind of wide-eyed optimism about what the future, and the future of my own body, could entail. I had to believe that feeling, intense feeling, was not only important but also potentially life- and world-changing."[52] We trans people are makers. Not just makers of new selves, but makers of optimism.

I first balked at Awkward-Rich's unabashed cultivation of "wide-eyed optimism," especially as a potential model for daily living, so trained am I toward skepticism and criticality. Optimism signals hope as we vault confidently toward future selves and future worlds. But, unfortunately, hope has come to be conflated with neoliberal naivete, willful ignorance, or blinding privilege. While there are, of course, justified critiques of optimism (I write more about hope in chapter 5 and the conclusion), I also ardently believe we deserve to speak joyfully of our futures. Transgression is not a sustainable or radical model of living for most. And it should never have been requisite for queer and trans people. The desire for marriage, family, even wealth, is the desire to live freely according to one's horizonal desires. So, I stand with Awkward-Rich in believing that we cannot surrender our queer futures. Our younger and current selves depend on us reaching new days. In this way, hope subverts: we can reject the cynicism placed on us and our lives. Awkward-Rich imagines a future and a body to *feel himself* beyond mere survival. The goal is to exist into futures *we* have had a hand in making. In so doing, shyness (as one possibility) insulates us from implacable futures so we can continue to dream.

I am trans. I *know* this only because I *feel* this. Though my future still beckons, my future need not be pocked with perfected explanation. Shy, for me, means fumbling through faltered, fluxing expressions of gender, an unintelligible feeling that drives my desire and sometimes stymies it. My body shifts with confusion so that feeling, rather than knowing, lets me linger, to just be. This delay has real psychic effect on my wellbeing. My body knows. *Our bodies know.* But our bodies also inhabit diaphanous states of dreaming, doubt, and speculation. This too is knowledge. Not only does shy subvert medical and cultural demands for arrival, but it dilutes the spectacle put on trans people. Quiet narratives of life lived, of being alive and trans, give us the quotidian and assembled. Shy moves beyond the scenes of clinics to instead leave open the possibilities of trans life, to account for the breadth of wonder, nerve, desire, joy, disappointment, fatigue, pain, and love we experience as (trans) people.

Six weeks after my top surgery, my doctor cleared me for light cardio exercise. That same afternoon I laced my running shoes and, for the first time since childhood, pulled a T-shirt over a bare chest. I started slow, lightly jogging down to the park and its familiar trails. The rhythmic punch of my shoes on soft dirt told my heart where to go, how to find pace. But not even a half-mile in, I caught my toe on a root and pitched shoulder-first into the ground. As I stood up to survey my body for injury, I placed my skinned palms to my chest and exhaled. I sensorially scanned my body for duress, dusting dirt from my kneecaps and out of the slim cuts on my hands. And then I kept going. I've been running for a decade, having first picked it up when I came out as gay and was getting divorced in my late twenties, desperate for the serotonin. Years later, in my late thirties, when I began to reckon with my trans feelings, I started running ultra marathons—thirty-one miles and thousands of feet of elevation gain, in Pennsylvania's Laurel Highlands and Orcas Island in the Puget Sound. Between my first ever jog around the block and the last finishing line, between these two timestamps, are innumerable training runs—pained and grinding, easy and fluid, and those on the brink of forgotten. Taken together, they fashion an unfinished whole. I return faithfully to this sport because it gives me a way into myself. Running allows me, even if for an hour at a time, to fully inhabit my body without requiring it do more than move. No grand argument is being made; rather, running is just steady motion, the quiet flex and release of muscles.

For me, running is a shy practice within trans storytelling. Running teaches me to relinquish finish lines as the sole source of pleasure. Running sets me into a flow state as I charge toward a challenge that constantly renews and evades. I am exiled. While I feel strong on some runs, others offer only suffering and exhaustion, side cramps and tight IT bands. Even as I become "a better runner," I only define "better" as more adaptable and understanding, more inside the process. While running offers me the material possibility of euphoria—the tightened abs and flatter chest—this is only one piece of how I experience my body. Running is also the escape from articulation. Instead, I move, make, be. I tune into my body—what it says when it hurts or what it needs when it weakens—and make ongoing adjustments, to stretch longer or front-load hydration. Even on bad runs, I practice failure until that word loses its freight, becomes falter, becomes process. Running reminds me that desire is temporal, not an arrived-at destination. It is often just a goddamn grind. Indeed, a common mantra for runners is *run the mile you're in*. Meaning, do not fixate on what you have left to achieve, but focus on your needs and ability in the very moment—more water, a gel, a quick stretch. My mantra is *keep going*. If I keep going I find that by focusing my attention to present need, I move further than imagined into new landscapes, beyond my own understanding of myself and my possibilities.

Descriptions and translations of trans life must work toward re-narrating the scene of marginalization and precarity to account for more. By so doing, alongside Kevin Quashie, we protect those "whose consciousness is not only shaped by struggle but also by revelry, possibility, the wildness of the inner life."[53] Because even as I feel pain in my body, I also find joy in the way it moves over a technical trail. We can, and should, honor our desire for coherence and euphoria, but at the same time also resist external demands for the same. While we long to feel good in our skin, we are justified in our aches and pain too. After decades of embodied unease, running allays my shame as I relearn myself. I experience this reinvention as sensation, not intellect. In this way, my body *feels possible*, this ability to live into the edges of my skin, to break toward horizons with an acute sense of imagination. I know myself while not knowing myself. I am alive in the question. I am alive in the question that is my body. I take on pain without rehabbing it, lingering in the quiet space of exile. I run the mile I am in. I am just a speck raking my way against an immense sky.

Refusing, Revising, Rewriting

My shyness refuses to participate in mastery, in accumulation, in rhetorical economies. Shy is a feeling I have and a move I make to navigate my worlds—whether under the canopy of Douglas firs, trekking alone across a wildflower ridgeline, or in the waiting room of my doctor's office. The discomfort in having to name something that cannot be named, or that loses itself in the naming, is relieved in forgoing or postponing the ritual altogether. While shy still privileges some inscription, this form of language-making occurs alongside or emerges from acute sensitivities, attention and care, and process. Holding back has not dimmed the vibrancy of my life, but on the contrary, has let me waylay with a greater appreciation for its complexity. Like Geryon, I am a fuckup, riddled with mistakes, my heart broken by believing in good when there was only danger. Like Geryon, I am most at rest not when I try to make up for the mistakes or pain, but when I write my autobiography in the blurred states.

In order to receive top surgery I sat in cold rooms, showed my chest to strangers, answered questions about time and dysphoria (how long have I felt my "wrong body"?), questions about transitions (will I take hormones? why or why not?), and affirmed that yes, I have a mental health professional who will "verify" and "recommend" me for the procedure. Practitioners requested "before" photos. They build their portfolios from skin, reproducing visual allegories about trans experience. What is inside is outside. I long for privacy, to be taken at my word, for my quiet desire to cast louder than medical lexicons. Malatino writes, "So often, we must rely on relationships with people and institutions that interpret us as subhuman, or at the very least misrecognize us so profoundly that the 'I' conjured in interaction barely resembles the 'I' we understand ourselves to be."[54] In this way (though, of course, not in all ways), dysphoria is an outside force, not an internal, buried feeling. Though we feel it as both.

After more chest X-rays and a hospital discharge, I returned home and curled into my mastectomy pillow for days. My wife helped me shower and replaced my bandages, walked our dog and felt my chest for air pockets. While the physical pain was minimal, much less than I expected, my emotional pain was devastating. I careened into a depression that took months from which to slowly emerge. Later, through online trans forums, I learned that post-op depression is common and its impact is greater the longer one's under anesthesia. Often, expectations of gender-affirming care compound the trauma: we believe we should come out the other side of surgery euphoric and closer to how we dream ourselves to be.

During this grief and fatigue, I received an insurance claim refusing to cover my preauthorized procedure. The double mastectomy was denied. When I called my insurance company, they clarified I was covered for a breast reduction, not the bilateral mastectomy, which was how the hospital coded the procedure. The cost was over $16,000. "Did you have a double mastectomy or a breast reduction," the insurance representative asked me. Wanting to avoid these charges, I deflected and demurred, claimed ignorance around the semantics of medical coding and terminology. "I don't really know the difference," I said, lying. "Well, do you still have tissue left in your breasts?" she asked. "Yes," I said monosyllabically and truthfully, since most surgeons leave tissue behind for realistic contouring. While I believed my response punctuated an end to our conversation, the rep then asked, "Can you fill a bra?"

This conversation repeated itself many times over the next year as I fought for my case to go back to claims, desperately explaining that the issue was simply the result of a wrong code, a couple numbers out of order. I worried about my medical documents, covered with the language of trans care: "gender dysphoria" and "mastectomy," "identifies as . . . " and "no HRT." I worried a $16,000 decision would come down to evidence produced by the most vulnerable part of my body—my bruised chest. I worried a decision would be made from the literal shape of my skin, but also from how I identified and described that ostracized piece of myself. Shy emitted from the feeling of exposure, from "Can you fill a bra?" Shy was also deployed, as strategy, my deflection and semantic withholding, so I could end those calls without disclosure, breaking into sobs as soon as I hung up.

While readers of *Autobiography of Red* are told Geryon is a monster, we never know if it's true, whether those tucked wings and red skin are literal or an allegory, an embodied projection of shame and alterity. But knowing the "truth" of Geryon's body is irrelevant to the poetics of his story, because it is precisely this doubt that makes Geryon. He's a wallflower; despite all his body says and reveals about him, it is not the scene of his full meaning.

> Once Geryon had gone
> with his fourth-grade class to view a pair of beluga whales newly captured
> from the upper rapids of the Churchill River.
> Afterwards at night he would lie on his bed with his eyes open thinking of
> the whales afloat
> in the moonless tank where their tails touched the wall—as alive as he was
> on their side
> of the terrible slopes of time.[55]

Geryon absorbs a whole world of meaning, his small body soaking into a singular moment as he pays witness to these beautiful animals, these captive belugas full of life yet trapped in tanks. Geryon is in pain. Some of his pain is heartache and trauma; but his sensitivity and shyness are also ongoing, strained and pained responses to difference. Little Geryon, standing under the enormity of the whales but separated by a glass plane, recognizes himself in the reflection—he is just as naked, captive, and surveilled, with time slipping away. He is just as alive but trapped. Vibrant but exposed.

I've fully recovered from top surgery. But I am considering revision options because some tissue remains, the areolas have widened, and my chest is asymmetrical. My wife tells me these blemishes are negligible. But the body is known for symmetry and my differences are hard to accept. I'm still processing the post-op depression, working out the gendered questions the procedure summoned. I am deeper into the pain of my body's doubts, and yet at the same time relieved of its repressive hold . . . sometimes. Trans lives happen inside the clinic, but those hours are modest compared to the many spent in our apartments mincing garlic, at work stocking boxes, in bed with our partners, on the street walking our dogs, at the bar with friends, alone on single-track, switchbacking trails. Our lives are happening everywhere. As one who loves language and poetry, who studies rhetoric, I regularly abstain from words. It is both caution and patience. I will wait, and in the meanwhile hold close the words of T. Fleischmann: "I would like to be uninscribed by language, like an uninscribed piece of paper. . . . It's taken a lot of resistance, that I want to leave my gender and my sex life uninscribed—that it took me years to consider the fact that I did not have to name my gender or sexuality at all."[56] They go on to say also, "The uninscribed . . . is a site of change." The site of change is a creative moment, a rupturing that occurs in revision, where imaginations not explanations are nourished.

I started testosterone the day my daughter turned one. Tight fist of lemon poppy-seed birthday cake clasped in her hand, she offered it to me with one word, "Dada." I apply my T gel to my shoulder and chest each morning, the alcohol burning small fissures in my skin. When the doctors at Planned Parenthood asked my goals for hormone therapy, I was honest. "I don't know. I just know how I feel right now is precarious." A few months prior, a lump appeared in my chest that required a biopsy. I first laid shirtless on a table for an ultrasound, cold goo across my right pec, and then one week later on the biopsy table, where the radiologist and surgeon pressed fat needles directly under my areola. "I don't care if it's cancer or not. I want the lump gone," I told my wife. Of course I cared;[57] but the pain flaring up from the thick biopsy needle was a simulacrum of another pain: being born female, the breast swelling, my body in excess of my control.

Geryon's autobiography is a live work of translation undergoing constant revision. "This is when Geryon liked to plan / his autobiography, in that blurred state / between awake and asleep when too many intake valves are open in the soul."[58] He tries, fails, and tries again to express the shifting eros and ethos of his inner life. To express is to express difference, not by fault of his own aesthetics, but because Geryon's world was never meant to understand him. Even so, his projects are not dire in their repetitions or opacities, because resolutions are not compulsory to his art-making. Geryon writes his autobiography as he lives it. We all do. The revisions help us make sense of our own mess even as we are muddled by it. This is the conundrum of language—even as we use it we misuse it. Just as we describe, we take away. We rewrite the same sentences, return to the same reckonings.

Even if our shy registers do not reform others'—our families' or our doctors'—notions of trans selfhood, even if all we do is enter the fray of the aspirational and mumble our way through the intakes, even if "I don't know" fills a room with difficult energy, we might still find respite in these murmurs. We withhold the "I" that will go unrecognized despite our efforts. We craft a story of our own making, whether it is "ours" or not, to weather what harms us. Because all the while, this conservation of selfhood and reservoir of energy means we prioritize what matters—writing our autobiography in the blurred states and reveling in the wildness of our interior lives. Inside is ours.

4

Nostalgic Potential

The Mixtape Is an Archive, and the Archive Is a Feeling Thing

Got bitten fingernails and a head full of the past
And everybody's gone at last . . .
Don't get upset about it, no, not anymore
There's nothing wrong that wasn't wrong before.

—Elliott Smith

Located south of downtown Eugene, Oregon, House of Records is a one-story house with sloping wood floors and shelves crowded with used and new vinyl. To walk through is to gently shift and pivot: indie in what was once a dining room, classic rock in the living room, hip hop in the hallways. I was thirty, a broke barista pulling espresso shots for minimum wage, going through my divorce from Michael and blowing my tip money on records. One rainy day I lingered in the store's indie section, flipping through vinyl sleeves until my fingers softened from films of dust. I worked my way into Elliott Smith's catalog, lined up under the east-facing window. Just arrived to my thirties yet arrested by student loan debt, a divorce, and vocational stasis, I stood holding *Either/Or* and was seized by nostalgia, flush with the feelings of my adolescent self. It had been over a decade since I'd listened to Smith's music, since I sat in my childhood bedroom with headphones on, neck bent over a notebook, replaying *Either/Or*, looping it front to back. "Speed Trials," "Between the Bars," "Angeles," "Say Yes"—some of the best songs in his entire catalog appear on this album, and yet I had forgotten about Smith and the quiet magnitude of his voice, his music slipping away into an archival ether.

Spending the last of my cash, I walked home in the rain with *Either/Or* under my jacket, wondering what it would feel like to return to this important artifact, wondering what such a synaptic charge of memory might summon.

The Pain of Home: Nostalgia's Roots

It's right there in the word: *algia* translates to "pain" and *nostros* to "return home." Nostalgia, then, is to return to the pain of home. Or, there is pain in returning home. Or, simply home is pain. In all senses, nostalgia is return and this return hurts. When Swiss medical student Johannes Hofer first named "nostalgia" in 1688, he described a homesickness that manifested through the skin—as fervorous heartbeats or hot fevers—and constructed an illness that always, in some degree, signaled home, toward *nostros*.[1] We cannot cleave home from nostalgia. Home makes the feeling and makes it painful. It comes as no surprise then that the same name reappears over and again in the genealogy of nostalgia studies: Odysseus. Symbolizing the long journey back, the struggle and hustle it requires to navigate toward home, Odysseus gives us the conventional conceits of nostalgia: home awaits, home is worth the pain of getting back to, home offers respite, familiarity, family. But I want to trouble this orthodox idea of nostalgia, because I suspect its conventionality in homelands and home families continues to reinforce simplistic narratives that overly politicize this achy affect and diminish its potentialities for queer returns. More on that soon, but first.

Home is complicated. For many, home fails to protect us or provide respite and is instead a site of pain and obligation, a sore, overworked muscle chronic in its injury. Yet this pain is not always the same as violence, but more complex and formative. I left home forever at eighteen, by which I mean I left my small house on Anita Street in suburban Detroit and have never returned to cross its threshold. Despite this estrangement, home still lives in me, as memory but also through relationships, scent and sound, even dreams, as my subconscious tries to reconcile such abrupt abdication, such fast abandonment of the only space I ever knew. Home is pain, and still a pull exists. Ann Cvetkovich gives us an important intervention on home, one with which I closely identify, and one that better nuances the desire to feel, think, and touch backwards:

> I don't want to naturalize or romanticize home, especially since I consider
> dislocation to have been a productive force in shaping me. I have found other
> ways of being at home or in the body besides "going home," especially be-
> cause I know there is not always a home to return to. But I sometimes feel the

need to touch the land of my childhood in order to remember myself in myself. I'm not recalling a lost paradise; I'm acknowledging the troubled history that led to my departure as part of figuring out what it means to go back.[2]

What then does it mean to *long* for return, knowing that return might deposit us directly into pain? Why do we "*feel* the need," as Cvetkovich writes? Why would we bring this upon ourselves if there were not more to this achy affect than mere solipsistic pleasure or political claim, the two reigning interpretations we have of nostalgia? What does it mean to "remember myself in myself"? We return because we feel the need, and that need is worth our attention. While we never go back, not literally, we find other routes of return, through feeling, music, and language. It is archival but also the remaking of an old want into agential energy. Adrienne Rich wrote, "Re-vision—the act of looking back, of seeing with fresh eyes, of entering an old text [the self, perhaps?] from a new critical direction—is for us more than a chapter in cultural history, it is an act of survival."[3] Through nostalgia, we are empowered.

I join Cvetkovich to reckon with why we might feel the need to go back, specifically arguing that a form of creative literacy ("figuring it out") flourishes in our returns. Throughout these pages, I've tried to guard agency in precarity, to hold them at the same time, to argue that one does not negate the other. In nourishing our nostalgic desires we come to see there is more to know about the self, that we are the makers of that knowledge, and we always have been. Returning to Elliott Smith's music in Eugene, while coming out and enduring some of the more painful years of my life, was my nostalgic impulse, a feeling but also an intention, an act of archival survival. While I did not know this when I bought *Either/Or* at House of Records, I'd soon learn that the nostalgic attention I gave his music was, simultaneously, nostalgic attention I gave myself. I turned back and saw a fourteen-year-old kid who needed help. Even more devastating, this kid saw me at thirty and saw that I needed help too. I was, at thirty, grieving through the process of coming out, confronting the new truths of myself. Smith was both part of the confrontation—he reanimated unfinished desire—and yet also balm to its pain. The replay, the loop of the tape, is not terminal but a Möbius strip: trace what's outside and find yourself in the interiors of an infinite spin. The nostalgic motion of Smith stirred up the knowledge I needed—that queer and trans desire lives in music, in sensation and memory, not just in knowledge. I listened to *Either/Or*, to "Between the Bars," and felt this kid's unfinished longings rise to the very surface of my skin. What was kept in the interiors at age fourteen found its way out.

Maggie Nelson's gentle advice on returns is, in many ways, advice on one's literacy of the self, that is, how we learn and relearn our lives as we life them: "Sometimes one has to know something many times over. . . . One may have to undergo the same realizations, write the same notes in the margins, return to the same themes in one's work, relearn the same emotional truths, write the same book over and over again—not because one is stupid or obstinate or incapable of change, but because such revisitations constitute a life."[4] Our bodies are a form of literacy that never culminates.

Who hasn't replayed the same sad old songs, found relief in hitting repeat, in the echo? "It is tempting," writes Cvetkovich, "of course, to suggest that 'cure' or 'healing' or 'recovery' comes from finding or returning home."[5] But, as we know, cure can be manipulated into a farcical landmark. Recovery—as a singular, linear model—fails us when not also braided within the realities of return or relapse. Nostalgia encourages us to take ownership of those limits, of how we know and compose ourselves; but it also flips the traditional script of capital time (that we must move further into our authentic selves, and therefore farther away from some specious version of an old self) to instead embrace the past in its present inflammations. Our archives formed us, and they continue to form us, puncturing our personal literacies to affirm us in our changes. Our archives emphasize how *we* make ourselves—despite external forces saying otherwise—and therefore how we will continue to make ourselves, ensuring our futures are solely ours to compose.

In this chapter I analyze the potential of nostalgia because I believe it is possible to feel nostalgic for a place and time that hurts, that we go back, not to retrieve a lost object or return to a lost time, but for the relief, even pleasure, in return*ing*. What if nostalgia is not the desire to go back and stay, but to revisit and rave? What if nostalgia is not about destinations (the past, the home, the family) but about the feeling of return in and of itself? That is, nostalgia is not reinstatement of what's lost, but the feeling of moving back and what that feeling opens, and specifically how it deepens our own sense of agency, literacy, and possibility. We are empowered by nostalgia, to speak on behalf of a younger self or to gain narrative authority over a past that claimed us. We learn more about ourselves by going back, by entering our archives to study the past self and retroactively fulfill our need for recognition or voice. When we take them together—this agency and literacy—we find (and feel) there are many ways of understanding and describing our lives. Just as we are makers of our past selves, through our nostalgic and archival attentions, so also are we makers of our future selves.

Before we explore any of that, we'll honor nostalgia by investing in our own series of returns, into nostalgia's history, its legacy as pathological attachment, its right-wing appropriations, but we'll also consider why escapism—so often conflated with nostalgia—is disparaged, and why we are taught to mistrust this affect. These returns will then open toward archives to explore the importance of feeling backwards. This chapter will also follow my own nostalgic pangs, as I return to the music of my youth, to Elliott Smith, not only to indulge in the gratification of returns, but to also make sense of that troubled time, and to thereby demonstrate how knowledge moves backwards, how nostalgia is, in that way, counterintuitively even, a form of growth. This chapter is therefore for anyone who has struggled to put into language their queer longings and has felt those longings drag out in time. It is for those who experience literacy as embodied, and experience both the pain and desire this reality bears. It is for those who are committed to learning and relearning themselves, even if that means coming out late, maintaining our youthful attachments, and adding the same damn song to every new playlist.

Making Our Escapes

"Between the Bars," the most known track on Elliott Smith's *Either/Or*, is presumably about leaving the past self, even as this is always impossible. "People you've been before that you / don't want around anymore."[6] If this isn't a trans lyric, I don't know what is. "Between the Bars" is my favorite song and has been since I was fourteen. Our favorite songs make so many playlists, are played at the end of so many days. We eagerly share them—a gesture of intimacy, a way of pointing inward as we point outward. They become part of us, art as ontological accessory, and so we take them everywhere, lease them out, inhabit them, return to them again and again. This is what the best art does—it repeats and regenerates in new spaces. Which is also how I might describe being trans—in the process of myself, full of nerve but also wonder. Renewing.

I listened to Smith a lot as a teen, hidden in my childhood attic bedroom, surrounded by tapes of his, but also by my sketchpads, notebooks, Walkman. Fresh to high school, I was a sinewy kid in headphones, wearing Smith's tapes thin, walking the halls in my own world with Smith's voice a shy guide into sadness and solitude. In the late nineties, I did not know I was queer. Even as I felt the unyielding ache, even as I endured the pain of difference, I could not articulate my humming desires into language; I could only sense their untuned vibrations. Not only did his music give me a way into such inchoate pain—a delicate space to sit with the unnamed grief—it offered relief when that pain became too acute. Smith's sad-boy sound, both tender and brooding, helped me express my embryonic trans self through projection: I couldn't make sense of myself, couldn't come out, but I could look to this shy, shaggy-haired boy singing about exclusion, rejection, and isolation, and see my own outlines.

Nostalgia vibrates with possibilities of reclamation. Meaning, we should take seriously this affect, to reclaim nostalgia and extend its potentialities beyond the realm of psychology and politics. It is a resource for survival. Why do we "*feel* the need," as Cvetkovich writes, to go back? Why are we are driven into our own archives, especially when those archives hold dark chapters, bad objects, cruel feelings?

The past is not welcoming, but the scene of impossibility and hostility. As I wrote early drafts of this chapter, *Roe v. Wade* was overturned and dozens of bills targeting trans youth proliferated through the marbled halls of congressional buildings. "Groomers" reentered the discourse on queer culture, calling back to the lavender scare and gay panic of previous decades. Florida can't say gay and white supremacists organized riots at pride festivals across the country. With the present so violently regressive, we are right to distrust the past even more. For many to most of us, we cannot go backwards without terror. But I echo Cvetkovich and start with this question—on why we return—to undermine a cornerstone assumption of nostalgia: that it is a literal desire to go back, that back is better. That to go back is to make something great . . . again. To dilute this toxic conceit of nostalgia, I will look at nostalgia's history as a medical diagnosis turned psychological disorder, and as a political opportunity, but then also the critical interventions made by scholars such Badia Ahad-Legardy to redefine this important affect away from medicine and politics.

Johannes Hofer, a seventeenth-century medical student, classified nostalgia in 1688 as an epidemic roiling through the ranks of the Swiss military: homesickness brought about by occupying and fighting in foreign lands. The diagnosis was medical, with physical symptoms—including fever, heart palpitations, insomnia, weakness, and loss of appetite—that required intervention.[7] Framed as the longing for home, nostalgia signified one's patriotism for their land of origin, meriting this affect with honor. Homesick soldiers were perceived as loyal to the nation, to the family, and to their homelands.

But, at the same time, as an embodied medical ailment, this made treatment compulsory and cure a prescribed destination. Cure was home. Doctors especially pressed this diagnosis if such sad feelings interfered with military performance, which they were said to do.[8]

Hofer's symptoms—loss of appetite, racing heart, lack of sleep—seem like trauma response; maybe he failed to consider the brutalities of war on a troop's psyche. Or, if he did, such nuances were buried under rigid diagnostic practices that privileged simplified explanations and singular interventions focused primarily on external pathologies. This changed later when psychoanalysis established greater authority within the scientific-medical fields in the nineteenth and twentieth centuries. During this time, nostalgia shifted from the physical to the mental, and thus from the spatial (home) to symbolic (the past). Nostalgia was, in this way, linked to melancholia, indicative of pathological attachments to a lost object, and relegated to disorder. One suffering the psychological plight of nostalgia was believed to be obstinately clinging to a lost childhood, for example. They couldn't let go; they obsessed over loss and were infatuated with the greener pastures of the past. Consequently, this psychological framing meant one suffered from nostalgia, that one was in psychic distress when confronting the irreversibility of time.[9]

Nostalgia is still often regarded as the experience of a singular subject, as it was in its earlier iterations as a medical and psychological disorder; but today nostalgia has also expanded into the public square. This conceptual shift from physical to mental, spatial to symbolic, made nostalgia vulnerable to today's right-wing political appropriation and mobilization. With a new focus on lost time, this idea of nostalgia has been retooled for the purpose of political gain. Calling on aggrieved crowds donning red hats and decrying some supposed lost greatness, US conservative politicians (but also pundits, extremists, organized militia) promise ridiculous returns based on reductive, faux histories—before green energy destroyed coal industries, before trans kids played sports, before the global demand to demilitarize our police, before award-winning documentaries on glacier calving deepened our understanding of the dire climate situation. Lauren Berlant criticizes nostalgia for this complicity in right-wing populism, specifically in Reagan Republicanism[10] (and, of course, reproduced later in today's current iteration of the GOP), arguing that nostalgia engenders nationalism by manipulating the citizen's supposed desire for a singular cultural identity. Herein, nostalgia is exploited affectively by stimulating anxiety around unknown futures, by linking current crises to cultural change, by framing the past with allegiance and the present with conspiracy. Indeed, one can identify nostalgia's active role in Brexit, in Trump's rise (and re-rise) to power and the organized establishment of his base, in the growth of Christian nationalism, in current SCOTUS decision-making (Justice Thomas wants to reconsider contraception and gay marriage rights with the overturning of *Roe v. Wade*), in censoring critical race theory throughout US public schools, and more.

Sara Ahmed extends Berlant's argument even further to follow nostalgia through "promissory forms of happiness" and into the market.[11] The promise of the good life, of happiness and prosperity, sits on an ever-receding horizon toward which we anxiously and relentlessly labor. This labor energizes the economy, even if (or all the while) depressing our affective spirit. Ahmed links happiness and nostalgia by defining the latter as "affective conversion . . . an affective state that registers the presence of a happy object that is no longer or that imagines something as being happy insofar as it is no longer."[12] But she also argues that the compulsion toward happiness, even if that compulsion sends us backward, is not innate but curated. Happiness keeps capital in circulation. Importantly, Ahmed calls out the racial undercurrent to the politicization and marketization of nostalgia: persistent whiteness. "The nostalgic vision of whiteness is at once an image of racial likeness or sameness. In mourning the loss of such a world, migration enters the narrative as an unhappiness cause."[13] Difference, then, is made the site of unease.

I agree with Berlant and Ahmed in that the past is co-opted by conservatives to expand political power on the pretense that progress is somehow dangerous (this danger is based on futurity's feeling of uncertainty and change). But rather than center nostalgia as the object of critique, I argue instead that these entries are not nostalgia but political suppression and violence, the retention of power at the cost of lives, the environment, our world. This is attachment to retainment, not renewal. This weaponizes nostalgia for the purpose of fearmongering and othering, with the goal of maintaining traditional (white) structures and legacies of power. We can clearly see the political territorialization of nostalgia when we scrutinize *who* is allowed to feel nostalgic. We don't have to look long to see nostalgia is for the party, not the person, that nostalgia is praised in the polis and criticized in the individual. The legacy of psychoanalytic pathology lives on for the person, especially for those not invested in right-wing reversion; our individual attempts to refigure or reimagine (or even just play in) nostalgia are quickly denigrated as solipsistic or narcissistic, the ultimate indulgence in escapism. We are condemned as opting out of the realities of the world for the selfish purpose of comfort or (even more nefarious) pleasure.

One might hear in these criticisms the echoes of Derrida from previous chapters. Our cultural discomfort around escapism is seen in his words on the user of drugs, how "he cuts himself off from the world, in exile from reality, far from objective reality and the real life of the city and the community; that he escapes into a world of simulacrum and fiction."[14] In Derrida's thinking, but also widely embraced by the broader social imagination around US drug use, escapism is the root of addiction's pathology. It's selfish and interior. In seventeenth-century Switzerland, Hofer intimated a similar condition with nostalgia, that it prohibits one from immersing themselves in the present moment and place.[15] Badia Ahad-Legardy, who informs much of my understanding of escapism, nostalgia, and the racialization of these affects, writes: "This early proscription of nostalgia corresponds to contemporary critiques that argue that nostalgia possesses no productive or political purchase because it fosters escapism rather than an active engagement or reckoning with either the past or present."[16] Ahad-Legardy challenges these condemnations of nostalgia by exposing the historical undertones of escape and escapism. She reveals these condemnations as rooted in racism, defending the drive to escape as also the drive toward another kind of world and world-making. She reminds us of a simple yet essential truth: escape can mean survival.

Drapetomania—a disease of the mind that encouraged enslaved peoples to flee—was coined by Dr. Samuel Cartwright in 1851 to pathologize, penalize, and criminalize enslaved peoples daring to escape their brutal conditions in Antebellum America. By diagnosing this will toward freedom as disease, Cartwright upheld an argument for systemic slavery while also naturalizing white logic through the production of scientific knowledge.[17] Drapetomania illustrates medical science's relentless and rooted commitment to racialized thinking, to upholding white supremacist regimes of violence and control through its discourse on health, bodies, pathologies, mental illness, and more. Ahad-Legardy's arguments reveal how one is both invalidated and erased while also shaped into pathology, coerced into a grammar of meaning.[18] Specifically, she explains how concepts like drapetomania excluded Black folks from accounts of nostalgia and instead joined their desires and behavior to aberration. Doctors scripted the need to flee as illness rather than as part of the human condition: "The slave psyche emerges as a point of fascination only to highlight the extent of black peoples' perceived inferiority and, by extension, to normalize white psychic life."[19] On top of this, the perception that enslaved folks could not access nostalgia originates from racist incredulity (how could one long for their West African homelands) and the violent refusal to see one's interiority as deeply infinite, unknowable, and untouchable.

Contemporary rhetorical studies on nostalgia criticize and claim it as a white feeling.[20] But of course, in so doing, they claim it as a white feeling. This excludes alternative discourses and analyses of this complex affect. William Kurlinkus, who is also influenced by Ahad-Legardy's work, writes, "Without exploration of nostalgia's diversity, white longing becomes normalized, other 'normals' are kept aberrant, and the majority's rule in this rhetoric (their nostalgic crux-hood) vanishes."[21] This legacy continues; we are still apt to think of nostalgia as pathological, that it is too saccharine or regressive. We've since struggled to free ourselves from these taut descriptions, internalizing nostalgia as an unhealthy disposition to one's self and future. It's no wonder why we're cautious with nostalgia, hesitant to look too close, wary of a pleasure that might also bring pain, wary to be thought of as navel-gazing, an inward wallflower seeking escape.

Escapism has been linked to pathology, and pathology has been a solvent source for authenticating racism under scientific imperialism. If we're trained to question our desire to escape, to feel ashamed of our need to flee or disengage, then we're trained away from our very selves, trained to doubt the intricate workings of our interiorities, to doubt our intuitions and instead concede to institutional authority. Sigmund Freud famously cleaved mourning from melancholia when defining the latter as a pathological attachment to a lost object (a person, lover, or sense of the self).[22] By returning over and over to the object, he argued, we refuse to process the loss and instead obsess in the interiors, press the bruise. When my poetry mentor told me elegies do more than memorialize, he insinuated beyond melancholia, beyond static homage or fixed memories, some item forgotten in a closet. But Freud made pain surmountable; he made overcoming our aches compulsory and all other versions of lingering and holding a kind of pathology, the failure to let go.

But what if we want or need to opt out? What if, in so doing, we also long to feel our escape as generative, maybe even fulfilling? Cvetkovich's work on depression influences some of my own thinking on public feelings, especially her privileging of impasse over progress. "We don't create a fantasy world to escape reality," Cvetkovich writes, quoting Lynda Barry. "We create it to be able to stay."[23] Staying requires endurance, strategies for rest, resilience in the face of relentlessness. In order to stay, we sometimes need to escape. Despite its seeming contradiction, the ability to escape, the will to escape, is of the same desiring drive to stay, to see to our survival. Sometimes this is by whatever means possible.

Into the Archives

There is a wearied, hungover affect to Elliott Smith's music, a tenor of trying to get through the day. "So sick and tired of all these pictures of me," sings Smith with fatigue, how he longs to escape a world that won't recognize him for who he is.[24] Trapped within his repeating anxieties, he sings of "speed-trials while standing in place." Smith was notoriously pained by spotlight. Interviews are difficult to watch, as he shifts awkwardly from the attention. He was also known for perfectionism, restarting songs on stage until he got them perfect. When he plays his cover of "Jealous Guy" on *The Jon Brion Show*, Smith shyly asks, "Are you ready?" To which Brion laughs and replies, "By the looks of things no, but I'm going to force you to play it."[25] Smith wears all brown, blinks sleepy eyes, and murmurs quietly. He starts the song over because he messes up, twice. He mumbles an apology. He mumbles an explanation. He hesitates and balks. But when he finally gets into the song, his voice is clear and striking. It takes up space. "I was dreaming of the past. And my heart was beating fast."[26] This quiet transformation from falter to song is everything. Smith summons out of himself a feeling that is at once his own and collective (shared, borrowed from John Lennon and brought to this audience, which now includes me and whoever else finds the YouTube clip). I fall into it. Despite all the strain, witnessing Smith sing is listening to beauty find its way through the imperceptible. This is desire, what we long to do, to cleanly translate a feeling. And yet this work so often evades us. Desire as elusive—this is being trans and closeted in the nineties when you not only lack the language but the imagination for something else. "No one broke your heart. You broke your own because you can't finish what you start," Smith sings in "Alameda."[27] It would take me years to finish what I started. Even then, the end was just another beginning, another return to the same lesson, the same lines, the Möbius strip wrung and released.

As a teen I obsessively kept journals, writing and sketching to stay busy through the school day, then late at night when home alone. In those years, the first few of the new millennium, I wrote constantly, relentlessly digging into the soft pages of spiral-bound notebooks. Headphones on, I often worked in my brother's room, a practice I got in the habit of doing since he left home the previous summer, days after my dad also abruptly split to leave our family for another. The house was unmoving, my mom working, at her boyfriends', or sleeping into the afternoon. I woke myself each morning and poured cereal into a bowl; I showered and walked to school in the dark. When I came home I would make dinner, watch TV, and do my homework. And then I'd write late into the night with minimal light, crowded into the feeling of alone. The batteries were constantly dying in my Walkman, so I dropped myself in its elegy to ask who will see this hurt kid, alone and writing, and just generally being a good fucking kid. My journals became an endless archive—poems and verses and sketches to catalog a day, but also a calling-out without response.

I also found myself drawing the same portrait over and over in the margins: shaggy hair covering vacant eyes, messenger bag slung around slouched shoulders, dark turtleneck, and bulky headphones—a nineties boy. I drew them anonymous and androgynous, even writing next to the reiterating figures, "Who is this guy I keep drawing?" Looking back, I laugh at the earnestness of a question I've now answered, an answer into which I awkwardly grew. He's the boy I wanted to be, the boy I was. He was me. My quiet diligence, sitting alone with a notebook and headphones, listening to my favorite albums on repeat, ceded me space to loiter in my interiors. All those boys, these boys who look like Elliott Smith . . . I was drawing (and redrawing) a feeling, outlining a vision of desire that I could not yet articulate through language: the boy I dreamed of being.

As explored in earlier chapters, capitalism invests in linear constructs of time to enforce designated outcomes: profit, reproduction, progress, but also health and happiness. Anything less is cataloged as obstinate delay. We are only meant to look forward, with the exception of regret. But even a remorseful backward gaze serves to reinforce a "better" future, the rock bottom foil to brighter days. We are trained into Freeman's chrononormativity, the expectation that we grow up, get educated, secure jobs, reproduce, and increase our assets.[28] We are trained to conflate personal development with economic productivity. In the second chapter, we explored the concept of "stuck" in the context of addiction, that those *not moving on* with their lives are somehow idling, forfeiting their standing as "productive members of society." The pathology of stuck reduces the human to terms of growth. How do we not internalize ourselves as failures if we're not "moving up" or "moving on"?

We remember Kathryn Bond Stockton's words on the queer child, that "there are ways of growing that are not growing up. The 'gay' child's fascinating asynchronicities, its required self-ghosting measures, its appearance only after its death, and its frequent fallback onto metaphors (as a way to grasp itself) indicate we need new words for growth."[29] Stockton's request for language around growing and growth is foremost rhetorical—we literally need to curate and circulate new language—but it is also imaginative. She wants us to understand the queer child (or perhaps just the child) beyond linear conceits of development, to know there are other ways of growing. Growth moves sideways, or it lingers, drags. Or it even move backwards, doubling over itself. Jack Halberstam invites us into imaginative habits that resist mastery. He calls this "knowledge from below," knowledge that is more concerned with unsettling (the killjoy) than resolving.[30] Unsettling mimics the practice of archive, digging into the past as recon or as rescue, to illuminate ways of dragging time so we might dream into past knowledge that is, in this very moment, re-creating itself. It allows us our agency without requiring mastery. And if we imagine it this way, going back and folding over itself, we imagine growth outside of linearity: as an assemblage, as thick and tactile and complex. We return to the same books and lessons. We write the same lines, poems, essays, and draw the same portraits. We replay the same sad songs. We look through old boxes of journals and sketchpads and photos.

I'm not an archivist, in profession or in theory. My archival pursuits consist mostly of me sitting on the floor, leafing through old notebooks and washed-out photos from disposable cameras. So many others do better at explaining the life, function, and potential of the archive (see Saidiya Hartman, among others, for example).[31] But if we're going to talk about nostalgia, it seems irresponsible, if not plainly undesired, to extricate the archive from the work we're trying to do. Freud wrote that while mourning allows us to move on after the loss of an object, melancholia hampers our emotional growth as we languish in stubborn attachment to that object. I don't take issue with the distinction between melancholy and mourning so much as with the pathologization of the former. If we are *meant to move on*, then we are coerced into elegy without consent. Ahmed challenges Freud to recuperate melancholia in queer terms. She installs an ethic in attachment, writing that "keeping the past alive, even as that which has been lost, is ethical: the object is not severed from history, or encrypted, but acquires new meanings and possibilities in the present."[32] Ahmed offers a significant contribution to the genealogy of nostalgia in that, for her, loss is not just transferred between the external and internal, because "for the object to be lost, *it must already have existed within the subject.*"[33] She describes a "withness" that presses our bodies upon one other in "a dynamic process of perpetual resurfacing."[34] We shape one another. Maintaining our attachments to the lost loved one is a way of grieving in which we keep impressions of the other "alive" even though they're gone. There is an epistemological function to loss in that how we respond "requires us to rethink what it means to live with death."[35] In maintaining our attachments to a lost self, we keep ourselves alive.

For Ahmed, living alongside death takes on heightened meaning for trans and queers folks, for people of color, for those who live in constant proximity to loss (material death, but also emotional, gendered, psychic loss), and for whom a regenerating attachment to loss creates a sense of possibility and community.[36] Traditional mourning effects closure and sentimentality; it closes like an urn, putting to rest. But when mourning is diffuse, a climate in which one lives,[37] the feeling of such total immersion creates a problem for language—it is difficult to describe our reoccurring aches when we are crushed by diagnoses and resolutions. Archives, however, grapple with this very urgency to name the lost without closure, to drag out the knowledge of the past to insist on uncontained futures. For each of us with our personal archives, by taking up Ahmed's vision we give ourselves permission to mourn melancholically, to obsess over what hurts us until we might finally give that hurt a name. And only then if we so desire (see previous chapter).

Archives immerse us in a state of both interminability and temporality— the present imbued with the past and braced against the future. Meaning, we call bullshit on Freud. Freud's demand that we mourn every loss depends on those losses as appearing unconnected. But this is not the reality of our enmeshed, assembled lives. New pain triggers the memories and even the physical manifestations of old pain. While Freud argues that mourning properly disposes us of these re-triggering events, we should resist such expectations, as these expectations are rooted in fraudulent conceptions of emotions, our bodies, our social lives. Instead, we witness what's lost while, simultaneously, resisting memorialization. If queer, trans, drug-using, and BIPOC folks live within violent conditions—both the tiny cuts and the systemic injuries— then the demand to mourn is, implicitly, a demand to see our losses as random or arbitrary, not the result of systems of catalog and control. There's a reason why I didn't have the language for being queer and trans as a youth.

I am especially interested in how nostalgia delivers us into our archives to offer more creative ways of knowing ourselves and our pasts, through which we might gently protect (escape into!) our futures. I join Ahad-Legardy and Kurlinkus to also explore nostalgia's diversity, its potential for feeling into the illimitable landscape of the self. We are always revising; this is not only beautiful but it affirms us as powerful agents and world-makers. Composers. Specifically, I want to extend Kurlinkus's and Ahad-Legardy's work to focus on agency found in our archives. As in, how does practicing nostalgia not only soothe us as we experience vulnerability and otherness as queer people, but how also does it reveal our agency to ourselves? How does it nourish our relationship to empowerment? How is this felt in the body? And how does it deepen our literacies of ourselves?

Archival Possibility: Our Bodies Were Made to Remember

Winter in Eugene, Oregon, is mild and melancholic: flat gray skies, slate rain, but also the foothills on the north and south ends of town are reminders of more wild; it doesn't take one long to reach higher ground and its rushing waterfalls, hot springs, clear rivers, and snowfall. It's why I moved from the Midwest in my late twenties. Some small thing ached in me, hinted I might need all that green to endure something dark.

Coming out later in life disassembled my sense of being, my identity.[38] Dissolving my known self while trying to cultivate the new self felt impossible. The only thing that brought me peace at that time was Smith's music. In those wrought winter weeks of separation, when Michael was at home packing up his stuff, I would walk for hours around Eugene listening to Elliott Smith's entire catalog, finding endurance through the familiar feelings of solitude and worry. "Tired of being down, I got no fight."[39] His songs made the liminal space between one life and another tolerable. This is not to say his art (or, any art, really) saved my life, but it sustained my survival, gave me an echo within which to rest. I walked the neighborhoods of my mossy town, a town just two hours south of where Smith grew up, with a raincoat to my throat and earbuds in my ears, following pavement the color of rain and trying to keep the fear at bay. Knowing if I did, then I might exist into a future I had some hand in making.

I walked a lot as a teen too, with curated mixtapes comprised of Elliott, the Smiths, Bright Eyes, Modest Mouse, and Splender. I ambled barefoot through my suburban Detroit neighborhood alone at night to feel, counterintuitive as it seems, less vulnerable, which is what I felt all day at school and home— vulnerable, that though I was invisible, a shy kid against the slamming of lockers, I was also a flame of difference. I buried myself under hoodies and stayed quiet in class. I avoided my mom's resentments and my stepfather's alcoholic diatribes. I learned to walk the eggshells. So at night I would take to the sidewalks to take up space in the world without being noticed, without others privy to my crushed, queer feelings. No one ever noticed I wasn't home and I said "it's OK" more than I heard my own name.

"Don't get upset about it, no, not anymore / there's nothing wrong that wasn't wrong before," Smith sings in "No Name No. 5."[40] Many of Smith's songs are left untitled, a sign not of indifference or indecision, but of refusing definitives. "Between the Bars" confirms as much. "The potential you'll be that you'll never see" tells us we are already our full selves, even as so much remains unknown.[41] This is Rilke, living the questions and taking on the pain of it. We are who we are, but we are also on our way to ourselves. We are between the bars. The past self is maybe haunting, but the pain of that truth does more than just burn.

My adolescent desire to feel Smith was my desire to be Elliott Smith, to cross those gendered boundaries in the obvious, embodied way, to be the boy. But also, my longing traces the lines of affect; I followed feeling, Smith's shyness, his sensitivities, and his exiling sadness. I tracked him into familiar spaces of alienation and isolation, where the interior brings respite, where we, as Smith sings, "forget all about the pressure of days," where we drive away those images of ourselves that are stuck in our heads.[42] We imagine "otherwise." It is not just to be the boy, then, but to be allowed all the feelings and movements of that boy, to feel my body crawl inside of that hunger and grow.

Nostalgia is pleasurable. It somatically feels good to remember: whether we're with college friends laughing about unforgettable house parties or with our partners poring over details from the first date. These are intentional memory punctures, collectively embarked upon and relationally spurred into warm feeling. But memory also moves without mandate, surfacing without notice. And this feels good too, the unsolicited recovery of something once lost.[43] There is a stun to nostalgia in this, when we are not looking for our histories but those histories surface in our daily lives nonetheless—a long lost song, a found letter, a flashback. *Flash* back. Nostalgia is sensory and sensational. While much of what we feel can be quickly intellectualized, nostalgia snaps swiftly away. Think of how smell transports us, sometimes to an undetermined past, our synapses fired but our recall dragging. Think of how our favorite songs from adolescence still animate us, how our bodies know so intimately the sonic progression. Our senses are tied to memory; our bodies hold them. What we hear, smell, taste—our bodies catalog events *through* the sensory feeling of that event. Our bodies were built to remember through somatic retrieval. Why are we *not* talking more about nostalgia in affect studies when it brings the body and imagination into such deep unification.

The pleasure in nostalgia, so often conceived as basking in better times, bears more than "good" memories. We retell a story to inoculate it with humor, rather than anxiety and stress. We retell a story to infuse it with anger, rather than confusion and capitulation. Nostalgia is as much about imagination and storytelling as it is about feeling. Nostalgia, then, can be nurtured, even deployed. "Nostalgia isn't only something that happens to us; it's also a universally available tool people deploy to resist over-innovation and capitalist burnout," Kurlinkus argues, "here, nostalgia becomes the power to imagine *otherwise*."[44] Against the relentless call to produce, nostalgia justifies our need to stall or hide.

While "otherwise" offers few details or directives, Kurlinkus indicates an excess of opportunity for us—as writers, artists, dreamers—to rethink ourselves. This has tangible outcomes in how we participate in world-making. For example, nostalgia resists the gentrification and whitewashing of neighborhoods, legacies, and histories. Sarah Schulman's *Gentrification of the Mind* is a call for remembering things *as they were*, without amnesia or reduction, to hold ourselves accountable to our compositional methods.[45] Nostalgia, much like shyness, possesses political purpose, as antidote for neoliberal gentrification of minoritized experience. "As we become conscious about the gentrified mind, the value of accountability must return to our vocabulary and become our greatest tactic for change," she urges.[46] Gentrification of our neighborhoods (or minds) displaces not just peoples, but their cultures, families, and communities, commodifying each under the facade of renewal and better futures. But I also hope in better futures. I have to and I want to. Kurlinkus writes, "Nostalgia's uncontained temporality, its critique of the present on behalf of the past in hopes of making better futures, is definitionally a training ground for world-building."[47] We mine the past, not to remake it but to remake what's ahead, to interrupt a future forced upon us.

Our interruptions need not be polite, apologetic, or explanatory, but instead, creative. We're "not to relive the past as it 'once was' but rather to reframe" it,[48] to approach pain under our terms. We cannot escape the systems within which we are embedded, but we can disrupt or scramble those systems, rescripting their narrative code. Nostalgia is this act of sensorial collage, as we unbury past artifacts to remake ourselves, for survival or for the simple purpose of awe. We go into our archives to witness ourselves as strong when, at the time, we felt only ruined by our weaknesses, to turn toward a version of the self that still moves within us, that still requires some attention.

Backward care for forward endurance, the archive bonds to futurity while being informed by the past. As Derrida once wrote, "There would indeed be no archive desire without radical finitude, without the possibility of a forgetfulness."[49] The will to archive, according to Derrida, derives from our death drive, our will to be and our will to be remembered. But beyond our desire for legacy, we do more than preserve the past through archives; we disrupt the present. Archival excavation, even if it means opening old journals or uncovering old mixtapes, is the work of rupture: both an epistemological and aesthetic labor in which we trouble conventional notions of loss.[50] This is a withness of loss, that we sense our object not as gone, but as always in a state of slipping away. It makes the archive porous, where we bend memory, releasing ourselves from the pressures of "working through" or "getting over" the past. In the previous chapters, we explored discursive strategies for surviving both a drug-phobic and transphobic world, that being shy offers one way to dodge, divert, and redirect, that we mobilize our own agency as storytellers (and human beings) to, in essence, talk our way through those structures determined to silence us.

Nostalgia, then, meets us in the question of how we might describe vulnerability, especially the vulnerable body, without also at the same time constraining one to precarity. How do we talk about what's difficult, the grit, without relying on spectacle, or what hurts without relying on pathology? While nostalgia describes the achy enjoyment of the return, the archive offers the material space in which our artifacts affirm us as creative, agential beings. We do the work in order to feel—to feel the pain of loss when numbness beckons us into burnout; to feel ease within a beloved's memory; to feel angry or outraged; to collage and curate and then, maybe, to feel some sense of control. It is, for example, how we might meet our trans childhood with kindness, not only regret.

While innumerable pressures—the psychoanalytic legacies of Freud, neoliberal calls for optimization, even crucial issues like the climate crisis—have us constantly looking forward, we still look back, for an array of purposes and pleasures. "Growing memories and the ability to access memory is a skill that allows access to eternity," writes Joy Harjo.[51] Trans folks, for example, are encouraged to look forward, but when and if they must approach the past to do so through narratives of incredulity (look how obviously queer I was with that bowl cut and tucked flannel!), narratives of crossed thresholds (the "liberation" in coming out), and siloed accounts of disjointed desire (the unfulfilled longing for the right adolescence). This is not to say those washed-out polaroids of fourteen-year-old me don't scream gender confusion. Oh they do. While looking back brings up the pain of difference and my inability to advocate for myself—the proverbial eggshells and a disappeared family—I see also my self-ghosting measures and nascent agency, the inked pages from my torn-up sketchpad, my brother's hand-me-down hoodies, mixtapes that gave me community. It wasn't much, but I worked with what I had, and it took me into viable futures.

Either/Or, the Song of My Body

After college, inexplicably, I didn't listen to Elliott Smith for more than a decade. Maybe I was distracted by the influx of indie music in the early aughts—Bon Iver, Sufjan Stevens, Death Cab for Cutie, more shaggy-haired boys—or maybe life overtook me in the way it does in one's early twenties. While I'm not sure what prompted my hiatus with Elliott Smith's music, my return to it—when I was thirty, far from my Midwest homeland and thumbing through his vinyl collection at House of Records—is more understandable. I bought *Either/Or*, walked home with it under my raincoat, and immediately put needle to black and listened to its whirr, hum, then the first strum of a C chord. I listened with my eyes closed, flipped the record and was still. Then, as the needle returned to its hold, I went into my closet, shuffled through boxes of old hats and belts and shoes. I pulled out my Sambas, my beloved sneakers from middle school that, though worn, fit me still. The impulse was innate, an instinct I was wise to trust.

My return to Smith's music was of course nostalgic, a pleasure also pocked with ache as I remembered being a teen. But as I receded into memories, I fell back into my unformed adolescence, my nascent trans childhood calling out to me. I returned to my stuck fourteen-year-old self, walking my neighborhood listening to his music, trying to put distance between myself and home, trying to imagine a future that felt intoxicating, not scripted. When Cameron Awkward-Rich writes that he had to "cultivate—actively cultivate" optimism for his future and the future of his body,[52] he's describing adolescent dreaming, how he learned to install futurity with hope, and how there was no other way than wide-eyed. We cannot forfeit the future. Our fledgling, queer selves deserve survival. I know my young queer being depended on future possibility, just as they depended on me reaching adulthood (a milestone I was sure I'd never reach) and finding joy, feeling widely, desiring deeply. Both current and past selves need one another. Because they are the same self, colliding into a shaken whole.

Framing nostalgia as an archival enterprise shows us just how useful nostalgia is in narrative reclamation, in feeling our agency as essential. A nostalgic narrative form, for example, prompts alternative ways to explain ourselves, describe our needs, to speak with self-given authority, nurture our agency, or even just play the system. A nostalgic narrative form refuses to cast the past only through regret. It also locates authority in the ordinary, not in the elite. We do not need, say, the credentials presumed by scientific research, or its emphasis on outcomes, to construct the story of ourselves. Rather, nostalgia provides a different set of discursive opportunities. We manipulate language, withhold it, fabulate it.[53] We do not have to follow the same scripted move, from the hurting to healed self. Instead, we stay with the body itself, we stay with the body and its desire for scent and song. We use poetics, scraps of journal entries, or historical archives to go back and give voice. Nostalgia attenuates Freud's pathologization of melancholia by shoring up the political and aesthetic (as well as personal) potentialities of attachment (and reattachment). We bend time away from colonial and capital constructions of linearity. But more than anything, we give ourselves permission to be weird, queer, fabulous, and feeling as we think about how time inflects on us, and how we inflect on time. We describe the world as it is to queer communities: painful, if not immediately dangerous. But this cannot be the whole of it. We also experience beauty and how beauty does not erase the reality of our losses, mournings, or melancholies. It's not one or the other, but an enmeshment, embracing ourselves as in pain and more than our pain. We are always more.

I am particularly invested in understanding pain beyond spectacle (see chapter 5), which means an investment in agency and assemblages, in seeing ourselves as complex creatures who are both ensnared in systems and free of those systems, who live on despite constant loss and losing. I am interested in how this shows up as archival composition, wherein we speak beyond the demanded lines of marginality that make us readable to others. Nostalgia allows us to insist that our pain not be normalized. Or categorized. Or, worst of all, elegized. Nostalgia helps us see loss not necessarily in isolation, but as contingent. As climate. But also as escapable.

By imbibing nostalgia, in talking openly about the past with purposes other than explanation, by listening to that song that immediately pulls us back to a contained memory, we feel ourselves as we were then (whenever "then" was). So often when I speak of my early twenties—the decade I understand as the repressed fallout of my tattered teen years—I find myself relying on discourse that explains, that makes sense of a withheld self, that arcs from closet to freedom. But this is always forced. Rather, in my own nostalgic dreaming, I go back and remember that, even in my stunted, scared, stalled years, I was making. I was composing, listening to my headphones and drawing in my notebooks and full of futural wonder. Nostalgia disrupts the linearity demanded of me. I'm not a more evolved or better person now, now that I'm out and have gained a deeper literacy of who I am and what I want. This is an especially plaguing idea of how we've come to understand being trans: that *before* holds only regret. Rather, I'm still myself, but with more of a sense of how to protect my ongoingness: writing poems and traversing long ridgelines, but also feeling my way into bodily autonomy by living the questions. By writing myself into those questions.

When Elliott Smith died in 2003, I sat in my car in my college parking lot, stunned with grief. This young person, whom I never knew but whose art guided me through difficult high school years, was gone. He did not make it. How then could I? What horrible confirmation, that such interior pain, with which I had so resonated, ends in tragedy. I could not access Smith the way I do now: bootleg footage from small shows he played, clips from pained interviews, even renderings of his Ferdinand tattoo—they're now all available online, artifacts that, when gathered, give us some of Smith but not everything. The archive is never everything. His cause of death was ruled inconclusive despite two non-hesitating knife wounds to the chest. I was halfway through college when he died, still drawing my boys. I had left home while my family broke into separate parts—my brother playing Nintendo in a gray apartment in California, my dad on a Michigan shoreline, my mom trapped in a ranch house in gridded suburban Detroit. So much distance between all our same skins. I burrowed into books and music, tried to make friends, but always felt myself estranged. I saw Smith's future as my own; we were the same boys on the same path, I thought. I could not name my pain then in the way I do now—the pain of suppressing an urgent, surfacing thing. But equally, I could not name the desire as queer—a projection of wanting to be him, of hair in my eyes, T-shirt tight across my broad chest, baggy cargo pants and black Sambas. My need to be the quiet moody guy was a trans desire. In the moments when this feeling breached, all I could do was put my headphones on and wait.

There's a reason why music is such a potent courier of nostalgia. It strums our senses, stores memories through vibrations and chords, licks and tones. While I'm not sure music, poetry, or art at large saves the world, I do think our attentions toward *saving*, as opposed to nurturing or retreating or witnessing, misguide the conversation on aesthetic possibility. It's not whether a poem or song mends the trenchant pains of being alive. They do, of course, expose those truths. But rather, the song helps us know ourselves.

My favorite album by Elliott Smith, *Either/Or* is a nod to Søren Kierkegaard's first work of the same name. And it is not lost on me that both portend a binary.[54] For Kierkegaard, aesthetics and ethics are oppositional forces: subjective art (*either*) counters an objective good (*or*), feeling counters logic. The question, for Kierkegaard (but presumably also for Smith) is not which side you choose—art or ethic—but why you choose what you do, and what it means for who you become. If I must choose, then I choose art. I choose beauty, desire, seduction, drama—the "either" in *either/or*. But I also don't buy into the coercion of this choice. And, as it turns out, neither does Kierkegaard. In fact, this was his whole point. It took me many years of reading and *returning* to this text to realize this, that the either/or construction is a fallacy, a rhetorical technique used to persuade one into believing that only two options (among an invisible many) exist, and only one is correct. This is also called the false dilemma. Once we make visible those invisible choices, we open ourselves toward hidden alternatives, through which we become more creative thinkers, knowers, and feelers. Kierkegaard is arguing for beautiful ethics. Or ethical beauty. He proves that the dissolution of the binary forges infinite possibility.

Elliott Smith in my headphones singing about his poison arms sheltered me as I suffered through high school, hidden under bulky clothes, trying to take up the least amount of space possible. Protection but also projection; Smith helped me envision a future outside of East Michigan through the kind of affective connection that happens with our favorite music. Because I could *feel* Smith's music, I felt beyond my own scope of limitation. I am *either*. My body is either. My gender is either, how I long for Smith's casual fashion, for that slouched shyness he exudes on the album cover. "Either" intimates the noncommittal, occurs in the moment before we make a decision. "Either" opens casually toward options, not out of a will to withhold, but out of a resistance to prematurely answer any question of the self. And I am *Or*. My body and gender are or. Or reminds us that a pivot is always possible, that veering doesn't always lead to a crash.

Being trans non-binary has required a serious relinquishment on answers and dis-attachment from the obdurate idea that we must know all of ourselves. And it has me standing with Kierkegaard to reject the false dichotomy of two choices. This is a decision I am constantly making and remaking, like a vow reclaimed in the quotidian motions of everyday life. Or like a song one constantly returns to or puts on another playlist. As I wrote in previous chapters, I do not, of course, reject binaried gender. We all have a right to our gender compositions. Rather, non-binary emerges as one of the many fragments salvaged from the either/or ruins.

The final track on *Either/Or* is Smith's popular love song "Say Yes." It begins simply, quietly: "I'm in love with the world / through the eyes of a girl."[55] Is this not how desire often feels, waking us to a buzzing world, our senses brimming with wonder? Desire motors us forward, through the mundane, so that when we're sitting in a dark living room on a gray day, when the world shrinks down to the size of an apartment, we still sense our own futurity. We are still wide-eyed in our optimisms.

"Say Yes" is not definitive about its futures. Indeed, for the whole track we are waiting on an answer, on whether the girl in the song sticks around. "It's always been wait and see." The album culminates in this two-minute piece of music. After all of Smith's wandering through streets, bars, parades, the sleepwalking and waking up in unknown places, "Say Yes" does not present a tidy ending to *Either/Or.* And why should it? This was not Smith's way. Instead, the song underscores an either/or moment: a choice is made (the girl) but the future remains mystified (will she stay), clouded by the opacity of that question. There is an unease, a pain even, to this kind of "wait and see," wherein Smith articulates an unavoidable truth of being alive and having a body: there is so much we don't yet know about ourselves. He describes this as a happy day followed by all "that gets fucked up," making you "pay" for good moments.[56] Collapsing happiness into melancholia, Smith makes them one.

Elliott Smith was a lyrical musician. He not only wrote beautiful songs, he created an archive of music that quietly vibrates in deep feeling. In poetry's long written and oral traditions, lyricism dates back to the ancient Greeks to describe short poems marked by emotion and imagery; lyrics are moved forward by the sense of wonder and feeling, rather than narrative. "One definition of the lyric might be that it is a method of searching for something that can't be found," writes Fanny Howe. "It is an air that blows and buoys and settles. It says 'Not this, not this' instead of 'I have it.'"[57] The lyrical, in this way, is a radical alternative to the Greek epic, to Odysseus's search for home.

I am *not this, not this.* My trans body says *not this, not this.*

When I first heard Smith's music, I was on the brink of an emotional abyss, alone with my headphones in an empty house. Smith's songs, as they circle around ambiguous ache—a constant pain that cannot be made sense of— became crucial to my own sense of waywardness as I navigated high school, shopped at the mall with friends, hid my body in the locker room. This then repeated itself a decade later. When I returned to his music at thirty, living in Eugene, amidst a painful divorce and an even more painful coming-out, I remembered these unfinished adolescent feelings. Through the complex chord progressions, the minor tones of the piano, and his lonesome lyrics, an old feeling began to hum again. I brought *Either/Or* home from House of Records, and a buried imagination began to awaken. It was a return to Smith's sound, to a nostalgic state of wonder that cultivated the awakening. Which is one way to say, nostalgia advocates for a future, even if and while that future changes shape.

It wasn't just that my return to this sad-boy music proffered a safe place to mourn, and therefore a way further into my attachment to pain, what we might call sulking. That wasn't why I went to Smith's catalog of waltzes and ballads as an adult. It wasn't why I pulled my old Sambas out of the closet. It was recovered agency, the feeling of first falling in love with this music when I was fourteen, of claiming a tiny space for myself through these albums. That return to adolescent agency helped me suspect I could survive the unraveling of my adult life—of coming out, breaking up with Michael, losing family. Against all odds, I was an agent of myself then, to whom I could return to attend to that boy-child as they so deserved.

Smith's music tells the story of struggle without cure. Because that is the reality of quotidian ache—there is often no fix. So instead, Smith gives us temporal attentions (wait and see), helping us release our needs for teleological ends. Smith gives us the right to ache without requiring recovery from that pain. We can be both sad and happy, stunned in wonder or fatigued by nerve. We don't have to choose.

I wish as a teen I was privileged to some cloudy horizons. I wish I could go back and imbue the unknown with desire, not dread. But returns are not possible, at least not through the ligaments of linear time. But by putting *Either/Or* back into my headphones, by returning to the words and measures in these twelve songs, I do feel a way back. Smith helps me remember I am always myself, even as I am figuring it out and in process. This is the founding principle of existentialism, the home field of Kierkegaard, that we exist *within* our becoming. We never get to the end of ourselves.

As a kid I anguished in difference but was enlivened by wonder. As in, I wonder what can be, I wonder what's next, I wonder what's possible. This is still true; and it brings us full circle, back to the first chapter, where wonder sustains us in crisis. In these chapters I've attempted to describe pain beyond the spectacle—the trans person in dysphoric despair, for example. My return to sweet Elliott is a trans nostalgic move that says yes to pain, but also more than pain: the delight in stealing my brother's baggy sweaters, in the many minutes it took to download a song off Napster, in drawing endless portraits of the same aching boy. I was waiting. I was waiting for language to appear through the haze of feeling, for when I could compose my own red autobiographies. Now, here I am, forty, still writing into the mess while re-realizing that vulnerability does not summon danger but feeling, re-realizing this because my wife told me on day one that there is not love without risk. Our relationship was born from our shared love of music. We spent our first weeks together curating countless playlists, attending concerts, and listening to records in her bedroom. Ten years later, our daughter who just turned two years old calls me "Dada." I answer her back with the name my wife and I always knew we'd give her. "Yes, Elliott, my girl?"

5

Wild Ache

Composing in Crisis

I opened *Achy Affects* in the wilds of interior Alaska, where I held to Rainer Maria Rilke to sustain myself through change and pain: live the questions. As in, stay within the present quandary with patience and presence. When Michael and I visited Denali National Park, the mountain was still called McKinley, after President William McKinley, who campaigned under the slogan "Commerce and Civilization" and promises of expanding land capture. After one hundred years of bearing its colonized title, President Obama skirted congressional obstinance to restore the mountain's name back to "Denali" in 2015, meaning "Tall One," named by the Koyukon people who have lived along the Yukon and Koyukuk Rivers for thousands of years. The tall one, the tallest in North America, is the heart of a park of over seven thousand square miles, 6 million acres of taiga lowlands, tundra passes, and glacial plains.

"I need more wild," I said to Michael, as we booked our tickets to Anchorage and reserved a shuttle to the park. "Wildness names, while rendering partially opaque, what hegemonic systems would interdict or push to the margins," write Jack Halberstam and Tavia Nyong'o.[1] Meaning, wildness gives us some language, but never enough. Or, perhaps more to the point, wildness scores the pain of our limitations against our hungry perseverance;

despite failure, we will keep trying to say the thing, to capture a sublime moment lost within 6 million acres of possibility. But "capture" has the capacity to evoke disparate reflexes—aesthetic or colonial—from those who wander daunting new landscapes.

Halberstam and Nyong'o continue, "Wildness has certainly functioned as a foil to civilization, as the dumping ground for all that white settler colonialism has wanted to declare expired, unmanageable, undomesticated, and politically unruly."[2] Wild—its physical topographies but also its epistemic potential—has been malleated by the hands and imaginations of imperialism across histories, taming difference through word. Colonizers assuage their discomfort by naming—venturing into the new to christen craggy peaks and claim for themselves legacies marked by conquest; venturing into proximate neighborhoods to dispense elite solutions for community enhancement. "The power to name, then, comes to signal a mode of masterful relation in which the one who names is also the one who can bestow, classify, and possess," writes Julietta Singh.[3] We're not fooled. These legacies are motivated by fragility—the fear one will be forgotten, or even worse, bested by the mysteries of life and death with nothing to show. Those undone by their fragility must own or master what undoes them, even though owning turns luminous desire into insipid acts of power. Do we name the mountain McKinley or instead describe her in relationship to her world—the Tall One.

As Michael and I roamed the quiet non-silence of Denali's backcountry, I inhabited an uninterrupted state of nerve. Always vigilant and never at ease, nerve kept me going while wearing me down. The hiking was technical; the bear spray fell out of my pack, lost to the rocky riverbeds on the second day; glacial sediment clogged our water filter and left us thirsty; a six-foot moose stared us down through thick brush as her calf tremored behind her tall legs. But that is the reason to go into the wild: to become unsettled, to stand under the Tall One and embrace what intimidates us. We do not overcome; we immerse.

I hold this trip to Alaska with my ex-husband Michael as the beginning of the end of our marriage, an unclean tear between one life and another, in which the internal bleed drained into the unforeseeable. Michael and I walked out of the backcountry affirmed by the strength of our partnership. We endured the grind of the northern tundra, yet it was not enough. It would never be enough—this matrix of love and impossibility exposed the inevasible injury that would reassemble my life. But first, I staved off divorce for the next year to attempt to rescue our relationship by the force of intellect. I told myself we could make it work, reasoning through strained days on how this could be so: I would mourn desire as a felt connection to the body, instead convert feeling into conceit; I'd seek out queer community, bridging an old world into new geographies; I'd queer our relationship into new chapters. In all attempts, I was a casualty of the will to know, forcing a telos to stifle desire and all the wild questions my desire inflamed. By the following summer, we were too exhausted by all that epistemological effort.

To endure life's ongoing eruptions and enraptures is to drive the line of nerve, to endure life broken and remade. Or, as Halberstam writes elsewhere of our queer selves, we "revel in the detours, twists, and turns through knowing and confusion."[4] When I read and reread this, I habitually hear "knowing" and "confusion" as cognates, that they impel one another. Or, just as possible, vivify one another. Confusion means to mix and embroil. There is no "knowing" without a vertiginous body seeking foothold, without an affective vibrato asserting itself into the quandary. Halberstam then offers, "It is knowledge that does not seek to explain but involve."[5] I longed to make sense of desire solely through intellect, by naming. I was standing in the wild but rejecting her promises.

When we finally dissolved our shared life, when Michael found a small studio apartment of his own, my capacity for language abated simultaneous to the increasing pressure to make sense—why the hell was I blowing up my life for an uncertain feeling. My words conferred only explanation to account for failure, the ingress of divorce, the slough of social and familial disappointment. I tried to quickly "move on," trimming the transition from marriage to divorce down to the quick, to keep it clean. I was tidying the story, all the while leashing myself to legibility. This showed in my writing as much as it did in my life. At the time, my poetry mentor explained my work as "pristine, white lumber, precariously and meticulously assembled." For years, I tried to write myself out of this emulsifying era of life, tried to understand how my own body availed me, even as I availed it. It would take years (is still taking years) to realize I had to write into, not out of. I did not have to move on.

This project, specifically this chapter and even down to this paragraph, brings me to the brink of expressive impossibility, where language, knowledge, and the feeling body converge. How do I write about knowledge as felt, or the imagination as flourishing through the skin? How do I write about the harm in naming while naming harm? This nearness to impossibility, however, is not unviable but rather an invitation into the wild, where, yes, we seek capture, but we can also express ourselves without eroding the land. From my own story of heartache, I am learning that we all deserve to not know, to instead feel it out, to make revisions and returns. We can be and become under our own volition and imagination. This is true during personal crisis. But in our current, alarming political condition? Still precariously true, but also a truth we're working toward, where, for example, trans people are trying to live their lives like everyone else—at the farmer's market, in job interviews, on the porch with friends—while also fighting (in varying forms) for equal care, job security, streamlined legal recognition, and a moment free from explanation. *Why are you blowing up your life?* This line repeated daily to the point I no longer knew its origins, whether the words were internally formed or externally imposed.

I want to begin this chapter (and end this book) by explaining our pain problem, how harm reduction helped me in my own crisis to think and write away from the sensational, to destigmatize how we know (or not know) ourselves. Just as we do not need to be in recovery to recognize ourselves as full, feeling agents in our lives, we do not need a formed thesis to write. We don't need to explain ourselves to describe ourselves. We don't need to know the future to work toward it. Just as harm reduction recognizes the nonlinearity of need—that we "take steps" forward and back, but also sideways and inward—so also might we call this the process of imagining, creating, and revising. Writing. I then carry this conviction into the walls of my university, wherein meaning sources the pained subject and makes academic futures, and wherein the subject provides solvent incentive for producing more pain.

I then attend to ache as a corporeal experience of chronic, systemic harm, but also a way to imagine beyond binaries, explanations, and spectacles. We need not declare an object good or bad, or a feeling positive or negative, to describe our felt selves. What we need is writing that dilates from a focal subject, even if in so doing, light rushes in, stunning our vision and disorienting our paths. To create better worlds—in which queer, trans, BIPOC, drug-using, low-income people have more freedoms, which means more access to aid, support, and community—we must nurture the relationship between feeling and knowledge. This nurturing occurs through compositions committed to reducing harm.

The Problem of Pain

When I left my street clinic outreach role in Oregon to pursue an academic career in Pennsylvania, I worried the transition would require leaving one world for another. Some of this anxiety was projection fostered by stark geographic difference: wildflowers, fir trees, and mossy roofs to row houses, humidity, and street litter. But also, I worried theory and practice operated as distinct disciplinary categories, that the intellect and body would slowly disband into independent parts. Working syringe exchange is an affective experience for me: the rake of the knuckles down my sternum to describe how to wake one from an overdose, or how perfectly a box of Narcan fits in my palm.

I worried also that academic work would consume all my time, causing my communities to shift and homogenize. Then I started teaching and faced even more intimidating unknowns: curriculums, lesson plans, and teaching philosophies. I struggled to find my place at the front of the college composition classroom. I was anxious, but weren't we all? With the introduction of AI and dropping enrollments in our humanities programs, the low retention rates of young faculty of color and the anemic job market, our composition programs (and humanities writ large) carry on in crisis. Add to this the affective, how the classroom vibrates with an imbalance of power, how its organization into teleological markers (grades, finals, teacher evaluations) precipitates anxiety in both student and teacher, how these markers are driven by the will to know. At the end of my first term teaching in Pennsylvania, when I was grading final reflection essays, a student asked me in the final lines of his paper what my sex is. Not my gender or my pronouns, but my sex. Part of being in the academy is confronting (in others and ourselves) the belief that all knowledge is ours for the taking, that if we summit a mountain, it is ours to name.

Capital has formed and informed the space within which theory is most often produced—the university—in ways that are innumerable and constantly felt. We labor and create product. We protect our futures by our performances in the present. We optimize ourselves. We accrue debt. We speak up to earn participation points. Much of American higher education is underwritten by the imperialist bid to prove ourselves as experts who can commodify our expertise. Undergraduate, grad student, TA, tenure-track professor, adjunct—all of us, the academy quite explicitly trains us to become knowledgeable, neoliberal subjects committed to productivity. D. K. Seitz explains this training as valorizing who "can 'connect' across multiple spheres, 'reflect' on past learning and future goals, and 'project' short- and long-term career plans, functioning as self-managing, initiative-taking, bits of human capital."[6] Urged to subjugate our subject, conquering difference means naming difference. What is most exposed—the pain and marginality—takes on that difference. That is, composition that is locked into the promises of mastery creates theory that capitalizes on the exigency of marginalization and provides security and prestige within the institution, turning complex issues, peoples' bodies, ongoing crises, and the long-term, everyday work of radical and transformative practices such as decolonization or harm reduction into mere metaphors. When scholarship can be commodified, our communities are rendered into objects of knowledge, knowledge for the taking.

More than ever, writing students enter my composition classroom with acute anxiety about academic performance, with the presumption that we should be knowers rather than learners. They (like many of us young scholars) were trained under the ethos of No Child Left Behind and through relentless calls to achieve success through grades, as well as extracurriculars, internships, and volunteer experience. Burdened by outcome, taught to fixate on futures, composition students are not only taught toward mastery, they are rewarded for its performance. And they are trained to consider composition as the punctuated articulation of knowledge: an introduction with an argument, followed by supporting evidence, and concluded through teleological pacification. The formula effects clarity but does little to stimulate one's desire to keep writing. This is why Fred Moten sanctions cacophony,[7] to dispel the illusion of harmony (what Eve Tuck and Wayne Yang call "settling"[8]). If harmony is indicative of success, ethics gives ground to knowing, wherein failure to know is not just epistemological failure, but moral failure too.

Critical of academic pressures to produce new work for the sake of professionalization and advancement, D. M. Keeling cautions against the commodification of our compositional models when she writes, "Scholars are perpetually preparing for the next turn, commenting on the next turn, declaring the next turn, and in each iteration, contributing to an entanglement of turns that are used in the production of further publications and disciplinary histories."[9] In a moment in which the humanities face existential trouble, the uncertain horizon foments a productive present—publish or perish, right? "There is no point in trying to hold out the university against its professionalization," argue Fred Moten and Stefano Harney. "They are the same."[10] We sense this urgency early and in reiteration. "Academic scholarship, for one, has become a form of human capital that offers rewards and status—including foundation grants, money, and prestige—that isolate the intellectual from those struggling to remain alive," writes Steven Osuna.[11] When the pain problem bankrolls scholarship, stakes are high.

While the field of affect studies composes close readings of the body to understand somatic sensations and their political relationships, it is the sensational I am moved to undermine. While sensationalism stimulates necessary attention at times,[12] it just as often manipulates, persuades, and obfuscates, constructing harmful narratives with calculated timing. Sensationalized news stories or state bills do not intend for us to look deeper (or longer) at crises; the intoxicating stimuli is a diversion. Working syringe programs was when I first understood the gravity of a publicized body, how much harm it endures under capitalism, how much it must contribute to definitions of crisis in the American imagination, and how it reifies the responsibility of the individual in times of crises.

As an eighties kid, I remember well the infamous public service announcements from Partnership for a Drug-Free America (PDFA): a man drops an egg into a hot, cast-iron frying pan and as it sizzles, says, "This is your brain on drugs. Any questions?" Later, PDFA intensified their message. This time the PSA shows a woman smashing the eggs raw with same pan; she then goes on to destroy the whole kitchen, blasting through a pile of kitchen plates while screaming, "And this is your family on drugs."[13] Today, the "meth mug shot" calibrates the same provocations—the before and after of meth use decomposing one's face to elicit alarm.[14] The former campy and the latter gratuitous, both produce visual histrionics of addiction despite the history of medicinal drug use and domestic diversion in the United States.[15] The PSAs cast fear, and by so doing cast criminalization as a natural response to such extreme risk. This is the problem of pain; the dichotomy between normal and pathological further deepens by sounding the alarms on difference.

At exchange sites, what one actually witnesses is a temporal collection of energies and moods, verve and ephemera, the smell of cigarette smoke and the pixelated sonics of interstitial conversations; people come and go, relationships form, and laughter takes up space alongside pain. Inside the crevasse of crisis, life persists in its dailyness. "Just another Friday," Gabby tells me, signaling that their expectations for frenzied conversations and busy lines have been met. The parking lot clears out as we pull the "Get Narcan Here" sign back into the van. Harm reduction is not only efficacious health policy but a way of thinking against the onslaught of overcharged, overdramatized images of vulnerability. Meaning, harm reduction may have something to offer composition studies.[16]

These spaces of rehab and the page (or academia or the classroom) are not separate. They are not the same, of course, but both operate under similar systems of demands. Both scenes (and the communities therein) bear expectations for deliverables, whether a published product or days sober. I don't mean to make oversimplified comparisons. The differences between them really are many. Rather, I mean to highlight the influence of capitalism on all scenes of life, how it finds and fills every crack and how pressure mounts as futures cloud over from crisis. The crises are real, of course. But by auditing the reality of what crisis engenders—the recursions and regressions, which is to say, the dailyness—then alterations to community-building practices clarify themselves. It starts by (and is continued by) embracing relapse to call it revision. It starts with the recognition that our compositions are chronic in their composing.

Sensationalized pain maintains one's marginal status, relegating one to their injury and identity modifier, wherein the modifier must keep modifying. Stories are simplified and bodies exoticized. When we are expected to express first from a place of pain, it implies that universality is left to everyone else. Universality meaning precisely that, the universal—our smoggy sky and muddy lawns, our home on Earth, our joy at birth, our frustration at the dinner table when our toddler throws her food, our unrequited love and requited love, desire materialized into aesthetic choices, dark coffee and walking the dog, all that consecrated dailyness issued by a sunrise.

The Pain in Being Stone

Like so many young, shy butches before me, I read *Stone Butch Blues* by Leslie Feinberg and saw myself in language, in literature, for the first time. Notoriously difficult to find, I was browsing the tall stacks of a used bookstore in Eugene, Oregon, when I spotted this out-of-print, lesbian-cult classic. I had just come out and was in my first relationship with a woman after my divorce. Amid raw grief, I was also falling in love, sleeping each night naked next to this new animal who would go on to become my wife. So, this is to say, all my feelings buzzed just under the skin.

Stone Butch Blues is the autofictional story of Leslie Feinberg, named Jess Goldberg in the book, a working-class, gender nonconforming, queer butch trying to make their way in the world, specifically Buffalo, New York, in the mid-twentieth century. The story begins in Jess's unsettling childhood, where they suffer constant bullying from peers and parents alike. As they become a teenager, leaving home to flee violence, they find solace and community in Buffalo's queer bar scene, forming relationships with other lesbians, including Theresa. Theresa is a femme and Jess's first love. But as the two navigate a tumultuous relationship energized by passion and conflict, Jess grapples with their gender identity. In the end, Theresa breaks up with Jess as they begin to pursue medical gender care, including top surgery and HRT.

Stone Butch Blues recounts relentless police raids and jail time. Jess works the factory line, unionizes, survives multiple instances of sexual assault, pursues long-term relationships, starts taking T, has top surgery, stops taking T, endures heartache, attends protests and marches, gets in fights, and generally lives a life marked by both struggle and vitality. Jess knows homelessness; Jess knows good sex and good love. *Stone Butch Blues* is the story of a life.

During my first read, so absorbed by Jess's familiar feelings of shyness, shame, and desire, I overlook the gender quandary motoring the narrative along. Only after I finish *Stone Butch Blues* do I then also read discourse on the novel, how Jess symbolizes subversion, the kind now expected of and inseparable from trans experience. Readings of *Stone Butch Blues* often rely on allegorical analysis, that Jess and Jess's journey capture some crucial, painful notion of gendered meaning. These analyses—based in methods from literary theory and gender studies—track the trans masculine body to the point where we shed Jess for the meaning and metaphors Jess carries.

We might be tempted to describe Jess, the stone butch in *Stone Butch Blues*, as gender troubled, or snagged by bodily incongruence and contradiction. We wouldn't be wrong. They often describe themselves this way. But whether Jess is in pain is not the question. Whether their pain emerges from their body is also not the question in which I am most interested. Jess "begins" to transition with testosterone and top surgery, only to then interrupt their transition by halting hormone therapy. The question of why has been most urgent for critics, among them Jay Prosser. It is this urgency I challenge, because we are meant to take it as compulsory. This urgency emanates from a disrupted timeline, that narrative linearity we've come to expect of transition: Jess delays telos for feeling, convoluting the pain central to being stone. Is it gender? Trauma? Surveillance? Almost always, the figure of a stone butch—the top who refuses to be touched—is interpellated through dysphoria: because they reject their sex, they must also reject sexual reciprocity. Prosser claims it could very well be this detail that differentiates butch from trans.[17] The stone butch is said to be stifled by "insufferable" shame and thus inhibited from consummate sexual, sensual connection with another. While Prosser argues that a strap-on only further displaces the stone from their bodily sex,[18] other readings—especially those not presupposing that gendered and sexual pain colors every moment of our lives—go unexplored.

My favorite sex scene in all of literature occurs in *Stone Butch Blues*, when Jess wears a strap and slowly brings their date, Annie, to orgasm not once but twice. It is deep and present sex, as Jess is a sensitive lover who knows the sensual significance in creating security between partners. "Then she said something to me I knew took a lot of courage. 'I've always wanted to come before I fuck.'"[19] And Jess gives Annie exactly this, going down on her until she comes. After a brief respite, they continue, their breathing clamorous again as Jess uses their strap to put their cock inside Annie, slowly thrusting then holding back, waiting, then more slow thrusting. Annie comes for a second time.

Their sex is guided by Jess's passionate patience, always waiting for Annie's body to relax into their togetherness, for Annie's body to relax onto Jess's hips. Though Jess is alert to Annie's wants, the sex is profoundly mutual. "It's true I faked an ejaculation, but not my pleasure. Annie's body felt so good."[20] The strap does not negate Jess's sexed parts or even enable some dissociated displacement.[21] The strap is Jess's cock. Its meaning is simple in its actions (pleasure) and indecipherable in its feeling (pleasure). The full meaning of the strapped sex is unattainable to those beyond Jess and Annie, and perhaps Leslie Feinberg (though the reader is privileged to some of the sweet heat of their connection). One need not project shame and pain, displacement and dysphoria, onto a moment that gives no evidence of such. One need not lock Jess into an epistemic location bordered by sexed difference.

Prosser writes, "Shame is a profound grappling with the self's location in the world—the feeling of being out of place, of not being at home in a given situation, combined with the desire to be home."[22] Though reasonable to situate home opposite to shame (in many ways, the former incubates the latter), this juxtaposed relationship reinforces pain as surmountable, that shame must be disposed and home sought out. The fix, the cure, the feeling of congruence is in our hands. This aspirational model of thinking about our bodies is so compulsory I often forget to consider whether it is even possible. My question is both personal and political. But when I do brake the trans trajectory inertia, I wonder at the harm it inflicts and why we must locate the precise boundaries of our pain. Perhaps because in so doing, when our pain is explainable, the crises around us feel intelligible (i.e., manageable) too?

The urgency of why—why does Jess stop HRT—presumes that knowledge predicates feeling, that we know ourselves a priori. Often, though, we develop deeper literacies of ourselves by traversing into the unknown and recalibrating along the way. If we read Jess's decision to stop HRT as reversal rather than revision, we reinscribe linearity and aspiration to the body. What if instead of asking "why" we asked "how": how does Jess navigate the brutal, gendering world? Even as we feel gender to be a fundamental part of the self, we sometimes also disidentify. We might long, instead, to disassemble singular, teleological constructions of the body, not just for the sake of theory but for our lived lives. We might, counterintuitively, need to live a bit longer in our pain, whether the reasons are clear to us or not. Regardless, the reasons are ours alone. When Prosser writes that "the point of every narrative" is to return home,[23] he summons Odysseus to endorse narrative as best suited for describing the feeling and gestures of transition (see chapter 4 on nostalgia and homelands). Prosser uses Feinberg's *Stone Butch Blues* to analyze the trajectories of transition when home is a moving target. And while he takes up affect—specifically shame—to examine Feinberg's stone butch, he stabilizes the goal of the body as getting home, wherever that might be.

For many trans people, belonging and security are not just embodied desires, but cairns marking survival. I'm uninterested in prioritizing non-binary embodiment at the cost of others. This is not a question of what opaque or illegible gendered-ness reveals to us about being gendered beings. We all have a right to our gender. Many of us are fighting—physically, emotionally, and legislatively—for this right. Rather, I'm challenging why and where we lay our stakes, what we call urgent and where we beam the spotlight.

Literary scholars, archivists, and readers alike call Feinberg's novel a transgender story, which it of course is. But class also gives *Stone Butch Blues* its texture, narrative propulsion, landscapes, and its stone butch. The novel is as much characterized by class trouble as it is by gender trouble. One should not eclipse the other, as Jess is shaped by both the constraints of money and body, employment and sex. When the sexed parts of our bodies are probed and theorized, assumed to be in pain, they of course respond in pain to the instrumentalization. When the conclusion is written before the story, the telos established before the research question, so much hermeneutical possibility is preemptively foreclosed.

While critics such as Prosser attribute stoniness to trauma, the resistance or refusal of vulnerability, and while this might be true at times, the ache of living without privacy, of life overexposed, also constructs the hardened exterior. The stone butch, contrary to their title, is deeply feeling (I speak from my own skittish skin here). Jess explains, "I clamped my emotions like a tourniquet. I had no privacy here, no space anywhere in the world where it was safe to grieve."[24] The clamped tourniquet cuts off one's lifeblood to keep one alive. So much of *Stone Butch Blues* is about feeling. Jess struggles in shame, but their passion—for sex, relationships, friendships, unions—also forms their identity. This is not to underplay Jess's pain, but to not insist on it either.

My commitments to affect—on behalf of Jess and my self—are commitments to materiality, to take up the sensations of the skin and remind us that all of this is felt, and that feelings offer equally interesting, if not equitably studious, ways to explore trans experience. To be fair to Prosser, he also writes, "Materiality is our subject, but the body is not our object. The body is rather our route to analyzing power, technology, discourse, language."[25] I wish it could go without saying that I adore *Second Skins* and appreciate how Prosser gives new life to *Stone Butch Blues*. I intend not to disparage Prosser or his interpretations of such an important text, but to pivot from them and gesture toward other readings, those unconcerned with the anatomical. Together, Prosser and I compose part of the trans assemblage, but in veering from the material locations of pain into broader considerations of unattainable feeling, I defect from traditional queer analysis into poetical forms of composition.

Honoring Venus and Venus

"Although critics in queer theory appeal to the social location of the cultural texts they cite, they offer little analysis of how social relations are inscribed therein, and virtually no examination of the institutional mechanisms in which these texts are produced nor those in which they emerge and circulate," offers Viviane Namaste in *Invisible Lives*.[26] She is, in particular, critical of queer theory and its erasure, overexposure, and theoretical exploitation of trans people. Queer studies has often elevated subversive incoherence at the expense of those whose lives depend on legibility. Indeed, the queer, the racialized, the classed (i.e., humans living in vulnerability) depend explicitly on composition, on being composed, which renders incoherence or risk as acts of privilege. Namaste argues that because "queer theory emerged within American departments of English, film studies, cultural studies and the humanities,"[27] and given the fields' commitments to textual or object analysis, these fields often fail to scrutinize those institutions managing trans lives across public and private terrain. As the background recedes further into the background—with its layers, detail, and relationships—the singular object, the "body," fills the foreground. By attaching pain to the single body, we will understand one another through difference as it manifests physically, not as it does systemically.

What does Venus Xtravaganza want to tell us in *Paris Is Burning*? She, a Latina trans woman and sex worker, longs for a husband, a house, and money.

What does Judith Butler tell us about Venus Xtravaganza? That, given her body, she should instead aspire toward transgressive rebellion against state definitions of family. Venus Xtravangaza is murdered during the making of *Paris Is Burning*. Not only does Butler dismiss the unequivocal needs Venus articulates to her audience, but Butler composes her arguments in the fallout of violence and death.[28] Jules Gill-Peterson tells us Butler "wanted Venus Xtravaganza to become one of a million wayward souls caught up in the vast ocean of racial and gendered violence in the Americas," and so becomes "an object lesson to the reader."[29] The myopic framing of Venus (the object lesson) ingrains our expectations of trans life as risky; but even worse, it exacerbates the material condition of those lives.

As I summon Venus here, as many scholars and archivists and documentarians have done, I summon her to make a point about pain. But Venus should not designate only loss—her short life was one lived. Venus was born in mid-May, like my wife, when geraniums, azaleas, and bleeding hearts bloom, when rain in the Northeast gives our city roads a soft sheen and hints of imminent humidity. She grew up in Jersey City and took the name Venus as a teen. She walked against the Jersey skyline and the Hudson riverbed, then moved to New York, winding the lines of the East River and the streets of Greenwich Village. Venus loved performance and fashion, and she was adamant about her autonomy, that she would do and get what she wanted. Exercising a sharp sense of poetic shade and read, Venus gave pointed commentary on modern life—women in the suburbs prostitute themselves too, for new appliances, she says in *Paris Is Burning*.[30]

Pain is not just composition's problem, but one in the archive too—what is retained or lost, and who oversees its artifacts and, therefore, the stories the artifacts together tell. Another Venus and another speculative archive: Saidiya Hartman asks in her essay "Venus in Two Acts," "How can narrative embody life in words and at the same respect what we cannot know?"[31] Her Venus is a young Black girl who reappears throughout the Atlantic slave-trade archives, a palimpsest of loss, in which undoing the violence of those who came before—reinscribing Venus into death—is an impossibility we must accept.[32] Hartman asks us to brave this impossibility by practicing narrative restraint and abandoning closure.[33] We hold back rather than fill in unnameable gaps, and we complicate resolutions to indicate the perpetuity of our work. I augment Hartman's recommendations to also make a claim for the chronicity of ache.

I am unsettled about the rifting estrangement between the university and the lived experiences of people who live proximal to that university—notably how the former approaches the latter. Which is not to say there is not breach, especially between the scenes described in this chapter. The boundaries are always porous. So, to be very clear, this is not about the difference among groups of people, but the difference of scenes and motions, and the sensations transmitting across our particular social webs. Indeed, it is how we tell the story of difference. If I'm looking to part with compositional alliances preoccupied with simplification and professionalization, if I hope to refuse capital's insistence on outcome and product and its influence on our imaginations, if I wish to rescale crisis into daily life, how do I resist these pulls as a writer? Part of my process has had to do with punctuation, whether I write relentlessly forward into argument or instead linger in feeling, narrative, and relationship. I, admittedly, in trying to write an academic text, have performed the former. Because, as Keeling says, argument can be produced faster. But over time I have learned to slow down, to recognize myself within the upheavals. I have learned to spurn object lessons to instead describe the world and her miry backgrounds.

Rather than further engrave one-dimensional accounts of oppression into my writing on vulnerability—particularly among drug-using folks and trans people—I focus on ache to reveal why we are persuaded into such imaginations foremost, but to also nuance pain and underscore other compositional options: to dream of alternative expressions; to relinquish the expectations (for our ourselves and others) for a pain-free life, even as we deserve it; to creatively curate new narratives of selfhood, and therefore new futurities of informed hope. All of which kindles our sense of agency and world-making. This to say, ache recognizes (reckons with) the impossible and the complex to then describe it: to compose.

Writing into Ache and Resisting Traditional Elegy

When I say "composition," I mean the literal, not disciplinary, definition: the mix and fusion of ingredients and the methods of its alchemy. Like con-fusion, the emphasis is on *how* rather than *why*. Writing through the valence of the singular, pained subject deflates our compositions, while ache spills out in illimitable iterations; its possibilities are everywhere. I want to explore how ache—as a paradigm for writing about marginalization, vulnerability, and pain—reduces harmful practices in composition studies: first, an achy heuristic reconceives crisis beyond faux transience and into the integrity of its longue durée, freeing us from the trap of solution-based writing and, worse, the notion we should get over or move on. Second, ache attenuates the spectacle made from marginalization, and in so doing unbinds the binary of negative and positive emotions. Our writing re-enlivens with life itself—with forbidden subjectivities, deconstructed timelines, untamed accounts of feeling, collaged and hybrid forms, and more.

We are all, in this moment, enduring some crisis or another. Climate change grips our lungs, or divorce papers have been signed. It is, of course, in our human nature to long for pain's terminus; but we cannot get over what we keep losing. "Crisis" organizes our conception of time to reinforce its linearity and require us to protect the future through reclamation of the status quo. I remember the bell curve in early COVID, how we tracked our location, studying our proximity to a possible end (that has yet to arrive). The opioid epidemic is in its third decade, exhibiting little sign of slowing. Christina Sharpe calls this a wake, wherein mourning is diffuse and grief an ongoing, irreconcilable pain.[34] Sharpe refuses to prescribe the conventional tonic for crisis: rehabilitation. She instead invites us into the wake. To work. Sharpe writes that wake work—specifically, the epistemological and aesthetic labors, expressions, and embodiments of being Black in America—troubles traditional notions of mourning because of the wake's interminability.[35] But "wake" is also to wake, to rouse again and face another day despite what comes after us. Wake is strength; it is how we write into loss that keeps losing.

"You are looking / at your child, turn your head, / then, poof, no more child. // that feeling. that's black."[36] That is the feeling of unrelenting violence and loss, the acute subsumed into ubiquity. These lines appear in "Short Film" by poet Danez Smith. "Short Film" is a long poem indexing the Black men, women, and children murdered by our state and its citizens. Though Smith longs to archive Black mourning, they also resist the archive's hold—its capture and closures—by organizing this indexical poem into "not elegies" and insisting on life within loss. Not an elegy for Trayvon Martin or Michael Brown, not an elegy for Renisha McBride or John Crawford III. Smith refuses memorial because, as they write, "all black people die. / I believe when a person dies / the black lives on."[37] The elegy cannot be written, because mourning reiterates endlessly in an anti-Black world. The elegy should not be written, because the elegiac displaces its subjects into contained and coherent pasts.

Danez Smith's poetry reevaluates elegiac expressions of mourning to account for loss that keeps losing. Traditional elegy fails; it envelops the subject, memorializing them, and thus forms the subject and the loss of the subject as understandable and articulable. But what about those who become part of the brutal matrix, wherein death is rendered predictable (statistical) through constant violence? When crisis is a wake in which one lives, the experience of total immersion is difficult to express. Smith's poems grapple with this difficulty to name the dead without giving closure to their death.

> I've trapped
> so many boys in poems.
> My mouth is an unmarked grave above which flowers bloom
> to sing the dead
> or it is just my mouth.[38]

Smith refuses to turn their poems into mausoleums. The boys, men, and women of Smith's poetry are gone but the pain is outstanding. There's "no more / room for grief // for it is everywhere now."[39] By expressing the ineffabilities of totality through its particularity, Smith inverts pain to position the subject not as returning to the site of loss, but as returned upon. Otherwise, pain enacts viral energy; it collects and expands. We take those names into "Politics of Elegy," readied by Smith's staging for an archive with no wrong answers except for stasis: "No more elegies / bring the fire."[40]

Most days when I sit down to write, I don't have fire to bring. Or, at least, its flames are not immediate but beckoned through breath. Heat and burn, blue into orange, fire destroys. First it smolders into suffocation then scorches into oblivion, like the wildfires I never grew accustomed to when I lived in the Pacific Northwest, some of which occurred naturally, many of which ignited from dry needle beds and arrogant human contact—a cigarette butt or a campfire during a burn ban. What always amazed me: the ferns and wildflowers that emerged through blackened dirt. When I attended an artist residency after finishing my doctoral program, I found an old note hidden in my studio desk: "In times of destruction, create something." It took me some time to locate the source, but I hunted around the internet to find these words come from Maxine Hong Kingston's book *The Fifth Book of Peace*: "In times of destruction, create something. A poem. A parade. A community. A school. A vow. A moral principle. One peaceful moment."[41] This is her antidote to war. Not because a poem or principle is a solution, but because it is a seed that blooms in a deadened forest floor.

I grew up at the edge of the metal ring of an ashy firepit, hot dog on a stick I carved with a pocketknife gifted from my father. We camped every summer in the Northern and Ontarian woods of Michigan and Canada. I helped pitch the heavy canvas tent, my short arms holding an aluminum pole over my head. Not until I was twenty did I make fire for the first time by myself. A friend and I were on the coast of California, the Sierras a day's drive behind us and the evening upon us. I struggled; the kindling wouldn't catch. I tore it down and reshaped the tiny twigs and re-piled the dead pine needles over and over, and still only ember and smoke. The air was cold. Condensation formed on the tent walls as I laid on my bag, having called it quits. As I thought about my breath catching against the nylon fly, then about oxygen as fuel, how it needs space, I went back to firepit, this time laying less kindling, this time blowing softly onto the pea-sized ember until it grew and grew. Since then, I have made hundreds of campfires, sometimes struggling against wet conditions, other times watching the flames catch immediately. This isn't a metaphor. Or, it can be. But it is an image of work and building. It is a literal example of how wonder made flame.

Affective attention to ache will insist on reiterative enactments, indexical organization, and hybrid cataloging. We will rewrite and remake. We will collage, because our lives emulate the shaken boxes full of scraps. Rebecca Macmillan argues that this form, "a mode of literary assemblage and inquiry," attunes audiences to "the politics of knowledge, memory, and efforts to account for the contemporary moment—especially those aspects of the present in crisis."[42] Macmillan also underscores the material centrality of archival forms, urging us to "reassess our systems of documentation and expand what counts as documentary form to include accounts of ordinary feelings and their material dimensions. These steps underwrite our capacity to lay bare the conditions of ordinary crisis of racialized violence and inequality that shape our present and our ability to work toward structural change."[43] This also is a kind of relationship with language, the reapplications and returns. Maggie Nelson names this pleasure "the pleasure of ordinary devotion" when we rewrite, remake, and revisit.[44] We may name this undertaking a poetics, or leave-no-trace, or life inside the questions where the future is undecided.

In addition to delaying time, writing into ache allays our subject from sensationalization. "Writing has nothing to do with signifying," write Gilles Deleuze and Félix Guattari. "It has to do with surveying, mapping, even realms that are yet to come."[45] In elucidating otherness without othering, ache—first as a heuristic, then as a writing principle—maintains human life over muted representations of oppression. By better portraying the quotidian cuts of marginality, we might, for example, demand both representation and privacy, knowing that despite this contradiction, our longing for such is not too much to ask; we more aptly capture what it feels like to survive the hostility of the day.

Throughout *Achy Affects* I have described each affect comprising this project—wonder, shame, shyness, and nostalgia—beyond their conventions, that we punctuate wonder for its revelatory commodity; that we overcome shame to harness pride; that we expel shyness for the moral call into sociality; that we spurn nostalgia for the sake of futurity. Each of these scripts relies on mastery, on mastering the antisocial emotion to reform it into something palatable. But in that way, we bisect affects into positive and negative feelings; and it is this binaried heuristic that undercuts our agency to insist on arrivals, disallowing dissonance so that we must rehabilitate what hurts. To think so categorically, and in terms of opposites (sick or healthy, normal or pathological), has done little to redress the multiple crises within which we find ourselves. It has done even less for serving the acute needs of our communities. If the margins are held captive to the center, then the center still regulates the margins. Often in our efforts to destabilize its power, we actually fortify that center by claiming the margins as marginal. Inhibited by such tautological frames, the "marginalized" either assimilate toward the center or else remain fixed in painful deviance. Instead, ache, because it can stem from desire or pain and everything in between, attenuates the concept of binaried emotion. I would love to see affect theory move beyond the dualism that restrains our theoretical creativity. We are not situated in either hope or despair, but within life itself, where hope and despair fluctuate through one another, where humor helps us mourn, where we cry in fear and cry from relief. Again, while I use the word "composition," what I mean are active forms of writing regenerating themselves. Again, this means a turn to poetics to illustrate how collaged forms imitate the sprawl of ache (even inside of urgency) and the multitudes of emotion (even inside of one pained person).

Love, An Index, by Rebecca Lindenberg, is a collection of elegiac poems organized through an archival form that at once honors and resists the elegiac tradition. The collection was published a few years following the disappearance of her partner, Craig Arnold, also a poet, who vanished on the Japanese island Kuchinoerabu, where he was participating in the US-Japan Creative Artists Program. While researching volcanoes pocked along the country and its islands, Arnold never returned from what he called his "pilgrimage." *Love, An Index* emerges from Lindenberg's loss. Though she initially started the project many years before Arnold disappeared, after his death the book, as she described, underwent a dramatic shift.[46] The details of the shift are not clear but presumable and quietly present in a poem titled "Illuminating."

Of all the experimental poems comprising *Love, An Index*—from the encyclopedic, eponymous index to the many shorter pieces delineated, at turns, as fragments, catalogs, and footnotes—"Illuminating" is the only that demands the reader physically shift the book in their hands; crossing the binding's threshold, it is the only poem Lindenberg lays out vertically down two pages like a centerfold. Supplementing the poem's central block of prose, ten brief notes, each less than fifty words and each in small print, float around this primary text. In this way, among others, "Illuminating" disorients readers; from the outset one handles the book differently and scans the page for a clear entry point, not knowing where to begin and end. "Illuminating" estranges one's reading experience through its material subversion of form while simultaneously enacting an intimacy that cannot be mistaken. The supplemental notes invite readers to reenter the central piece of the poem; and through this reiteration one senses the mimetic relationship between event and emotion, as well as the repetition, re-cataloging, and archiving that must occur when returning to the past through the film of loss.

The ten floating notes of "Illuminating" support the central text through aesthetic and structural reinforcement, hovering close while maintaining distinct distance. These floating notes, like rectangular life rafts drifting around a ship, are less invested in memory itself than they are in constellation. And in some instances, they veer explicitly into counsel and the confessional. Scripted in past tense, they look back while also pointing outward in varying directions. For example, in the top left corner, above the central text, Lindenberg writes, "you said when you were a kid, you'd say to yourself: I will remember this. and then you would remember it, whatever it was, in every detail."[47] Then, across the page on the right, also preluding the central piece: "I do not believe I remember any of this wrong, but there is a reason I have left bits out." One is not certain which note to read first, as the text on the right rises higher on the page, though the small font of both could render them endnotes, addendums, even afterthoughts. The mimetic toggle between the central poem and its hovering notes underscores mourning's need for extrapolating and reiterative language.

The main text of "Illuminating," the block of prose anchored to the center of the page, recounts the memory of a shared road trip Lindenberg and

Arnold took across the American West: "The car is warm, but its window is cold against my bare forearm."[48] From buffalo burgers to Devils Tower, a "gang of hogs" to pink gold, Lindenberg relays the memory from object to object, facilitating a constellation of loss, lost memory, and the fraught work of remembering. "The index suggested itself as a solution to a series of problems," Lindenberg responds in an interview about the book.[49] Skeptical of that which reflects order, a "whole story," and informed by what she calls her "own unfortunate subjectivity," Lindenberg overlays diverse emotions to unify them as a collection of loss.

"Illuminating" is thick with feeling: grief ("we press the heels of our palms into the soft gray rock of the Dakota Badlands, leaving a print we don't know how long wind and rain will need to erode"); wonder ("the Middle ages, for this reason called Dark though in fact it was a time of great transformation whose texts we call Illuminated"); anxiety ("Devil's Tower [*sic*] is teeming with venomous snakes") or perhaps that reflects wonder too; nostalgia ("you said something about the olden days"); humor ("You're harassing the prairie dogs"); resolve ("if you can recall how it felt at the time you can grasp that the end changes nothing"). Lindenberg's nontraditional aesthetic surface—the associative bundling of text—creates an endless reading experience. It demotes linearity and amplifies an openness wherein memory can be revisited, reinvested, and dialogically engaged. The very moment one turns the book to read the poem, shifts occur.

The illegibility of mourning is understood and felt through ordered disorder. Indeed, this poem is neat with its slim columns and contained spaces. But rather than instilling ease, the neatness of the poem affects a stickiness—each thing in the poem depends on the other. Lindenberg wrote "Illuminating" after being inspired by those medieval manuscripts that, she tells us, were copied by illiterate scribes who "traced the shapes of the letters, leaving two columns around the text—one for the errata of the master scribe, who proofread their work, the other for the scholia or interpretative commentary of the reader."[50] The significance of this interest in textual flexibility and partnership, Lindenberg offers in a note appended to the bottom of the page, is to foster a "conversation, which none may resolve but any might partake of."[51] In this case, who then is the master scribe and who the illiterate tracer? Lindenberg offers herself as the latter. Which makes us, the readers, the interpretative community (surely not the master scribe!) invited into a memory not our own, privileged with pathos for marginalia, and called to embrace the wildness of our own unfortunate subjectivities.

The Wild Ache

Writing into our ache lets us act out, to be-wild and bewilder (perhaps even while leaving no trace). I believe by studying ache, we can more generously describe the pain of living within crisis without sensationalizing ourselves or others. We name without giving a Name. Against legal systems, medical systems, media conglomerates, we write with ferality into the questions, because in so doing we become intimate with agency; it is born from wild desire. After all, we write because we love. We write for justice, which is an act of love. Or we write into a question, which is an act of passion. Cameron Awkward-Rich's provocation has carried me through this entire project, and I call on it again now: "What would it mean to do minoritarian studies without being driven by the desire to rehabilitate the subjects/objects of our knowledge? What kind of theories would we produce if we noticed pain and, rather than automatically seeking out its source in order to alleviate it . . . if we instead took it as a fact of being embodied."[52] Inspired again and again by his call to leave our subject untouched, I remember my responsibility as a writer is not to extract pain but to trace and describe its synaptic signals.

Ache is to want, pine, need—to need practical solutions, unconditional care, and better policies for healthcare, reproductive rights, affordable housing. To desire calm weather, fewer wildfires, and lower AQI numbers. To long for anonymity, or perhaps just neutrality, when waiting in line at the pharmacy. As I did. As I smiled at the pharmacist, paying twice as much for my prescription as I would at the other pharmacy. I paid for my prescription when it's free at the LGBTQ clinic. But I didn't know this yet. We need without knowing what exactly it is we need, or we have contradictory needs: to be heard but not required to speak. To take testosterone in the morning the way everyone else takes Lexapro, Lipitor, or Prilosec. That is, the meaning of applying the gel to my stomach is a parcel in my day, a fragment in a shaken box, a daily dosage of self-recognition and kindness. Incremental yet instrumental. And though at other times the testosterone is life-altering or lifesaving or full of poetic potential, most days, it is the former. It burns my dry skin after a hot shower in the morning. Then I forget about it.

Ache is also tender, crushing, craving. Unsatiated yet energized by hunger, we are horny and clingy. We make bad decisions when we ache. The drinks, the kiss, the texts—signals we send to give voice to and gratify our longing. We take important risks when we ache, like moving from our homelands or breaking up. Because, yes, ache will make you break your own heart. Ache is slow momentum, so that even when we feel stuck, we do not fully despair. Ache gets me down to the small Baptist church on a Tuesday morning to vote; and after I do, ache walks me home. In our best memories—which are often also the most quotidian, as when I pull a small plastic comb through my daughter's fine baby hair—we ache. We ache in vulnerability, and vulnerability sends pins through our skins all day. If we let it. I'm learning to let it. Ache is the broken heart that keeps breaking.

Ache is educating myself on the opioid epidemic only to find it dramatically shifted within days, because of a new policy banning exchange in a neighboring state or the introduction of tranq in the drug supply. Ache is there's always more to learn. Ache is 115 overdoses a day. Ache is stagger and stun. Ache is working alongside the syringe exchange manager who makes ten dollars an hour and is only part-time and how her quitting makes me want to quit too.

Ache is anonymity. Ache is the desire to hug someone after they told me their friend overdosed and died. But I can't—it's against volunteer rules. Ache is three hours in Eugene, Oregon, exchanging syringes, urging participants to come to the offices for HIV and Hep C testing. When they say it's too long and expensive a bus ride, too difficult to make it during testing hours, that, actually, being unhoused is pretty time-consuming, ache is saying "I understand" while handing them a pamphlet on safer injection practices. But actually I do not understand the exhaustion of finding bus fare, taking the 36 for a half hour down West Eleventh (which offers nothing other than sprawling parking lots and box stores), giving all your personal information (including years of sex and drug behaviors) to a volunteer (who may or may not be a young college student), waiting for results, getting results, which if they are positive only mean more bus rides on West Eleventh.

Ache is helping my ex-husband shop at thrift stores to furnish his new studio apartment during those first burning days of divorce. Ache is the blue, threadbare carpet in that studio where we have sex for the last time. Ache is riding my bike drunk through Oregon's night rain, pedaling fast, pressing lungs into ribs and raising my heart into fast percussion, closing my eyes through red lights, letting what will happen, happen. A car slams its brakes.

Ache is wanting more from my body, but also realizing that the want comes from a place of love, that *more* is potentiality, if also blockade. Ache is to live within that contradiction. Ache is failed explanation. Ache is considering failure a fine place to find myself. Ache is sleep and escape. Ache is depression. But ache is also the first apartment with friends, ant traps and rat traps and freedom, sitting on the floor and drinking green bottles of Rolling Rock, surrounded by unpacked boxes and particleboard furniture, marveling at the early summer sun setting in the kitchen window, how it flared downtown's church steeples, how we were finally on our own, how home was a thing I could have a hand in making. To ache is to desire—for relief, connection, extraction. But to ache is to also desire more—more joy, more justice, art, good food, better policy, inclusive care. Ache, then, is where we relinquish the expectations for a pain-free life even as we deserve a pain-free life, where we creatively curate new narratives of selfhood and therefore new futurities of informed hope.

How to represent in language the evasive forces that steam through us, wreck us, inspire us; how to answer the condition of our lives? Write a lot, then keep writing, write beyond failure, write beyond the pain of not saying what you hoped to say. Write until "good" is touched, then lost. Write until "good" falls away and something else rises to the surface. This too is ache, which requires us to stay hungry for those questions galvanizing our work and worlds, rejecting "good" as a static barometer of telos—as in, we're "done" with a piece because it is good—which is too easily absorbed by optimization, betterment for the sake of grade or advancement. "Good" becomes judgment, an ideation of aesthetic capture, not an experience felt as truce. I don't think a piece finished; I feel it, and that feeling aches, knowing there is still more to be done. This hurts, yes. Because desire hurts.

This brings us to the question of hope, which seems deeply and unnecessarily attached to solutions, whether we have them, whether we have the right ones, and whether we articulate them into perfection. But therein, one senses no room to relapse or rewrite. Perfection is a product of capitalism—turn it out, become the "productive member of society," "publish or perish." Cancel out everything else. This is labor, not work, not making.

What I'm trying to say is there are ways to lessen our collective pain. Grow good humans, vote, protest, volunteer, make art, donate, listen, witness, protect yourself, or whatever. It's about the assemblage, the assembling of these verbs into a life, perhaps even a poem.

CONCLUSION

Loving the Questions

Have patience with everything unresolved in your heart and
try to love the questions themselves as if they were locked
rooms or books written in a very foreign language

—Rainer Maria Rilke

I was the first to wake, opening my eyes with braced caution. On my back with
my wool hat pulled down over my eyes, I inhaled a quiet breath, exhaled, then
pushed the hat up to look through the opaque, orange nylon rainfly. Nothing
looked back at me. Which meant I was OK. I could shimmy out of my sleeping
bag, unzip the tent door, and sit with my legs out, forcing my warm feet into
frozen boots. Michael was still sleeping, so I stretched out of the tent and
headed toward the creamy glacial stream with our plastic water jug. The cold
water shocked then numbed my hands as I waited on the bank, scanning the
horizon and turning my back in a low squat to maintain a 360-degree vigil.
I heard one howl. It charged into the air with warmth, like I could touch the
soft beast origin of the sound. Then the echo back: a family of undulating
yelps and song. A pack of twenty wolves emerged from a deep overhang of
frozen dirt and spongy sedge. Together, we stood and stretched.

It took hours for the bus to traverse just a few miles on the washboard grav-
el road, the only road in Denali, coming to a full stop when a grizzly blocked
our path with her snout to the ground. Moments later the bus doors opened
to the abyss, and Michael and I stepped out with forty-pound packs on our
backs. Light yellowed in the late afternoon as we searched for camp, trying

to make good time through thick brush and taut branches. The Teklanika Glacier has receded nearly 500 yards and downwasted 300 feet over the past four decades, so that when Michael and I stepped off the green Denali school bus, we stepped on loose stones and matted grass, not ice; we hiked down into the valley in boots, not across on skis.

"How about here?" Michael asked, pointing his hiking pole toward a tangled grotto of arctic cotton and alpine sweetgrass. We were out of sight, but too much so. I wanted visibility, to see and be seen. We hiked on, picking up a game trail for a half mile before dropping back into brambles. Rounding a butte, we came upon a small rock spit wide enough for our tent and packs, and from which we could see the Tall One, Denali herself. I realized I was finding comfort in a shared, tamped space, that other animals had slept there, drinking from the nearby stream, just as we shared the same thin trails of bent grass and cracked branches. The proximity to life brought both danger and comfort, and this is what bewilders me, the felt paradox of the place. But Denali is bewilderment, its landscapes untaming every animal body passing through it, including my own. While today we might use "bewildered" to describe an internal state of confusion, its etymological origins suggest an external force: to be bewildered is to be wilded, some effort driving us into feral landscapes then abandoning us in our disorientations. Even as Denali's life continues its slow crumble or seasonal shifts crack the soil, even as the sun never sets or then never rises, the immutable tundra mutates. The freeze, hibernation, then the slough, melt, and rising rivers.

Increasingly so, Denali's transformations reflect settler-nation demand for production. The taming moves backward, and from afar. Fossil fuel, manufacturing, tech, and agricultural companies—most from the lower forty-eight states—contributing to worldwide climate change have touched the same tundra dirt under my boots. Denali receives more rainfall and less snow cover each year. Glaciers recede and annual temperatures rise. We know this. We know others know this. The question—the overwhelming, insurmountable question—of what to do upends us. We recycle, vote, use canvas rather than plastic bags, but pain persists. A causal question follows the first: how to practice (or even sense) hope when corporations such as Tyson, Boeing, Dow, and Amazon, or institutions such as the two-party government or a politicized Supreme Court, undo our work in a literal instant?

This is the crux of *Achy Affects*, describing how pain shapes but does not make us, writing into the complexity of living within crisis without being fully demoralized by it. En route to this crux, I came to understand this less as pain and more as *ache*, a chronic response to infinite stimuli catalyzing our sense of unease in a disordered world. In my own tiny nook in this world—a nook comprised of writing, a university, a needle exchange van—I asked myself into a question and therefore, into these pages: what does ache have to do with writing, or with the wilding we might pursue (intentionally, out of desire and opportunity, but also because we must) in our lives and work?

Getting divorced and then undertaking a long drive across the country to start "anew," I was tempted to spurn my past—the divorce, but along with it the Denali rock spits, the syringe exchange in downtown Eugene, and, well, my past self. No one in Pennsylvania would know about my divorce. No one needed to know shame was not just some theoretical foothold, studied in affect theory readers. Shame was of my skin and being. In earlier parts of the book, I describe how shame's taut feelings constrain us to abject narratives of who we are, determining what we can become and do; but also, shame constricts our imaginative hope, making horizons a demand, not a desire. I shared my own stories of shame and how "I should have known" became an echo in my life, a creed that repeated itself. But this reprise did little to serve my hope in futures; instead, I became wary of knowledge without punctuation, skeptical of knowledge that takes longer than a few minutes to unspool itself. I was stymied in the narrative of mastery and expertise—that to be a better human, I had to know all of myself, and I had to know best for others too, what they needed and how they needed it. But to live into the edges of life requires mess and mistakes, requires getting it a little wrong but leaning in with feeling nonetheless.

As it turns out, I am who I am and my origins are my origins. When I started writing *Achy Affects*, I let the tension collapse, risking academic illegibility for creative urgency. Not only did I let my past speak (my pain speak), but I began to pay witness to it, and in so doing realized that over time acute pain becomes enduring ache, and that pain cannot be undone but reflects the remnants of life lived. Ache illustrates how kinetic connections and the steep enmeshments of our shared lives mean that I cannot, for example, write earnestly about shame without describing and reckoning with its origins under my own skin. I will undoubtedly return to the same themes in my writing, whether through the filaments of a different trail or in an unbroken landscape, whether through new genre or hybridic revision. We choose to ache in this way and, in turn, the aches sustain our generosity and keeps us writing.

But also, ache—in stressing repetitious interminability rather than the spectacled individual—exposes the harmful structural practices embedded in our cultural and political systems. I wrote early drafts of *Achy Affects* between 2020 and 2023, when COVID took hold, Black Lives Matter uprisings took to the streets, and wildfires took down West Coast old growth. *Roe v. Wade* was overturned. Russia enacted war against Ukraine. The US Supreme Court limited the EPA's authority in curbing climate change. Florida was told not to say gay. Gun violence raged. Since then: more wars, more misinformation, more grief. We are overwhelmed and burned out, forlorn and outraged. I say all this not to claim that life is more acutely in crisis *now* than it ever has been (though it sure seems so), but to recognize that crises continue to propel our world forward, forming uncertain horizons and anxious futures.

At a recent speaking engagement, I spoke on this inertia of crisis. A small group of us gathered in a wood-paneled room where the windows to my back streamed spring sun. My brother flew in from Oakland, California, to attend. My wife cradled our six-month-old daughter in the back corner, bouncing and rocking her, changing her diaper in the hallway while she fussed and cooed. At the end of the event, I fielded questions from the audience. The final question, prompted by the moderator's timekeeping—"We have time for one more question"—was simple. "Are you hopeful?" I had just spent the warm spring months prior driving Midwest toll roads, reeling from one bad news week to another and returning to the homelands because my dad was recovering from open-heart surgery. But it was also during that time that I sat in the firefly meadows of Bennington, Vermont, where I had done an MFA ten years prior, remembering myself then, trying to will my past self to "lean in, feel everything, lean in and witness" as I wrote in a notebook, when my wife was going through her second trimester, little life blooming. I thought about the felt convergence of the past and future, how we occupy its centrifuge.

I thought about work, as in the labor we give by necessity as well as selflessly to make a life, to make a living; and I thought about feeling. I thought about how it feels to exist in upheaval, how it feels when better worlds diminish before our eyes because of merciless legislation, and how it feels to protect our sense of possibility against this current of crisis. And finally, I thought about how it feels to admit there are no ideal solutions but we work toward them, inspired by our ideals, nonetheless. As I wrote this book, I could not let go the question of how to envision and create better futures, as cliché as that sounds, while thoughtfully resisting all the ways "better" elicits harm and futures are held captive to predetermined demands of productivity. This question shaped *Achy Affects*.

I am a shy, queer kid processing the shame of a divorce, of what it means to not know, overwhelmed often by the many intersecting crises within which I currently live. *Achy Affects* is a direct response to understanding myself through the ebb and flow of feeling, through acute pain but also the quotidian slogs of getting by. These pages are a direct response to resisting telos, as a theoretical and methodological practice, but also as a lived experience of rejecting coerced futures and relinquishing the obligation to explain. "Yes, I am hopeful," I replied to my interlocutor. "I have to be . . . but I also want to be. I believe in desire, wonder, and pleasure." My baby screeched from the back of the room. I thought about taking her to the coast in the summer, playing in the tide pools—the gentle wonder of a sea star wrapping its body around her fingers and palm, the sharp barnacles we'd carefully avoid. I thought about offering this image to the audience, but balked at its naive inclination, that my hope delicately balanced on whether or not my daughter could touch a sea star. Tina Campt offers some solace in *Listening to Images*: "Futurity is, for me, not a question of 'hope'—though it is certainly inescapably intertwined with the idea of aspiration. To me it is crucial to think about futurity through a notion of 'tense.' What is the 'tense' of a black feminist future? It is a tense of anteriority, a tense relationship to an idea of possibility that is neither innocent nor naive. Nor it is necessarily heroic or intentional. It is often humble and strategic, subtle and discriminating. It is devious and exacting. It's not always loud and demanding. It is frequently quiet and opportunistic, dogged and disruptive."[1] In thinking about tense, Campt is thinking about time, but also grammar and composition. We remember that Anne Carson called adjectives "latches of being," while nouns name. I remember my poetry mentor teaching me to describe the world, because in so doing, I'm not trying to assert an idea, I'm captivated in sound and image. Most importantly, what we're all striving for anyways, is to be immersed in feeling. Which is much harder to achieve, especially as we grow in our writing, and especially as the world grows in its chaos.

I again turn to Rilke, who told us not only to live the questions, but love them. "Try to love the questions themselves. . . . Do not now seek the answers, which cannot be given you because you would not be able to live them. And the point is, to live everything. Live the questions now. Perhaps one day you will then, gradually, without noticing it, live along some distant day into the answer."[2] When I was in Alaska, Rilke's advice seeded courage when I feared what would stir me awake in the night. It nurtured endurance as I waded through glacial streams, braced against cold currents. It welcomed blissed wonder, as when I sat on my bear canister in the rain, watching wolves wake to the day, nudging one another into the misty morning. And it guided me into crisis: living the questions was both feeling—the breach of new awareness into the surfaces of my skin—and mantra, into which I pressed my abraded body. I was queer and I had to come out. Rilke's advice erupted me into pain while, simultaneously, offering solace.

In the first chapter I described the solace spurred by wonder when we mystify our destinations, then the relief of regress in chapter 2, the relief of remaining quiet in the face of confrontation (chapter 3), and the laudable indulgence in feeling backwards (chapter 4). But let's not forget: this all still hurts. There is real pain in our lives. Wonder reminds us of mortality, and not just our own but the places we call home. Earth herself. Shame traps, shy stands a thin line against erasure, and nostalgia calls out from distance and loss.

To love the questions is to embrace ache, to embrace the disappointing reality that we hurt, and we sometimes hurt one another. These hurts are not irredeemable. Once we embrace ache as a fact of being embodied, we become less motivated by simplistic solutions and therefore less overwhelmed by the problem itself. "It is precisely the recurrent, habitual, and mundane practice of showing up that makes us less and less willing to inhabit a world where we don't show up," writes Hil Malatino. "And where whole systems fail to show up for us."[3] As in, what else is this work all about?

Inspired by the scene of syringe exchange and my ongoing work with harm reduction advocacy groups, while also endlessly buzzing in my own embodied experiences of being trans and queer, I've come to thread all the pieces, feelings, scenes, connections through the unanswered question. By living *and* loving the questions, we evade those outcomes forced on us, the tidy conclusions that constrict us into narratives not of our own making. We embrace the discomfort of returning to and relearning the same truths. It means believing we are always, beautifully ourselves while we are on our way to ourselves, no end in sight. Here we are. *We are here.*

NOTES

Introduction: Healthy Markets

Epigraph: Waite, *Teaching Queer*, 15.

1. Rilke, *Letters to a Young Poet*, 27.

2. Narcan, the common brand name for naloxone, is a drug that when administered can reverse an opioid overdose. I vacillate between "Narcan" and "naloxone" throughout the text, just as I do in regular life, calling it both.

3. Siemaszko, "Ohio Sheriff Says His Officers Won't Carry Narcan."

4. Lorde, *Sister Outsider*, 114.

5. Derkatch, "Self-Generating Language of Wellness and Natural Health," 134.

6. Malatino, *Queer Embodiment*, 8.

7. Clare, *Brilliant Imperfection*, 105.

8. Foucault, *History of Sexuality*, 143.

9. Foucault, *History of Sexuality*, 141.

10. Foucault, *History of Sexuality*, 144.

11. Snorton, *Black on Both Sides*, 11. Snorton is also calling back to Hortense Spillers's essay "Mama's Baby, Papa's Maybe: An American Grammar Book," *Diacritics* 17, no. 2 (Summer 1987): 64–81.

12. Foucault, *History of Sexuality*.

13. Foucault, *History of Sexuality*, 138.

14. Hardt and Negri, "Biopolitical Production," 154.

15. Puar, *Right to Maim*, 16.

16. Thaca, "One Junky's Odyssey," 30.

17. Christian, "Race for Theory," 75, emphasis original.

18. Spade, "Mutilating Gender," 315.

19. Heaney, *New Woman*, 6, italics in the original.

20. Heaney, *New Woman*, 15.

21. Lorde, *Conversations*, 91.

22. Lorde, *Sister Outsider*, 114.

23. Aristotle, *Rhetoric of Aristotle*.

24. Eric Shouse cogently distinguishes feeling, emotion, and affect in marking feeling as personal, emotion as the external display of feeling, and affect as non-conscious sensation or intensity. See Shouse, "Feeling, Emotion, Affect." While I appreciate these separations, to feel is both intellectual and embodied. As in, feelings inspire thinking; knowledge inspires moods. Less intrigued by a cause-and-effect relationship, I am more inspired by this ongoing collapse itself—and what we find within the mess of broken dichotomies. I write within feelings *and* affect to privilege the material, to center the life being lived within our questions, and to insist on that life as infinitely unknowable, yet no less compositional and expressive. This to say, I vacillate between the use of "feelings" and "affect" synonymously.

25. Leslie Feinberg quotes Bowen in *Trans Liberation* (65).

26. Awkward-Rich, "Trans, Feminism," 824.

27. Malatino, *Trans Care*, 41.

28. Wiman, *Ambition and Survival*, 57.

29. Quashie, *Sovereignty of Quiet*, 45.

30. See Ahmed, *Cultural Politics of Emotion*; Sedgwick, *Touching Feeling*; Goffman, *Stigma*; and Gould, *Moving Politics*.

31. For example, Eve Sedgwick argues that for those whose most accessible affect is shame, they are often "the ones called (a related word) shy." Sedgwick, *Touching Feeling*, 63.

32. Lindenberg, *Love, An Index*, 49.

33. Christian, "Race for Theory," 72 and 73.

34. Rilke, *Letters to a Young Poet*, 27.

1: Wonder Drug

Epigraphs: Quashie, *Sovereignty of Quiet*, 72; Walker, *Color Purple*, 234.

1. For people using drugs and those dealing with addiction, COVID only compounded problems—transportation, safe supply access, work, general levels of anxiety.

2. See Adler-Kassner and Wardle, *Naming What We Know*.

3. Tuck and Yang, "Decolonization Is Not a Metaphor," 6.

4. Tuck and Yang, "Decolonization Is Not a Metaphor," 4.

5. Tuck and Yang, "Decolonization Is Not a Metaphor," 7.

6. See Heaney, *New Woman*.

7. Tuck and Yang, "Decolonization Is Not a Metaphor," 20.

8. Szalavitz, *Undoing Drugs*, 157.

9. Glaveanu, *Wonder*, 4–5.

10. Racine, *Beyond Clinical Dehumanisation*, 54. Emphasis original.

11. Racine, *Beyond Clinical Dehumanisation*, 57.

12. Waite, *Teaching Queer*, 15.

13. Lorde, *Sister Outsider*, 123.

14. Cvetkovich, *Depression*, 81.

15. Cvetkovich, *Depression*, 81.

16. Wamsley, "Judge Orders Boy Who Started Oregon Wildfire."

17. Montegary, "Healthy Families, Secure Bodies," 142.

18. Montegary, "Healthy Families, Secure Bodies," 143. See also Berlant, "Slow Death."

19. Barry et al., "Understanding Americans' View," 85–93. See also Cook and Brownstein, "Public Opinion and Public Policy"; Sun et al., "Public Opinion about America's Opioid Crisis."

20. Cook and Brownstein, "Public Opinion and Public Policy," 1174.

21. Cook and Brownstein, "Public Opinion and Public Policy," 1174.

22. Steinbock, "Framing Stigma," 49.

23. Awkward-Rich, "Trans, Feminism," 824.

24. See Sharpe, *In the Wake*.

25. Quashie, *Sovereignty of Quiet*, 72.

26. Plato, *Theaetetus*.

27. Descartes, *Philosophical Writings*, 1:350.

28. Irigaray, *Ethics of Sexual Difference*.

29. Young, *Intersecting Voices*, 56. See also La Caze, "Encounter between Wonder and Generosity," 10.

30. MacLure, "Wonder of Data," 228.

31. MacLure, "Wonder of Data," 228.

32. MacLure, "Wonder of Data," 228.

33. Wiman, *Zero at the Bone*, 91.

34. Ahmed, *Cultural Politics of Emotion*, 180. See also Ramos and Roberts, "Wonder as Feminist Pedagogy," 36. They explain that Ahmed influenced their understanding of wonder as pedagogy, in that it moves away from colonial logics of capture and binaries to instead privilege "learning that disrupts taken-for-granted truisms and knowing as possession (of the 'known') in favor of knowledge as a relationship that is multiple, dynamic, and never complete."

35. Glaveanu, *Wonder*, 3.

36. Foucault, *History of Sexuality*, 77.

37. As of this writing, bill HB 1245, which would legalize all programs in the state, was advanced by the Pennsylvania House Judiciary Committee. We are waiting to see if it first passes the (Democrat-led) House floor and then the (Republican-led) Senate. But with the 2024 election results, we have reason to be pessimistic.

38. A 1:1 exchange allows participants to receive only as many sterile syringes as they returned.

39. A new report from the CDC shows that fatal overdoses increased 44 percent among Black people in 2020 (this is twice what white populations experienced). There is justifiable resistance against calling for help during an overdose, and it makes sense that people of color would be even more skeptical or fearful of calling emergency teams. See Kariisa et al., "Vital Signs."

40. Substance Abuse and Mental Health Administration, "SAMHSA's Strategic Plan," 3.

41. Wiman, *Zero at the Bone*, 91.

42. Muñoz, *Cruising Utopia*, 25.

43. Muñoz, *Cruising Utopia*, 22.

44. Muñoz, *Cruising Utopia*, 22.

45. On cultivating optimism, see Awkward-Rich, "I Wish I Knew How It Would Feel to be Free."

46. MacLure, "Wonder of Data," 228.

47. Mann, "Feminist Phenomenology," 49. Emphasis mine.

48. In 2022 we got reports of Xylazine (known as "tranq" because it is medically used as a horse tranquilizer) infiltrating the heroin supplies on the East Coast. But like fentanyl and most else, it made its way to Pittsburgh in time. Xylazine can cause skin ulceration, which can lead to necrosis.

49. See Carr, *Scripting Addiction*.

50. See Sharpe, *In the Wake*.

51. National Center for Health Statistics, "Drug Overdose Deaths."

52. Honig, "As Opioid Overdoses Bleed City's Budget."

53. Smith, Malinowski, and Ballou, "Public Perceptions of Naloxone Use."

54. Quashie, *Sovereignty of Quiet*, 72.

2: The Spectacle of Shame

Epigraph: Belcourt, *History of My Brief Body*, 40.

1. Ahmed, *Cultural Politics of Emotion*, 107.

2. Tomkins, *Affect Imagery Consciousness*.

3. I'm thinking here of Ahmed (*Cultural Politics of Emotion*) and Eve Sedgwick (*Touching Feeling*), notably. But also Gould's text, *Moving Politics*, among others.

4. Ahmed, *Cultural Politics of Emotion*, 103.

5. Rubin, *Intersex Matters*, 64.

6. Sedgwick, *Touching Feeling*, 36.

7. An important distinction: I do not use "shame" and "stigma" interchangeably. Shame is sensation

and feeling, while stigma is the institutionalization of that feeling. Stigma, as it circulates within the medical-therapeutic industry, is the rhetorical echo of shame, producing judgment on human behavior, discerning and delineating failure.

8. Donovan et al., "Beliefs Associated with Pharmacy-Based Naloxone," 367–78.

9. See Foucault, *Birth of the Clinic*.

10. Goffman, *Stigma*, 5.

11. Derkatch, "Self-Generating Language," 134

12. Puar, *Right to Maim*, 16.

13. National Harm Reduction Coalition, "Principles of Harm Reduction."

14. Derrida, "Rhetoric of Drugs," 25.

15. Freeman, *Time Binds*, 3.

16. National Institute on Drug Abuse, "Drug Overdose Death Rates."

17. US drug prohibition laws have a very long history of promoting and naturalizing zero tolerance, from the Rockefeller drug laws of the 1970s that established minimum fifteen-year sentences for possession to habitual offender laws ("three-strike" legislation). For more information see American Addiction Centers, "Guide to U.S. Drug Laws."

18. Health Policy Politics, "Purdue Pharma OxyContin Commercial."

19. Harvey, *Spaces of Hope*, 106.

20. These were deemed "conferences," but always took place in warm, tourist destinations. See Van Zee, "Promotion and Marketing of OxyContin," 222.

21. Van Zee, "Promotion and Marketing of OxyContin," 223.

22. Van Zee, "Promotion and Marketing of OxyContin," 223.

23. Van Zee, "Promotion and Marketing of OxyContin," 221.

24. National Institute on Drug Abuse, "Drug Overdose Death Rates."

25. Centers for Disease Control and Prevention, "Provisional Drug Overdose Death Counts."

26. Netherland and Hansen, "War on Drugs that Wasn't," 668.

27. Netherland and Hansen, "War on Drugs that Wasn't." See also Peterson, Gubrium, and Fiddian-Green, "Meth Mouth." And see Linnemann and Wall, "'This Is Your Face on Meth.'"

28. Netherland and Hansen, "War on Drugs that Wasn't," 666.

29. "Policy makers were more likely to introduce punitive drug-related bills during the crack scare and are more likely to introduce treatment-oriented bills during the current opioid crisis." Kim, Morgan, and Nyhan, "Treatment versus Punishment."

30. Netherland and Hansen, "War on Drugs that Wasn't," 669.

31. ABC News, "New Face of Heroin Addiction."

32. Puar, *Right to Maim*, 16.

33. Derrida, "Rhetoric of Drugs." 25.

34. Centers for Medicare and Medicaid Services, "Substance Use Disorders."

35. Oregon Health Authority, "Drug Addiction Treatment and Recovery Act (Measure 110)."

36. Hoffman and Gale, "Scenes from a City."

37. Hoffman and Gale, "Scenes from a City."

38. Hoffman and Gale, "Scenes from a City."

39. Hoffman and Gale, "Scenes from a City."

40. Ahmed, *Cultural Politics of Emotion*, 103–4.

41. Shaw, *Governing How We Care*, 140.

42. Shaw, *Governing How We Care*, 140.

43. Weheliye, *Habeas Viscus*, 46.

44. Des Jarlais et al., "Syringe Services Programs."

45. Spade, *Normal Life*, 2. Also see Spade's "Mutilating Gender."

46. *Oxford English Dictionary*, s.v. "wild."

47. Gerstler, "Bear-Boy of Lithuania," in *Medicine*, 4.

48. Belcourt, *History of My Brief Body*, 40.

49. Rilke, "Second Elegy," in *Duino Elegies and The Sonnets to Orpheus*, 13.

3: Painfully Shy

Epigraph: Carson, *Autobiography of Red*, 29.

1. Carson, *Autobiography of Red*, 7.

2. Carson, *Autobiography of Red*, 4.

3. Carson, *Autobiography of Red*, 23.

4. Gill-Peterson, "Feeling Like a Bad Trans Object."

5. Ahmed, *Cultural Politics of Emotion*, 103.

6. Carson, *Autobiography of Red*, 145.

7. Carson, *Autobiography of Red*, 55–56. Italics original.

8. A word here on differentiating "shy" from "introverted." I am both but understand introversion to indicate one's social battery—how it is drained or charged. Whereas, shy is a sensorial state of being, not necessarily drained or enlivened, but activated or mobilized. Definitively felt. Introversion is not so much temporal feeling as it is trait.

9. See Aizawa and Whatley, "Gender, Shyness, and Individualism-Collectivism," 7–25.

10. "You can killjoy when you don't laugh at an offensive joke or when you refuse to cover over the injustices with a smile. You can killjoy because of what you do not and will not celebrate; national holidays that mark colonial conquest or the birth of a monarch. You can killjoy by entering the room because your body is a reminder of a history that gets in the way of the occupation of space. You can killjoy by asking to be addressed by the right pronouns or by correcting people if they use the wrong ones. You can killjoy by asking for that panel or that plenary not to be all white men, again. You can killjoy by asking to change a room because the room they have booked is not accessible, again. *Killjoy Truth: We have to keep saying it because they keep doing it.*" Emphasis original. Ahmed, "Find Other Killjoys."

11. Both quotations are from Malatino, *Side Affects*, 1.

12. Malatino, *Side Affects*, 321.

13. Tomkins, *Affect Imagery Consciousness*, 387.

14. Darwin, *Expression of the Emotions*, 327.

15. Sedgwick, *Touching Feeling*, 63.

16. Lane, *Shyness*, 4.

17. Lane, *Shyness*, 8.

18. Moran, *Shrinking Violets*, 4.

19. Stockton, *Queer Child*, 11.

20. Stockton, *Queer Child*, 13.

21. Stauffer, *Ethical Loneliness*, 10.

22. Derrida, "Rhetorics of Drugs," 25.

23. Moran, *Shrinking Violets*, 4.

24. Wiman, *Zero at the Bone*, 118.

25. Malatino, "Future Fatigue," 640.

26. Malatino, *Trans Care*, 2.

27. Social media influencing is a pointed example of how money is acquired through branded narratives of the self-made.

28. Spade, "Mutilating Gender," 317.

29. Carr, *Scripting Addiction*, 3.

30. Carr, *Scripting Addiction*, 11.

31. Carr, *Scripting Addiction*, 11.

32. Malatino, "Future Fatigue," 640.

33. Milnes, *History of Euphoria*, 8.

34. Heaney, *New Woman*, 6.

35. Currah, "Transgender Rights," 443.

36. See Heaney, *New Woman*; and Snorton, *Black on Both Sides*.

37. Gill-Peterson, "Feeling Like Bad Trans Object."

38. Rubin, *Intersex Matters*, 64.

39. See Weheliye, *Habeas Viscus*, 4: "Bare life and biopolitics discourse not only misconstrues how profoundly race and racism shape the modern idea of the human, it also overlooks or perfunctorily writes off theorizations of race, subjection, and humanity found in black and ethnic studies, allowing bare life and biopolitics discourse to imagine an indivisible biological substance anterior to racialization." And then later, "What seems to have vanished from this description is the *life* in *bare life*," (131), emphasis original.

40. Gill-Peterson, *Histories of the Transgender Child*, 197.

41. Hartman, *Scenes of Subjection*, 21.

42. Gill-Peterson, *Short History of Trans Misogyny*, 81. Emphasis mine.

43. Gossett, Stanley, and Burton, *Trap Door*, xviii.

44. Vaccaro, "Felt Matters," 255.

45. Vaccaro, "Felt Matters," 255.

46. Vaccaro, "Felt Matters," 256.

47. Utilizing civil disobedience tactics to bring attention to people dying from AIDS, ACT UP (Aids Coalition to Unleash Power) exemplifies the power of affect (specifically, shame and anger) to enact political change. Their rallying cry is "silence equals death."

48. Quashie, *Sovereignty of Quiet*, 45.

49. Quashie, *Sovereignty of Quiet*, 9.

50. Heaney, *New Woman*, 6.

51. Gill-Peterson, *Short History of Trans Misogyny*, 7.

52. Awkward-Rich, "I Wish I Knew."

53. Quashie, *Sovereignty of Quiet*, 45.

54. Malatino, "Tough Breaks," 125.

55. Carson, *Autobiography of Red*, 90.

56. Fleischmann, *Time Is a Thing*, 67.

57. The biopsy tested negative for malignancy. A cyst had grown, then ruptured. When I asked my nurse, "Would that be painful, a cyst rupturing?," she replied, "Oh, extremely." But I never felt it. I don't know what to make of that. Perhaps that some pains elide others.

58. Carson, *Autobiography of Red*, 60.

4: Nostalgic Potential

Epigraph: Smith, "No Name Number 5," *Either/Or*.

1. Batcho, "Nostalgia," 166.

2. Cvetkovich, *Depression*, 71.

3. Rich, "When We Dead Awaken," 18.

4. Nelson, *Argonauts*, 112.

5. Cvetkovich, *Depression*, 152.

6. Smith, "Between the Bars," *Either/Or*.

7. Batcho, "Nostalgia," 166.

8. Batcho, "Nostalgia," 166.

9. Batcho, "Nostalgia," 168.

10. Berlant, *Queen of America*, 3.

11. Ahmed, *Promise of Happiness*, 160.

12. Ahmed, *Promise of Happiness*, 241.

13. Ahmed, *Promise of Happiness*, 121–22.

14. Derrida, "Rhetorics of Drugs," 25.

15. Ahad-Legardy, *Afro-Nostalgia*, 11.

16. Ahad-Legardy, *Afro-Nostalgia*, 11.

17. Ahad-Legardy, *Afro-Nostalgia*, 103–4.

18. Snorton, *Black on Both Sides*, 53.

19. Ahad-Legardy, *Afro-Nostalgia*, 16.

20. See the comments from Ahmed above.

21. Kurlinkus, "Nostalgic Design," 424.

22. Freud, "Mourning and Melancholia."

23. Cvetkovich, *Depression*, 205.

24. Smith, "Pictures of Me," *Either/Or*.

25. Junk Bond Trader, "Elliott Smith."

26. Junk Bond Trader, "Elliott Smith."

27. Smith, "Alameda," *Either/Or*.

28. Freeman, *Time Binds*, 3.

29. Stockton, *Queer Child*, 11.

30. Halberstam, *Art of Queer Failure*, 2.

31. See, for example, Love, *Feeling Backward*; Hartman, "Venus in Two Acts"; Arondekar et al., "Queering Archives"; Stone and Cantrell, *Out of the Closet, Into the Archives*; Cvetkovich, *Archive of Feelings*.

32. Ahmed, *Cultural Politics of Emotion*, 159.

33. Ahmed, *Cultural Politics of Emotion*, 160, emphasis original.

34. Ahmed, *Cultural Politics of Emotion*.

35. Ahmed, *Cultural Politics of Emotion*, 159.

36. Ahmed, *Cultural Politics of Emotion*, 161.

37. See Sharpe, *In the Wake*. In this profound text, Sharpe describes mourning as a climate. Meaning, we are totally saturated by systemic violence, grief, and losing; and the systems (capitalism, for example) that create this ongoing endurance of mourning are inescapable. Sharpe argues that continual and reiterative loss for Black communities means living under occupation wherein "individual lives are always swept up in the wake" (8). Sharpe writes that wake work troubles conventional notions of loss precisely because of seeing loss in its interminability (19). The object is always lost and being lost, engendering a "total climate" (a withness) of living in and with death (21).

38. I have internalized this message that thirty is late to come out, that we should know at much

earlier ages whether we are "different." Ironic how this ingrained narrative on being gay or lesbian has yet to apply to children who know themselves to be trans. Either way, we come to ourselves when we do. It's all valid.

39. Elliott Smith, "Twilight," *Basement on a Hill.*

40. Smith, "No Name No. 5," *Either/Or.*

41. Smith, "Between the Bars," *Either/Or.*

42. Smith, "Between the Bars," *Either/Or.*

43. Of course, depending on what is recovered (or triggered), the unexpected arrival of memory can be painful as well.

44. Kurlinkus, "Nostalgic Design," 428. Italics mine.

45. See Schulman, *Gentrification of the Mind.* Schulman goes on to argue, "For in the end, all of this self-deception and replacing, this prioritizing and marginalizing, this smoothing over and pushing out, all of this profoundly affects how we think" (52). Schulman is therefore concerned not only about physical gentrification, in urban spaces and university buildings, but about the epistemological repercussions of this gentrification. She urges accountability, as it is always "in the interest of justice" and will protect minds, memories, and bodies from the commodification and control of neoliberal institutions (52).

46. Schulman, *Gentrification of the Mind,* 52.

47. Kurlinkus, "Nostalgic Design," 436.

48. Ahad-Legardy, *Afro-Nostalgia,* 33.

49. Derrida, *Archive Fever,* 19.

50. Hartman, *Lose Your Mother,* 19.

51. Harjo, *Poet Warrior,* 13.

52. Awkward-Rich, "I Wish I Knew."

53. See Nyong'o, *Afro-Fabulations.* He insists on a porous archive, one that resembles the non-neutrality of time, one that confronts the complex problem of how the archive names and contains while also being defined by its ephemerality. Nyong'o bends memory, releasing us from the pressures of either "working through" or "escaping" the past. Rather, he argues for disjunction, by which we foil "any effort to cohere the narrative of the past into a single, stable, and linear story." Nyong'o encourages us to tease out the rewards of fabulated archiving to spawn alternative temporalities, all the while envisaging "new genres of the human out of the fabulous, formless darkness of an anti-black world" (26).

54. Kierkegaard, *Either/Or.*

55. Smith, "Say Yes," *Either/Or.*

56. Smith, "Say Yes," *Either/Or.*

57. Howe, *Wedding Dress,* 21.

5: Wild Ache

1. Halberstam and Nyong'o, "Introduction: Theory in the Wild," 453. Emphasis original.

2. Halberstam and Nyong'o, "Introduction: Theory in the Wild," 453. Emphasis original.

3. Singh, *Unthinking Mastery,* 166.

4. Halberstam, *Queer Art of Failure,* 15.

5. Halberstam, *Queer Art of Failure,* 15.

6. Seitz, "It's Not About You," 5.

7. Harney and Moten, *Undercommons,* 135.

8. See Tuck and Yang, "Decolonization Is Not a Metaphor," 6.

9. Keeling, "Of Turning and Tropes," 317–18.

10. Harney and Moten, *Undercommons*, 31.

11. Osuna, "Class Suicide," 27.

12. ACT UP relied on sensationalized stunts of activism to force attention on people living with and dying from AIDS, for example.

13. Moreau, "I Learned It by Watching YOU!"

14. See Linnemann and Wall, "This Is Your Face on Meth."

15. Most drugs—heroin, cocaine, marijuana, amphetamine, LSD—were unregulated and utilized by the US medical industry in the nineteenth century, and even into the early twentieth century. Which is not to say earlier histories represent better drug policy, but that sensationalized representation of drug use can be tied to the origins of criminalizing drugs.

16. But also communications, rhetoric, and queer studies classrooms, among others.

17. Prosser, *Second Skins*, 178.

18. Prosser, *Second Skins*, 178

19. Feinberg, *Stone Butch Blues*, 207

20. Feinberg, *Stone Butch Blues*, 208.

21. Prosser, *Second Skins*, 178

22. Prosser, *Second Skins*, 179.

23. Prosser, *Second Skins*, 205.

24. Feinberg, *Stone Butch Blues*, 157.

25. Prosser, *Second Skins*, 13

26. Namaste, *Invisible Lives*, 20.

27. Namaste, *Invisible Lives*, 20.

28. See Namaste's arguments against Butler's reading in *Invisible Lives* (13–23).

29. Gill-Peterson, *Short History of Trans Misogyny*, 80.

30. Livingston, *Paris Is Burning*.

31. Hartman, "Venus in Two Acts," 3.

32. Hartman, "Venus in Two Acts," 10.

33. Hartman, "Venus in Two Acts," 12.

34. See Sharpe, *In the Wake*.

35. Sharpe, *In the Wake*, 19.

36. Smith, *Black Movie*, 21.

37. Smith, *Black Movie*, 30.

38. Smith, *Black Movie*, 32.

39. Smith, *Black Movie*, 27.

40. Smith, *Black Movie*, 32.

41. Kingston, *Fifth Book of Peace*, 402.

42. Macmillan, "Archival Poetics," 201.

43. Macmillan, "Archival Poetics," 201.

44. Nelson, *Argonauts*, 112.

45. Deleuze and Guattari, *Thousand Plateaus*, 5.

46. Lindenberg, "McSweeney's Book Q&A."

47. Lindenberg, *Love, An Index*, 20–21.

48. Lindenberg, *Love, An Index*, 20–21.

49. Lindenberg, "Interview."

50. Lindenberg, *Love, An Index*, 20–21.

51. Lindenberg, *Love, An Index*, 20–21.

52. Awkward-Rich, "Trans, Feminism," 824.

Conclusion

Epigraph: Rilke, *Letters to a Young Poet*, 27.

1. Campt, *Listening to Images*, 17.

2. Rilke, *Letters to a Young Poet*, 27.

3. Malatino, *Trans Care*, 72.

BIBLIOGRAPHY

ABC News. "The New Face of Heroin Addiction." YouTube video, 8:31. (2010). https://www.you tube.com/watch?v=cskq_zGVSZs.

Adler-Kassner, Linda, and Elizabeth Wardle, eds. *Naming What We Know: Threshold Concepts of Writing Studies.* Logan: Utah State University Press, 2015.

Ahad-Legardy, Badia. *Afro-Nostalgia: Feeling Good in Contemporary Black Culture.* Urbana: University of Illinois Press, 2021.

Ahmed, Sara. *The Cultural Politics of Emotion,* 2nd ed. New York: Routledge, 2015.

Ahmed, Sara. "Find Other Killjoys." *Feminist Killjoys.* December 31, 2023. https://feministkilljoys. com/2023/12/31/find-other-killjoys/.

Ahmed, Sara. *The Promise of Happiness.* Durham, NC: Duke University Press, 2010.

Aizawa, Yuki, and Mark A. Whatley. "Gender, Shyness, and Individualism-Collectivism: A Cross-Cultural Study." *Race, Gender, & Class* 13, no. 1/2 (2006): 7–25.

American Addiction Centers. "Guide to U.S. Drug Laws." Accessed October 18, 2022. www.recov ery.org/addiction/us-drug-laws/.

Aristotle. *The Rhetoric of Aristotle, A Translation.* Edited by John Edwin Sandys. Cambridge: Cambridge University Press, 1909.

Arondekar, Anjali, Ann Cvetkovich, Christina B. Hanhardt, Regina Kunzel, Tavia Nyong'o, Juana María Rodríguez, Susan Stryker, Daniel Marshall, Kevin P. Murphy, and Zeb Tortorici. "Queering Archives A Roundtable Discussion." *Radical History Review,* no. 122 (May 2015): 211–31.

Awkward-Rich, Cameron. "I Wish I Knew How It Would Feel to Be Free." *Paris Review.* June 11, 2020. www.theparisreview.org/blog/2020/06/11/i-wish-i-knew-how-it-would-feel-to-be-free/.

Awkward-Rich, Cameron. "Trans, Feminism: Or, Reading like a Depressed Transsexual." *Signs: Journal of Women in Culture and Society* 42, no. 4 (Summer 2017): 819–41.

Barry, Colleen L., Alene Kennedy-Hendricks, Sarah E. Gollust, Jeff Niederdeppe, Marcus A. Bachhuber, Daniel W. Webster, and Emma E. McGinty. "Understanding Americans' View on Opioid Pain Reliever Abuse." *Addiction* 111, no. 1 (2016): 85–93.

Batcho, Krystine Irene. "Nostalgia: The Bittersweet History of a Psychological Concept." *History of Psychology* 16, no. 3 (2013): 165–76.

Belcourt, Billy-Ray. *A History of My Brief Body.* Columbus, OH: Two Dollar Radio, 2020.

Berlant, Lauren. *The Queen of America Goes to Washington City: Essays on Sex and Citizenship.* Durham, NC: Duke University Press, 1997.

Berlant, Lauren. "Slow Death (Sovereignty, Obesity, Lateral Agency)." *Critical Inquiry* 33, no. 4 (2007): 754–80.

Campt, Tina. *Listening to Images.* Durham, NC: Duke University Press, 2017.

Carr, E. Summerson. *Scripting Addiction: The Politics of Therapeutic Talk and American Sobriety.* Princeton, NJ: Princeton University Press, 2010.

Carson, Anne. *Autobiography of Red: A Novel in Verse.* New York: Vintage, 1998.

Centers for Disease Control and Prevention. "Provisional Drug Overdose Death Counts." Accessed November 2024, https://www.cdc.gov/nchs/nvss/vsrr/drug-overdose-data.htm.

Centers for Medicare and Medicaid Services. "Substance Use Disorders." https://www.medicaid. gov/medicaid/benefits/behavioral-health-services/substance-use-disorders/index.html.

Christian, Barbara. "The Race for Theory." *Feminist Studies* 14, no. 1 (Spring 1988): 67–79.

Clare, Eli. *Brilliant Imperfection: Grappling with Cure.* Durham, NC: Duke University Press, 2017.

Cook, Amy K., and Henry H. Brownstein. "Public Opinion and Public Policy: Heroin and Other Opioids." *Criminal Justice Policy Review* 30, no. 8 (2019): 1163–85.

Currah, Paisley. "Transgender Rights without a Theory of Gender?" *Tulsa Law Review* 52, no. 3 (Spring 2017): 441–51.

Cvetkovich, Ann. *An Archive of Feelings: Trauma, Sexuality, and Lesbian Public Cultures.* Durham, NC: Duke University Press, 2003.

Cvetkovich, Ann. *Depression: A Public Feeling.* Durham, NC: Duke University Press, 2012.

Darwin, Charles. *The Expression of the Emotions in Man and Animals.* 1872. Oxford: Oxford University Press, 2002.

Daston, Lorraine, and Katharine Park. *Wonders and the Order of Nature 1150–1750.* Princeton, NJ: Princeton University Press, 2001.

Deleuze, Gilles, and Félix Guattari. *A Thousand Plateaus.* Minneapolis: University of Minnesota Press, 1987.

Derkatch, Colleen. "The Self-Generating Language of Wellness and Natural Health." *Rhetoric of Health and Medicine* 1, nos. 1–2 (2018): 132–60.

Derrida, Jacques. *Archive Fever: A Freudian Impression.* Translated by Eric Prenowitz. Chicago: University of Chicago Press, 1998.

Derrida, Jacques. "The Rhetoric of Drugs: An Interview." *Differences* 5, no. 1 (1993): 1–25.

Des Jarlais, Don, Ann Nugent, Alisa Solberg, Jonathan Feelemyer, Jonathan Mermin, and Deborah Holtzman. "Syringe Services Programs for Persons Who Inject Drugs in Urban, Suburban, and Rural Areas—United States." Centers for Disease Control and Prevention. *Morbidity and Mortality Weekly Report,* December 11, 2015.

Descartes, René. *The Philosophical Writings of Descartes.* 2 vols. Translated by John Cottingham, Robert Stoothoff, and Dugald Murdoch. Cambridge: Cambridge University Press, 1985.

Donovan, Elizabeth, Patricia Case, Jeffrey P. Bratberg, Janette Baird, Dina Burstein, Alexander Y. Walley, and Traci C. Green. "Beliefs Associated with Pharmacy-Based Naloxone: A Qualitative Study of Pharmacy-Based Naloxone Purchasers and People at Risk for Opioid Overdose." *Journal of Urban Health,* no. 96 (June 2019): 367–78.

Feinberg, Leslie. *Stone Butch Blues.* Los Angeles: Alyson Books, 1993.

Feinberg, Leslie. *Trans Liberation: Beyond Pink or Blue.* Boston: Beacon Press, 1999.

Fleischmann, T. *Time Is a Thing My Body Moves Through.* Minneapolis: Coffee House Press, 2019.

Foucault, Michel. *The Birth of the Clinic: An Archaeology of Medical Perception.* New York: Vintage, 1973.

Foucault, Michel. *The History of Sexuality: Volume 1, An Introduction.* Translated by Robert Hurley. New York: Vintage Books, 1978.

Freeman, Elizabeth. *Time Binds: Queer Temporalities, Queer Histories.* Durham, NC: Duke University Press, 2010.

Freud, Sigmund. "Mourning and Melancholia." In *Collected Papers* vol. 4, translated by Alix Strachey and Joan Riviere, 152–70. London: Hogarth Press, 1950.

Gerstler, Amy. *Medicine.* New York: Penguin, 2000.

Gill-Peterson, Jules. "Feeling Like a Bad Trans Object." *Post 45.* December 2019. https://post45. org/2019/12/feeling-like-a-bad-trans-object/.

Gill-Peterson, Jules. *Histories of the Transgender Child.* Minneapolis: University of Minnesota Press, 2018.

Gill-Peterson, Jules. *A Short History of Trans Misogyny.* New York: Verso, 2024.

Glaveanu, Vlad P. *Wonder: The Extraordinary Power of an Ordinary Experience.* London: Bloomsbury Academic 2020.

Goffman, Erving. *Stigma: Notes on the Management of Spoiled Identity.* New York: Touchstone, 1986.

Gossett, Reina, Eric A. Stanley, and Johanna Burton, eds. *Trap Door: Trans Cultural Production and the Politics of Visibility.* Cambridge, MA: MIT Press, 2017.

Gould, Deborah. *Moving Politics: Emotion and ACT UP's Fight Against AIDS.* Chicago: University of Chicago Press, 2009.

Halberstam, Jack. *The Queer Art of Failure.* Durham, NC: Duke University Press, 2011.

Halberstam, Jack. "Introduction." In *The Undercommons: Fugitive Planning and Black Study,* by Stefano Harney and Fred Moten, 5–12. New York: Minor Compositions, 2013.

Halberstam, Jack, and Tavia Nyong'o. "Introduction: Theory in the Wild." *South Atlantic Quarterly* 117, no. 3 (July 2018): 453–64.

Hardt, Michael, and Antonio Negri. "Biopolitical Production." In *Biopolitics: A Reader,* edited by Timothy Campbell and Adam Sitze, 273–310. Durham, NC: Duke University Press, 2013.

Harjo, Joy. *Poet Warrior.* New York: Norton, 2021.

Harney, Stefano, and Fred Moten. *The Undercommons: Fugitive Planning and Black Study.* New York: Minor Compositions, 2013.

Hartman, Saidiya. *Lose Your Mother: A Journey along the Atlantic Slave Route.* New York: Farrar, Straus and Giroux, 2007.

Hartman, Saidiya. *Scenes of Subjection: Terror, Slavery, and Self-Making in Nineteenth-Century America.* Oxford: Oxford University Press, 1997.

Hartman, Saidiya. "Venus in Two Acts." *Small Axe* 12, no. 2 (June 2008): 1–14.

Harvey, David. *Spaces of Hope.* Edinburgh, UK: Edinburgh University Press, 2000.

Health Policy Politics. "Purdue Pharma OxyContin Commercial." YouTube Video, 00:37. September 22, 2016. https://www.youtube.com/watch?v=Er78Dj5hyeI.

Heaney, Emma. *The New Woman: Literary Modernism, Queer Theory, and the Transfeminine Allegory.* Evanston, IL: Northwestern University Press, 2017.

Hoffman, Jan, and Jordan Gale. "Scenes from a City That Only Hands Out Tickets for Using Fentanyl." *New York Times,* July 31, 2023. www.nytimes.com/2023/07/31/health/portland-oregon-drugs.html.

Honig, Esther. "As Opioid Overdoses Bleed City's Budget, Councilman Proposes Stopping Treatment." National Public Radio, June 29, 2017. www.npr.org/2017/06/29/534916080/ohio-town-struggles-to-afford-life-saving-drug-for-opioid-overdoses.

Howe, Fanny. *The Wedding Dress: Meditations on Word and Life.* Berkeley: University of California Press, 2003.

Irigaray, Luce. *An Ethics of Sexual Difference.* Translated by Carolyn Burke and Gillian Gill. Ithaca, NY: Cornell University Press, 1993.

Junk Bond Trader. "Elliott Smith—Lennon, Jealous Guy cover [Live on *The Jon Brion Show*]." YouTube video, 4:40. January 18, 2013. https://www.youtube.com/watch?v=zunr2TmKZf8.

Kariisa, Mbabazi, Nicole L. Davis, Sagar Kumar, Puja Seth, Christine L. Mattson, Farnaz Chowdhury, and Christopher M Jones. "Vital Signs: Drug Overdose Deaths, by Selected Sociodemographic and Social Determinants of Health Characteristics—25 States and the District of Columbia, 2019–2020." *Morbidity and Mortality Weekly Report* 71, no. 29 (July 22, 2022): 940–47.

Keeling, D. M. "Of Turning and Tropes." *Review of Communication* 16, no. 4 (2016): 317–33.

Kierkegaard, Søren. *Either/Or.* Translated by David F. Swenson and Lillian Marvin Swenson. Garden City, NY: Doubleday, 1959.

Kim, Jin-Woo, Evan Morgan, and Brendan Nyhan. "Treatment versus Punishment: Understanding Racial Inequalities in Drug Policy." *Journal of Health Politics, Policy, and Law* 45, no. 2 (April 2020): 177–209.

Kingston, Maxine Hong. *The Fifth Book of Peace.* New York: Alfred A. Knopf, 2003.

Kurlinkus, William C. "Nostalgic Design: Making Memories in the Rhetoric Classroom." *Rhetoric Society Quarterly* 51 no. 5 (2021): 422–38.

La Caze, Marguerite. "The Encounter between Wonder and Generosity." *Hypatia* 17, no. 3 (2002): 1–19.

Lane, Christopher. *Shyness: How Normal Behavior Became a Sickness.* New Haven, CT: Yale University Press, 2008.

Lindenberg, Rebecca. "Interview." By Elizabeth Clark Wessel. *BOMB Magazine.* February 18, 2013. www.bombmagazine.org/articles/2013/02/18/rebecca-lindenberg/.

Lindenberg, Rebecca. *Love, An Index.* San Francisco: McSweeney's, 2012.

Lindenberg, Rebecca. "A McSweeney's Book Q&A with Rebecca Lindenberg, Author of *Love, An Index.*" By McSweeney's Books. McSweeney's Internet Tendency, April 23, 2013. https://www.mcsweeneys.net/articles/a-mcsweeneys-books-qa-with-rebecca-lindenberg-author-of-love-an-index.

Linnemann, Travis, and Tyler Wall. "'This Is Your Face on Meth': The Punitive Spectacle of 'White Trash' in the Rural War on Drugs." *Theoretical Criminology* 17, no. 3 (2013): 315–34.

Livingston, Jennie, dir. *Paris Is Burning.* Off White Productions, 1990.

Lorde, Audre. *Conversations with Audre Lorde.* Jackson: University of Mississippi Press, 2004.

Lorde, Audre. *Sister Outsider.* Trumansburg, NY: Crossing Press, 1984.

Love, Heather. *Feeling Backward: Loss and the Politics of Queer History.* Cambridge, MA: Harvard University Press, 2009.

MacLure, Maggie. "The Wonder of Data." *Cultural Studies, Critical Methodologies* 13, no. 4 (2013): 228–32.

Macmillan, Rebecca. "The Archival Poetics of Claudia Rankine's *Don't Let Me Be Lonely: An American Lyric.*" *Contemporary Literature* 58, no. 2 (Summer 2017): 173–203.

Malatino, Hil. "Future Fatigue: Trans Intimacies and Trans Presents (or How to Survive the Interregnum)." *Transgender Studies Quarterly* 6, no. 4 (2019): 635–58.

Malatino, Hil. *Queer Embodiment: Monstrosity, Medical Violence, and Intersex Experience.* Lincoln: University of Nebraska Press, 2019.

Malatino, Hil. *Side Affects: On Being Trans and Feeling Bad.* Minneapolis: University of Minnesota Press, 2022.

Malatino, Hil. "Tough Breaks: Trans Rage and the Cultivation of Resilience." *Hypatia* 34, no. 1 (2019): 121–40.

Malatino, Hil. *Trans Care.* Minneapolis, MN: University of Minnesota Press, 2020.

Mann, Bonnie. "Feminist Phenomenology and the Politics of Wonder." *AVANT: The Journal of the Philosophical-Interdisciplinary Vanguard* 9, no. 2 (2018): 43–61.

Milnes, Christopher. *A History of Euphoria: The Perception and Misperception of Health and Well-Being.* New York: Routledge, 2019.

Montegary, Liz. "Healthy Families, Secure Bodies." *Gay and Lesbian Quarterly* 26, no. 1 (2020): 140–51.

Moran, Joe. *Shrinking Violets: The Secret Life of Shyness*. New Haven, CT: Yale University Press, 2017.

Moreau, Joseph. "'I Learned It by Watching YOU!' The Partnership for a Drug-Free America and the Attack on 'Responsible Use' Education in the 1980s." *Journal of Social History* 49, no. 3 (Spring 2016): 710–37.

Muñoz, José Esteban. *Cruising Utopia: The Then and There of Queer Futurity*. New York: New York University Press, 2009.

Namaste, Viviane. *Invisible Lives: The Erasure of Transsexual and Transgendered People*. Chicago: University of Chicago Press, 2000.

National Center for Health Statistics. "Drug Overdose Deaths." Centers for Disease Control and Prevention, 2021. www.cdc.gov/nchs/hus/topics/drug-overdose-deaths.htm.

National Harm Reduction Coalition. "Principles of Harm Reduction." Accessed November 24, 2021. www.harmreduction.org/about-us/principles-of-harm-reduction/.

National Institute on Drug Abuse. "Drug Overdose Death Rates." Accessed May 17, 2024. www.nida.nih.gov/research-topics/trends-statistics/overdose-death-rates.

Nelson, Maggie. *The Argonauts*. Minneapolis: Graywolf Press, 2015.

Netherland, Julie, and Helena B. Hansen. "The War on Drugs that Wasn't: Wasted Whiteness, 'Dirty Doctors,' and Race in Media Coverage of Prescription Opioid Misuse." *Culture, Medicine, and Psychiatry* 40, no. 4 (2016): 664–86.

Nyong'o, Tavia. *Afro-Fabulations: The Queer Drama of Black Life*. New York: New York University Press, 2018.

Oregon Health Authority. "Drug Addiction Treatment and Recovery Act (Measure 110)." Behavioral Health Services. https://www.oregon.gov/oha/hsd/amh/pages/measure110.aspx.

Osuna, Steven. "Class Suicide: The Black Radical Tradition, Radical Scholarship, and the Neoliberal Turn." *Futures of Black Radicalism*, edited by Gaye Theresa Johnson and Alex Lubin, 21–38. London: Verso, 2017.

Peterson, Jeffrey Chaichana, Aline Gubrium, and Alice Fiddian-Green. "Meth Mouth, White Trash, and the Pseudo-Racialization of Methamphetamine Use in the U.S." *Health Communication* 34, no. 10 (2018): 1173–82.

Plato. *Theaetetus*. Edited by Benjamin Jowett. New York: Scribner, 1990.

Prosser, Jay. *Second Skins: The Body Narratives of Transsexuality*. New York: Columbia University Press, 1998.

Puar, Jasbir. *Right to Maim: Debility, Capacity, Disability*. Durham, NC: Duke University Press, 2017.

Quashie, Kevin. *The Sovereignty of Quiet: Beyond Resistance in Black Culture*. New Brunswick, NJ: Rutgers University Press, 2012.

Racine, Catherine A. *Beyond Clinical Dehumanisation towards the Other in Community Mental Health Care: Levinas, Wonder, and Autoethnography*. London: Routledge, 2021.

Ramos, Fabiane, and Laura Roberts. "Wonder as Feminist Pedagogy: Disrupting Feminist Complicity with Coloniality." *Feminist Review* 128, no. 1 (2021): 28–43.

Rich, Adrienne. "When We Dead Awaken: Writing as Re-Vision." *College English* 34, no. 1 (1972): 18–30.

Rilke, Rainer Maria. *Duino Elegies and The Sonnets to Orpheus*. Translated by Stephen Mitchell. New York: Vintage, 2009.

Rilke, Rainer Maria. *Letters to a Young Poet*. Translated by M. D. Herter Norton. New York: Norton, 1934.

Rubin, David. *Intersex Matters: Biomedical Embodiment, Gender Regulation, and Transnational Activism*. Albany, NY: SUNY Press, 2017.

Schulman, Sarah. *The Gentrification of the Mind: Witness to a Lost Imagination.* Berkeley: University of California Press, 2012.

Sedgwick, Eve Kosofsky. *Touching Feeling: Affect, Pedagogy, Performativity.* Durham, NC: Duke University Press, 2003.

Seitz, D. K. "'It's Not About You': Disappointment as Queer Pedagogy in Community-Engaged Service-Learning." *Journal of Homosexuality* 67, no. 3 (2020): 305–14.

Siemaszko, Corky. "Ohio Sheriff Says His Officers Won't Carry Narcan." NBC News, July 7, 2017. https://www.nbcnews.com/storyline/americas-heroin-epidemic/ohio-sheriff-says-his-over dosing-ohioans-my-guys-have-no-n780666.

Sharpe, Christina. *In the Wake: On Blackness and Being.* Durham, NC: Duke University Press, 2016.

Shaw, Susan. *Governing How We Care: Contesting Community and Defining Difference in U.S. Public Health Programs.* Philadelphia: Temple University Press, 2012.

Shouse, Eric. "Feeling, Emotion, Affect." *M/C Journal* 8, no. 6 (2005). https://journal.media-culture.org.au/mcjournal/article/view/2443.

Singh, Julietta. *Unthinking Mastery: Dehumanism and Decolonial Entanglements.* Durham, NC: Duke University Press, 2017.

Smith, Danez. *Black Movie.* Minneapolis: Button Poetry, 2015.

Smith, Elliott. *Either/Or.* Kill Rock Stars Records, 1997.

Smith, Elliott. *Basement on a Hill.* ANTI- Records, 2004.

Smith, Jordan O., Scott S. Malinowski, and Jordan M. Ballou. 2019. "Public Perceptions of Naloxone Use in the Outpatient Setting." *Mental Health Clinician* 9, no. 4 (2019): 275–79.

Snorton, C. Riley. *Black on Both Sides: A Racial History of Trans Identity.* Minneapolis: University of Minnesota Press, 2017.

Spade, Dean. "Mutilating Gender." In *The Transgender Studies Reader,* edited by Susan Stryker and Stephen Whittle, 315–32. New York: Routledge, 2006.

Spade, Dean. *Normal Life: Administrative Violence, Critical Trans Politics, and the Limits of Law.* Brooklyn, NY: South End, 2011.

Stauffer, Jill. *Ethical Loneliness: The Injustice of Not Being Heard.* New York: Columbia University Press, 2018.

Steinbock, Eliza. "Framing Stigma in Trans* Mediascapes: How Does It Feel to Be a Problem?" *Spectator* 37, no. 2 (Fall 2017): 48–57.

Stockton, Kathryn Bond. *The Queer Child, or Growing Sideways in the Twentieth Century.* Durham, NC: Duke University Press, 2009.

Stone, Amy L., and Jaime Cantrell, eds. *Out of the Closet, Into the Archives: Researching Sexual Histories.* Albany, NY: SUNY Press, 2016.

Substance Abuse and Mental Health Administration, U.S. Department of Health and Human Services. "SAMHSA's Strategic Plan FY2019–2023." April 11, 2022. https://facesandvoicesof recovery.org/resource/samhsa-strategic-plan-fy2019-fy2023/.

Sun, Diana, Amanda Graham, Ben Feldmeyer, Francis T. Cullen, and Teresa C. Kulig. "Public Opinion about America's Opioid Crisis: Severity, Sources, and Solutions in Context." *Deviant Behavior* 40, no. 4 (2023). Online. https://doi.org/10.1080/01639625.2022.2071656.

Szalavitz, Maia. *Undoing Drugs: The Untold Story of Harm Reduction and the Future of Addiction.* New York: Hachette, 2021.

Thaca, I. "One Junky's Odyssey." *Harm Reduction Communication* 5 (Fall 1997): 1–30.

Tomkins, Silvan. *Affect Imagery Consciousness.* 2 vols. New York: Springer, 1962.

Tuck, Eve, and K. Wayne Yang. "Decolonization Is Not a Metaphor." *Decolonization: Indigeneity, Education, and Society* 1, no. 1 (2021): 1–40.

Vaccaro, Jeanne. "Felt Matters." *Women & Performance: A Journal of Feminist Theory* 20, no. 3 (November 2010): 253–66.

Van Zee, Art. "The Promotion and Marketing of OxyContin: Commercial Triumph, Public Health Tragedy." *American Journal of Public Health* 99, no. 2 (February 2009): 221–27.

Waite, Stacey. *Teaching Queer: Radical Possibilities for Writing and Knowing.* Pittsburgh, PA: University of Pittsburgh Press, 2017.

Walker, Alice. *The Color Purple.* New York: Harcourt, 1992. First published 1982.

Wamsley, Laurel. "Judge Orders Boy Who Started Oregon Wildfire to Pay $36 Million in Restitution." National Public Radio, May 22, 2018. www.npr.org/sections/thetwo-way/2018/05/22/613374984/judge-orders-boy-who-started-oregon-wildfire-to-pay-36-million-in-restitution.

Weheliye, Alexander G. *Habeas Viscus: Racializing Assemblages, Biopolitics, and Black Feminist Theories of the Human.* Durham, NC: Duke University Press, 2014.

Wiman, Christian. *Ambition and Survival: Becoming a Poet.* Port Townsend, WA: Copper Canyon Press, 2007.

Wiman, Christian. *Zero at the Bone: Fifty Entries Against Despair.* New York: Farrar, Straus and Giroux, 2023.

Young, Iris Marion. *Intersecting Voices: Dilemmas of Gender, Political Philosophy, and Policy.* Princeton, NJ: Princeton University Press, 1997.

INDEX